Food and Agriculture Policy: Understanding the Decision Making Process for Agricultural Policy

Food and Agriculture Policy: Understanding the Decision Making Process for Agricultural Policy

Nekesah T. Wafullah

SOCIETY Publishing

www.societypublishing.com

Food and Agriculture Policy: Understanding the Decision Making Process for Agricultural Policy

Nekesah T. Wafullah

Society Publishing
224 Shoreacres Road
Burlington, ON L7L 2H2
Canada
www.societypublishing.com
Email: orders@arclereducation.com

ISBN: 978-1-77407-640-8 (Hardcover)

ABOUT THE AUTHOR

A skilled agriculture expert with extensive knowledge in project management, agricultural energy, various forms of fertilizer, their production, marketing, application regimes and policies; business development management services; cross border fertilizer trade policies; product registration and efficacy trials and assessment; legume production and marketing aspects; food safety advocacy and policy issues; partnerships in businesses; youth, and women empowerment, and volunteerism. She is adept at project planning and strategic management as well as creating simple solutions to complex problems. As mentorship is one of her key areas, she has dedicated time to journey with high school and college students advocating for better performance in Agricultural sciences. She writes and edits agricultural books and loves watching movies, cooking, baking, networking, reading and dancing during her free time. She is also a food and fashion enthusiast. Nekesah holds an M Sc. Agricultural and Applied Economics degree from the University of Nairobi with a major in International Trade and Policy

TABLE OF CONTENTS

List of Figures xi
List of Tables xiii
List of Abbreviations xv
Acknowledgment xix
Preface xxi

Chapter 1 Overview: Agriculture 1
1.1 Agriculture 2

Chapter 2 Overview: Policy 13
2.1 Policy 14
2.2 The Policy Cycle 15
2.3 Policy Evaluation 16
2.4 Policy Evaluation Methods 17
2.5 Policy Evaluation Challenges 18
2.6 Politics And Policy 18
2.7 Agriculture And Policy 19
2.8 Agricultural Sustainability And Public Policies 19

Chapter 3 Economic Analysis of Public Policies 45
3.1 The Neoclassical View of Market Economies 46
3.2 Fundamental Economic Theorems of Welfare 48
3.3 Market Failures and Government Involvement Explanations 50
3.4 Intervention by The Government In The Economy 52
3.5 Welfare Economics 53
3.6 Demand Functions and Consumer Surplus 53
3.7 Correct Measures of Welfare Change: The Equivalent and Compensating Variations 55

3.8 The Relationship Between Change In Consumer Surplus, ΔCS, EV, and CV 58
3.9 Marginal Cost, Supply Function, And Producer's Surplus 59
3.10 Aggregation And The Difference Between Profits and Rents 61
3.11 Comparative Advantages And Gains From Trade 62

Chapter 4 Process of Policy Analysis 65
4.1 Policy Analysis 66
4.2 Alternative Frameworks For Policy Analysis 66
4.3 Phases of Policy Analysis 68
4.4 The Policy Analysis Matrix (PAM) 73

Chapter 5 Agricultural Policy 83
5.1 Agricultural Policy 84
5.2 Sectoral Focus 84
5.3 Other Sectoral Policies 84
5.4 Economy-Wide Policies 85
5.5 Delivery Method 85
5.6 Agricultural Policy Rationale and The State's Role in The Economy 97
5.7 The New-Institutional View of Agricultural Policy 97
5.8 Efficiency Vs. Equity 98
5.9 The State's Function In The Market Economy 99
5.10 The Importance of Economics In Agricultural Policy 100
5.11 Agricultural Policy of Economic Goals 100

Chapter 6 Economics of Agricultural Policy 103
6.1 Development of The Economics of Agricultural Policy 104
6.2 The Farm Problem 104
6.3 The Economic Consequences of Aid For Markets And Related Policies 107
6.4 Political Economy Models 112
6.5 Economics of Quota And Price Discrimination Programs 113
6.6 The Economics of Government-Run Price Stabilization And Buffer Stock Schemes 115
6.7 The Economics of Government Policy For Subsidized Crop Insurance 118
6.8 The Economics of Agricultural R&D Policy 120

Chapter 7 Specific Agricultural Policy Analysis **125**

7.1 Specific Agricultural Policy Review 126

7.2 Trade Policies 129

7.3 Exchange Rate Policy 133

7.4 Sectoral Policies 135

7.5 Policies That Promote Access To Resources 141

7.6 Credit Policies For Agriculture And Rural Areas 146

7.7 Water Utilization And Irrigation Policy 151

Chapter 8 Case Studies **161**

8.1 Patterns In Agricultural Policy In Various Regions 162

8.2 Initiatives For Helping Producers 163

8.3 Policy Support Measures For Consumers 189

8.4 Policy Coherence, Integration, And Harmonization at National And Regional Levels 227

Appendices **247**

Index **251**

LIST OF FIGURES

Figure 1.1. Index of world population and production of cereals and meat, 1966–2009
Figure 1.2. Food supply in crops primary equivalent (kcal/cap/day, 2009)
Figure 1.3. Net exports of food by region, 2000–2012
Figure 1.4. World Bank global food price indices 2000–2013
Figure 1.5. Trends in mineral fertilizer use 1961–2001
Figure 1.6. Sources of growth in global agriculture, 1961–2007
Figure 3.1. The Edgeworth box
Figure 3.2. Demand function and consumer's surplus
Figure 3.3. The compensating variation of a reduction in price
Figure 3.4. The equivalent variation for a reduction in price
Figure 3.5. Change in consumer surplus Variation, equivalent Variation, and compensating Variation.
Figure 3.6. Marginal cost curves and producer's surplus
Figure 3.7. The transformation curve and the autarkic equilibrium
Figure 3.8. Production possibility frontier
Figure 3.9. Production possibility frontier with trade
Figure 4.1. Distribution of welfare in a multi-market model
Figure 4.2. The marketing channel
Figure 4.3. The exchange rate market
Figure 5.1. Time required reaching the market
Figure 5.2. For many farmers, transporting inputs and outputs is a major issue
Figure 7.1. The effects of subsidies on exports
Figure 7.2. The effects of a tariff and of an equivalent quota on imports
Figure 7.3. Minimum guaranteed price
Figure 7.4. A price band scheme
Figure 8.1. Percentage of countries with subsidies for inputs (2007–2012)

Figure 8.2. Percentage of nations adopting steps to increase smallholders' credit access (2007–2012)

Figure 8.3. Proportion of countries implementing Price stabilization and support schemes (2007–2012)

Figure 8.4. Fraction of nations with government insurance and catastrophe risk management programs (2007–2012)

Figure 8.5. Percentage of nations applying land policies (2007–2012)

Figure 8.6. Fraction of states providing direct food subsidies (including price control measures) (2007–2012)

Figure 8.7. Percentage of fuel-subsidizing nations (2007–2012)

Figure 8.8. Proportion of countries that distribute food (2007–2012)

Figure 8.9. Percentage of countries pursuing cash transfers (2007–2012)

Figure 8.10. Percentage of countries that accept export bans (2007–2012)

Figure 8.11. Percentage of nations with a national reserve of food in operation (2007–2012)

LIST OF TABLES

Table 2.1. Policy classification based on policy elements

Table 2.2. Policy stages and types of evaluation carried out

Table 3.1. Ranking of all possible consumption bundles of (x, y)

Table 4.1. The policy analysis matrix (PAM)

Table 5.1. Classification of policy instruments affecting the agricultural sector

Table 8.1. The countries reviewed

Table 8.2. Input subsidy schemes for selected countries (2007–2012)

Table 8.3. Major credit instruments adopted in selected countries (2007–2012)

Table 8.4. Examples of countries with public, partially public and non-governmental CGSS

Table 8.5. Countries of financial institutions for agricultural purposes

Table 8.6. Examples of countries with price support measures for staple commodities

Table 8.7. Different insurance and risk management project

Table 8.8. Examples of countries with policies related to land (2007–2012)

Table 8.9. VAT exemptions/reductions on basic food items (2007–2012)

Table 8.10. Food safety net implementation of services in specific countries (2007–2012)

Table 8.11. Recently introduced and extended or maintained cash transfer services in selected countries (2007–2012)

Table 8.12. Cash transfer typology in selected countries

Table 8.13. Variations in import tariff policies (2007–2012)

Table 8.14. Country level trade policy alignment vs. REC on selected staples (2007–2012)

LIST OF ABBREVIATIONS

ACGSF	agricultural credit guarantee scheme fund
ADB	Agricultural Development Bank
AERR	ASEAN emergency rice reserve
AFTA	ASEAN free trade area
AMIS	agricultural market information system
APBS	Andean price band system
APTERR	ASEAN plus three emergency rice reserve
ASALs	arid and semi-arid lands
ASEAN	Association of Southeast Asian Nations
AU	African Union
BM&F	Bolsa de Mercadorias&Futuros
BNDA	Banque Nationale de Développement Agricole
BNDES	Banco Nacional do Des envolvimentoEconômico e Social
CAADP	Comprehensive Africa Agricultural Development Program
CACM	Central American Common Market
CAN	Andean Community
CBA	cost-benefit analysis
CCE	crop-cutting experiments
CCT	conditional cash transfer
CEA	cost-effectiveness analysis
CEPT	common effective preferential tariff
CESs	commodity exchange systems
CET	common external tariff
CFA	Financial Cooperation in Central Africa
CFS	committee on world food security
CGE	computable general equilibrium

CGSs	credit guarantee schemes
CGTMSE	micro and small enterprises credit guarantee fund trust
CMA	cost-minimization analysis
CT	cash transfer
CU	customs union
CUA	cost-utility analysis
CV	compensating variation
DRC	Democratic Republic of Congo
DRM	disaster risk management
DUP	directly unproductive profit
EAC	East African Community
EAERR	East Asia Emergency Rice Reserve
EAGC	Eastern Africa Grain Council
ECOWAS	Economic Community of West African States
ETLS	ECOWAS trade liberalization scheme
EV	equivalent variation
FA–	Food and Agriculture Organization
FAPDA	Food and Agriculture Policy Decision Analysis
FAPRI	Food and Agricultural Policy Research Institute
FDI	foreign direct investment
FDIs	financial development institutions
FIRA	FideicomisosInstituidosenRelación con la Agricultura
FISP	farmer input support program
FTA	free trade area
GDP	gross domestic product
GIEWS	global information and early warning
GMP	guaranteed minimum price
GST	goods and services tax
GTAP	global trade analysis project
HLPE	high level panel of experts
ICT	information and communication technologies
IFAD	International Fund for Agricultural Development
IFPRI	International Food Policy Research
IMF	International Monetary Fund

INCRA	Instituto Nacional de Colonização e ReformaAgrária
INDAP	Instituto Nacional de Desarrollo Agropecuario
ISFP	initiative on soaring food prices
IVR	interactive voice response
LAC	Latin America and the Caribbean
LAO PDR	Lao People's Democratic Republic
LDCs	less developed countries
LEAP	livelihood empowerment against poverty
LURCs	land use right certificates
MAFAP	Monitoring African Food and Agricultural Policies Project
MAFISA	micro-agricultural finance schemes
MENA	Middle East and North Africa
MEPs	minimum export prices
MERCOSUR	Southern Common Market
MFIs	microfinance institutions
MISs	market information systems
MSP	minimum support price
NAFTA	North American Free Trade Agreement
NAIS	National Agricultural Insurance Scheme
NCPB	National Cereals and Produce Board
NCT	non-contributory cash transfer
NEPAD	New Partnership for African Development
NES	National Export Strategy
NFRA	National Food Reserve Agency
NG–	non-governmental organization
NIRSAL	Nigeria opportunity-based risk-sharing system for agricultural loans
NWRS	negotiable WRS
OECD	organization for economic co-operation and development
OM	open market
PAM	policy analysis matrix
PDTI	Program de Desarrollo Territorial Indígena
PMV	Plan MarocVert
PPP	purchasing power parity
PSE	producer subsidy equivalent

PSNP	productive safety net program
RAIP	regional agricultural investment plan
RECs	regional economic communities
SAARC	South Asian Association for Regional Cooperation
SADC	Southern African Development Community
SAFEX	South Africa Future Exchange
SAFTA	South Asian Free Trade Agreement
SCT	Social Cash Transfer
SFB	South Asian Food Bank Association
SH	shillings
SISPAM	Sistema de Información a la Producción y los Mercados Nacionales
SMEs	small and medium-sized enterprises
SSA	sub-Saharan African
STCs	surplus transformation curves
SURE	subsidy reinvestment and empowerment
TFP	total factor productivity
TRQ	tariff rate quota
UCE	Uganda commodity exchange
UNCTAD	United Nations Conference on Trade and Development
VAT	value-added tax
VUP	vision 2020 Umurenge program
WAEMU	West African Economic and Monetary Union
WB	The World Bank
WFP	world food program
WII	weather index insurance
WRSs	warehouse receipt systems
WT–	World Trade Organization
ZAMACE	Zambian agricultural commodity exchange

ACKNOWLEDGMENT

It was more fun to write a book than I ever expected and particularly satisfying. Without my loving husband, accomplice, and collaborator Charles, none of this would have been feasible. He was the first person I called once when I had this chance, and on this trip, we walked together.

Iam thankful tomy friend and sister, Anne, who has always set the pace and inspired me to take on new challenges in life and use a better picture to bring my thoughts into motion. My parents, close family, and friends who are always in my thoughts when I participate in a mission, making it better when I move forward.

Finally, I can't list all your names. I can't thank you enough for all those who were part of the journey, you know yourself!

PREFACE

The book provides an explanation of how to practice sustainable agriculture for livestock, its sub-sector, and how. It also reveals how agriculture is dealing with developments and obstacles and how monitoring is designed to achieve high-quality results for all actors. In addition to the above, the distinctive characteristics of agriculture and agricultural policy are discussed. In an attempt to gain an understanding of agricultural policy, standard policy and policy, methods were defined. Methods for studying economics and agricultural coverage are also discussed in the development and collaboration. It addresses government intervention's role and significance. A wide range of food safety and agricultural development options introduced in African, Asian, and Latin American and Caribbean countries, LAC, are also reviewed. The countries affected are 81% of the total population in Africa, Asia, and LAC, 90% and 98%, respectively. The work focused on reporting patterns, current activities, and emerging issues. Policies are continually designed to have an effect on domestic products' affordability and access.

1

OVERVIEW: AGRICULTURE

CONTENTS

1.1 Agriculture...2

1.1 AGRICULTURE

Agriculture refers to the many methods in which crop flora and domestic animals maintain the international human population via providing meals and other products. Agriculture is one of the oldest and top activities of humans. The records of agriculture began heaps of years ago. After gathering wild grains establishing at least 105,000 years ago, nascent farmers commenced to plant them around 11,500 years ago. Pigs, sheep, and cattle had been domesticated over 10,000 years ago. Plants had been independently cultivated in at least eleven regions of the world. Industrial agriculture based on large-scale monoculture in the twentieth century got here to dominate agricultural output, though about 2 billion humans nevertheless depended on subsistence agriculture in the twenty-first century. Despite growing industrialization and urbanization in the world, almost 50% working population nevertheless engaged in agriculture. In growing international locations, agriculture is a huge supply of employment and it is viewed as the spine of most African economies. The agricultural area may typically be divided into the following subsectors.

1.1.1 Crops Subsector

The crop production sub-sector is growing plants for food and fiber as a whole. Agriculture refers to the many methods by which plant flora and domestic animals provide food and other goods to the global human population. Agriculture is one of the oldest and most strong practices among human beings. Articles on agriculture started hundreds of years ago. After harvesting wild grains at least 105,000 years ago, nascent farmers started planting them about 11,500 years ago. Pigs, sheep, and cattle were domesticated around 10,000 years ago. In at least 11 parts of the world, plants were developed separately. Industrial agriculture based on large-scale monoculture in the twentieth century came here to dominate agricultural output, while about 2 billion people remained dependent on subsistence farming in the twenty-first century. Given the growing industrialization and urbanization of the world, nearly 50% of the workforce is still engaged in agriculture. In growing international locations, farming is a huge supply of jobs and is seen as the backbone of most African economies. Usually, the agricultural area can be divided into subsectors below orchards, groves, greenhouses, and nurseries, engaged in growing crops, plants, vines, or timber and their seeds in general. Cereals, pulses, fruits, and vegetables, nuts, oilseeds, sugars, and starches, fibers, beverages, narcotics, spices, condiments, rubber forages, grass, and green leaf manure are part of the crop production subsector.

1.1.1.1 Livestock Subsector

Livestock refers to domesticated animals raised for human use in an agricultural environment for labor production and products such as food, eggs, milk, fur, leather, and wool. Included in livestock are cows, pigs, sheep, goats, horses, mules, dogs, buffalo, and camels, chickens, turkeys, ducks, geese, guinea fowl, and squabs.

1.1.1.2 Fisheries and Aquaculture Subsector

Aquaculture is an aquatic species production that involves fish, shellfish, crustaceans, and aquatic plants. Fisheries are an enterprise that is engaged in the processing or harvesting of fish under the supervision of a certain authority.

1.1.1.3 Forestry

Forestry is the science and craft for people and the environment benefits to create, manage, use, conserve, and rebuild trees, forests, and other resources. Traditional forestry generally covers a broad range of issues, including timber supply, fuelwood, wildlife habitat, water quality protection, tourism, landscape, biodiversity preservation, watershed conservation, erosion control, and forest conservation as "sinks" of atmospheric carbon dioxide.

1.1.2 Role of Agriculture in Economic Development

Agriculture is the pillar of most developing economies. It accounts for a large proportion of gross domestic product (GDP) (ranging from 30 to 60%), employs a large proportion of the workforce (from 40% to 90% in most cases), represents a major source of foreign exchange (from 25% to 95%), supplies the bulk of basic food and provides subsidies to more than half of the population of developing countries. More support for growth and income generation is provided by good forward-looking and backward relations within the rural sector and with other economic sectors. Given the importance of agriculture for the economies of most developing countries, in these countries, both domestic and export growth has remained largely underdeveloped. Many reports show that there is a slow and gradual increase in agricultural production in these countries. Nevertheless, slow growth in food production and rapid annual output variations and the key causes of their growing deprivation and food insecurity for developing countries remain major and persistent issues. The proportion of undernourished people in developing countries rose from 38% to 40% (from 116 million to 235 million) in the mid to early 1990s. A number of challenges underpin the changing agricultural situation in developing countries. The problems are related to laws, systems, and growth.

1.1.3 Agricultural Production and Trade Patterns

Food supply has increased at the global level in line with the population over the past 50 years. As estimated from FAO data, between 1966 and 2009 (indexed to 1966 = 100) the corresponding Figure 1.1 trends in food production and population. The world population rose from 3392 million in 1966 to 6817 million in 2009 (nearly 7 billion people). Global cereal production increased from 461 tons to almost 1000 million tons per year, while meat production increased from 87 tons per year to 285 million tons per tonnage. The per capita production of cereals increased from an estimated 135 kg/person/year in 1999 to around 150 kg/person/year since it declined slightly and was around 146 kg/person/year in 2009. Over the same period, total global meat production increased from about 26 kg/person/year to 42 kg/person/year by an impressive triple and around 1.5 times per capita.

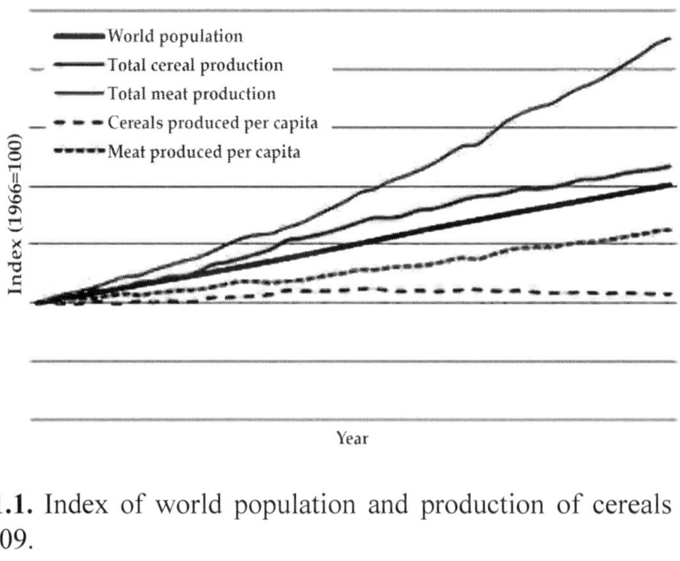

Figure 1.1. Index of world population and production of cereals and meat, 1966–2009.

Source: Calculated from FAOSTAT data on Total Population and Per capita Production.

Output levels, however, vary widely around the world. The map below shows estimates of per capita dietary energy produced from crops by the Food and Agriculture Organization of the United Nations (FAO) (Figure 1.2).

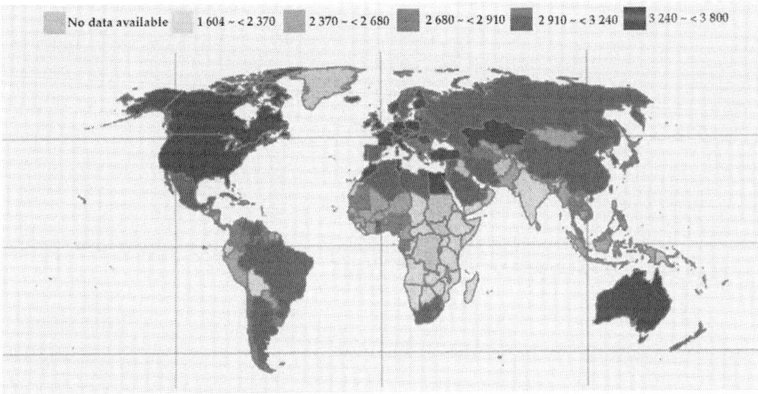

Figure 1.2. Food supply in crops primary equivalent (kcal/cap/day, 2009).

Source: FAO (2013a).

Trade may shift agricultural products from surplus to areas of deficit. Trade, however, only responds to strong demand (ability and willingness to pay), rather than need, and other factors, such as high transportation and transaction costs, may exist that prohibit goods from getting to where they are needed. Over the past 30 years, there has been very significant increases in global agricultural trade and export increases have outstripped production increases. Agricultural trade has dropped as a share of global trade overall (from nearly 25% in the 1960s to less than 10% in 2011), but that should be seen in the light of phenomenal increases in total trade—according to WTO (2012: Chart 3), the average 1950–2011 annual rise was 3.5% for agriculture, 7.5% for manufacturing and 6.0% for all trade. There are some 'blips' downward in exports, but there is a clear upward trend overall. According to Hawkes and Murphy (2010), food import bills as a share of GDP in developing countries more than tripled between 1974 and 2004, and the share of agricultural production exported between 1971 and 2003 grew from 19% to 40%. Cereals used to dominate international food trade, but now constitute a small share of the overall value, while exports of higher value such as meat and vegetables have risen rapidly since the turn of the century (FAO, 2013a). Import and export state trends are changing. Below is a regional overview of net trade. The picture, however, differs from resource to country (Figure 1.3).

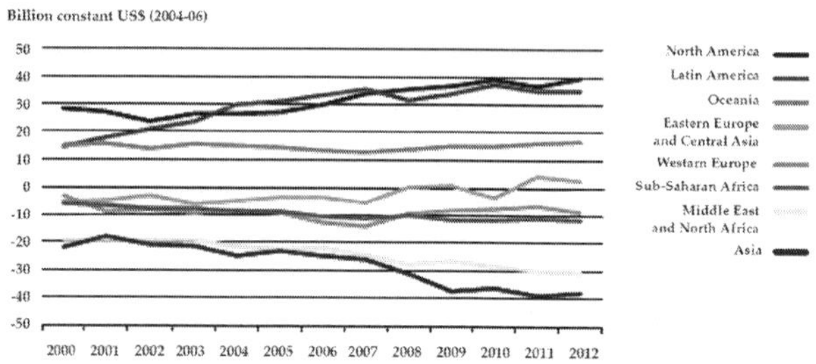

Figure 1.3. Net exports of food by region, 2000–2012.

Source: FAO (2011b).

China and other fast-growing parts of Asia have both increased domestic production and increased food imports (World Bank, 2014a). Africa's continent has also increased its net food imports very substantially (Rakotoarisoa et al., 2011). Wheat is the largest deficit product in the food basket of developing countries among commodities (FAO, 2013a).

Over the past few years, high and unpredictable food prices have hit the headlines in most countries, with ongoing discussions about long-term shifts and patterns (Figure 1.4).

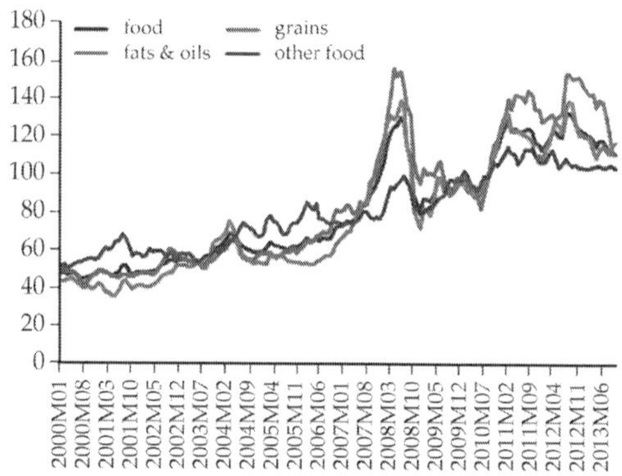

Figure 1.4. World Bank global food price indices 2000–2013.

Source: FAO (2011b).

For many countries, and particularly for global trade, large agribusinesses are rapidly dominant in production. According to a Global Bank report on the potential of agribusiness in Africa, the food market in Africa, estimated at around US$ 313 billion a year in 2013 could triple by 2030, with investments in infrastructure, smart business and trade policies and a competitive agribusiness sector connecting farmers to consumers in -urban areas. The goal is to incorporate small-scale farmers more successfully into markets so that they can improve the agricultural sector. Small and medium-sized enterprises (SMEs) are crucial in linking small-scale farmers to national markets, meeting food demand, and creating employment for tomorrow.

A few large firms are largely dominating world trade in both agricultural inputs and services (Dalle and Ruppanner, 2010; Hawkes and Murphy, 2010; Murphy et al., 2012), while the retail sector is increasingly dominated by supermarkets (Reardon and Timmer, 2007).

1.1.4 Factors Driving These Trends

Based on their price, demand, and risk perceptions, farmers, and traders decide what goods and how much to cultivate, harvest, sell, and shop. In conjunction with the reliability of their management, the actual conditions encountered (weather, price shocks, etc.) result in the amounts eventually generated, exchanged, and stored that year. Factors that drive these agricultural patterns can be categorized into three broad categories, i.e., Side factors of demand, side factors of supply and risk and uncertainties.

1.1.4.1 Trends in Demand-Side Factors

Agricultural production meets the demand of the market. Overall demand is driven by growth rates and is also heavily influenced by income/living standards. After the late 1960s, the world population has more than tripled to just over 7 billion people in 2014, but growth is rising: the projected demographic scenario of 'moderate fertility' is projected around 9.5 billion people by 2050 and 10.9 billion by 2100 (UNDESA, 2014). Typically speaking, as countries become wealthier, they consume more meat (kcal) in general, consuming more processed foods, meat, fats, and oils, and sugar. The underlying causes of these dietary shifts include (Kearney, 2010) increased urbanization, with many consequences including increased food intake away from home, increased economic growth and household wealth, increased global industry openness to trade, and an overall shift toward low-income food (although prices have risen in recent years) over several decades.

Increased global consumption of animal products has increased the use of grains and legumes as animal feed, especially maize, wheat, and soy. In developed countries, more grain is actually used for feed than for food (OECD/FAO, 2012). This trend is likely to increase, particularly if the production of livestock continues to shift towards industrialized units and away from open pastures and small family farms that feed their animals on by-products (FAO, 2012).

There is also a growing demand for non-food uses of agricultural products such as biofuels (Singh, 2010). Biofuels accounted for 20% for sugar cane, 9% for vegetable oil and coarse grains, and 4% for sugar beet for a significant share of global use in the 2007–2009 periods (FAO/OECD, 2011). Initially, much of the market for biofuels was driven by so-called 'mandates' and subsidies, but now that supply chains are in place, high oil prices could feed demand for biofuels also without mandates. Alexandratos and Bruinsma (2012) reported the combination of increasing population, higher incomes, shifting diets and energy demands to raise the global demand for agricultural products by 1.1 billion per year from 2005/2007 to 2050. Around the same time, according to the FAO, '842 million people were estimated to suffer from chronic hunger in 2011–13, or about one in eight people in the world, and frequently did not get enough food to lead an active life' (FAO, 2013b, p. i). This also points to a large amount of unsatisfied customer demand in addition to the legal issues that this poses. There is concern that increasing world demand for food crops for other uses such as biofuels can be slowly priced out of the market by the poorest consumers (Huang et al., 2012).

1.1.4.2 Trends in Supply-Side Factors

The total annual harvest for crops is equal to the crop yield per hectare multiplied by the area planted and crop frequency. While overall the most important factor has been increased yields per hectare, which according to calculations by the Organization for Economic Co-operation and Development (OECD) and FAO (2012) accounted for 78% of the increase between 1961 and 1999, all three factors have played a role in past production increases.

1. **Land:** Use of land for agriculture has expanded in some parts of the world, mainly by opening previously uncultivated areas of forest. Deininger and Byerlee (2012) calculate that from 1990–2007, the land cultivated expanded by 1.9 million hectares per year, concentrated in sub-Saharan Africa, South-east Asia, Latin America, and the Caribbean, mainly to produce vegetable oils (especially palm oil), soya, sugarcane, rice, and maize.

2. **Water:** Agriculture currently accounts for 70% of global freshwater use, ranging from an average of 90% in low-income countries to 42% in industrialized countries where irrigation can compete with urban and industrial uses, according to the FAO (2011b). WTO (2013) projects leading to an increase in agricultural trade, since water-deficient regions are increasingly being forced to import food.

3. **Infrastructure:** Advances in transport and refrigeration infrastructure have lowered travel times and costs and significantly facilitated trade, particularly for perishable products like meat, fruit, and vegetables. For example, between 1955 and 2004, air transport costs (measured in terms of revenue per ton-kilometer) dropped by 92% (WTO, 2008, p. 84). Sea freight, road, and rail have reduced costs and increased speed to varying degrees of extent (WTO, 2013).

4. **Fertilizers:** Use of mineral fertilizers has exploded since the 1960s, particularly in Asia; however, use in Africa is still very low. Pollution from fertilizer and other agrochemical runoff is a serious and widespread problem (FAO, 2011b) (Figure 1.5).

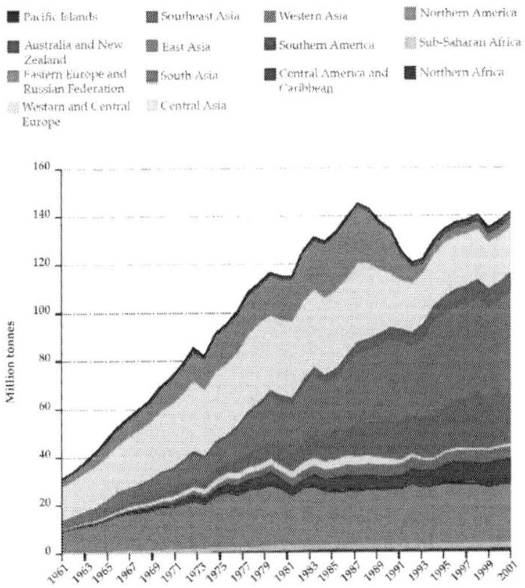

Figure 1.5. Trends in mineral fertilizer use 1961–2001.

Source: FAO (2011b).

5. **Energy:** The price of energy from fossil fuels directly affects farm input prices, for example, fertilizer, and diesel for tractors and irrigation, as well as the cost of transport and trade. The price of fossil fuels also feeds

into demand for biofuels and potentially vice versa. World energy prices have risen considerably (with some ups and downs) since 2000, but the 'fracking revolution' (new sources of fossil fuels and extraction technologies) poses questions as to whether the world will have a new era of cheap fossil fuel energy, or whether prices will go on rising. For this reason, Hertel (2013) describes energy prices as the 'wildcard' (source of major uncertainty) in the future of global agriculture.

6. **Technology, Skills, and Knowledge:** Figure 1.6 is taken from a Fuglie (2012) modeling study that shows the main supply-side growth factors in global agricultural production. Take note of key growth factors and total factor productivity (TFP) description. A companion modeling study (Evenson and Fuglie, 2010) illustrates 'technology capital' as the main driving force of TFP, a blend of research and development with training and growth. Fuglie's conclusion is positive that TFP still has room to grow to help rises in agricultural production to meet world demand, even though investments in machinery and inputs are not keeping pace. Nevertheless, productivity increases across countries have differed significantly, and other researchers (e.g., Ray et al., 2013) are even more doubtful about the ability of technology-driven development to satisfy global demand.

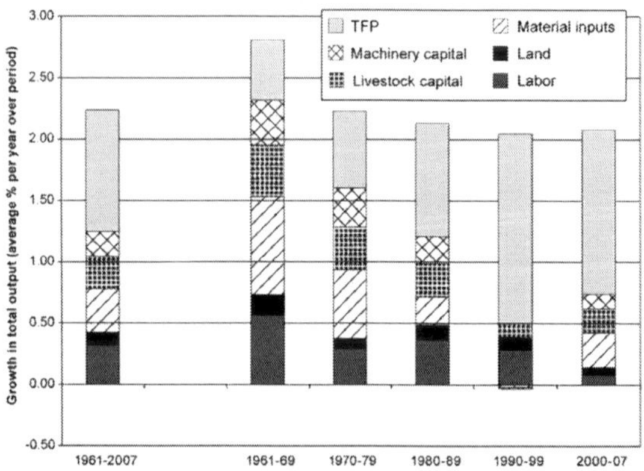

Figure 1.6. Sources of growth in global agriculture, 1961–2007.

Source: Fuglie (2012).

1.1.4.3 Risks and Uncertainties

Risks and uncertainties are very significant not only because of their direct effects, but also because of their influence on the decision-making of farmers and traders. Ceteris paribus is likely to reduce investment and development perceptions for higher risks.

- **Price risks:** In the last twenty years, food price volatility has risen over international markets (FAO/OECD, 2011)
- **Weather Risks:** Climate change is likely to increase, although it is still hard to predict exactly how and when. One recent modeling exercise forecast raises the real maize price by 40–45% in 2050 and the climate change price of wheat and rice by 20–25% relative to a climate change scenario (Rosegrant et al., 2014). Climate change can also increase the risks to human health.
- **Pest and Disease Risks:** Because of the globalization of agriculture, it has risen and is likely to continue to increase. This is not a minor technical point because pathogens like wheat rust or banana Sigatoka can wipe crops across large areas and pose a major threat to food security (Strange and Scott, 2005). Second, most crops are grown far from their centers of origin and have a small pool of genes that can increase pest and disease susceptibility (Marshall, 1977). The movement of pests and diseases around the world (often without the natural enemies that keep them in check at home) has been significantly enhanced by food trade globalization. Finally, the growing concentration of the top three companies on the global seed production market now supply about a third of the market (Dalle and Ruppanner, 2010) means, among other things, that more and more farmers and consumers rely on a few plant varieties with a narrow genetic base that are more susceptible to unexpected pests and diseases.

1.1.5 Challenges in the Field of Agriculture

Many developing countries' main objective is to create a supply chain that is both competitive and a demand boost. It is hindered by influences primarily resulting from the characteristics inherent in the elements of landscape, soil, and social economy. In most developing countries, many of the problems that impede agricultural production include.

1.1.5.1 Environmental Challenges

The climate change on earth at the time though is no good for anyone. Climate change can interfere with food availability, decrease food access, and affect the quality of food. The semi-arid areas are in danger of becoming arid and the arid zones have become so dry that they cannot conceive of any agricultural venture. As a result, climate change has intensified the cases of diseases and pests, culminating in new pests and diseases, and traditional pests and diseases are mutating and becoming more difficult to manage.

1.1.5.2 Economic Challenges

In most developing countries, the decrease for investment in agriculture has indicated a reduction in funding from the public sector in agriculture and a reduction in the supply of inputs and services to farmers. Lack of access to affordable financing in most developing countries is regularly cited as the number one obstacle to executing projects on the ground. This also means inadequate access to services and markets, unequal market conditions, inadequate access to advanced technologies, and high cost of agricultural goods for production and transportation. Considering that most farmers are small-scale in developing countries, compliance with sanitary and phytosanitary steps and agricultural product quality standards is difficult. In competitive international markets, it restricts the share of agricultural products.

1.1.5.3 Human Challenges

For human settlement, agriculture has been a major source of land. It has seen the loss to the urbanization of a certain proportion of arable land. Another problem with the ever-growing agricultural population is to foster the human capital available in the smallholding farms. Because of the lack of training programs, creativity, and a favorable political, economic, and regulatory environment, its money is currently being wasted. Food-related problems, wars, migration, and deforestation have become a threat to the development of agriculture in developing countries with the threat of joblessness.

1.1.5.4 Policy Challenges

The most legal and regulatory framework in developing countries is outdated or highly bureaucratic. These serve only to constrain agricultural development, trade, and effective competition. The challenge is to come up with policy and legal liberalization methods that empower regulatory institutions to deliver on their mandates efficiently, rather than being bottlenecks to agricultural enterprises.

2

OVERVIEW: POLICY

CONTENTS

2.1 Policy 14
2.2 The Policy Cycle 15
2.3 Policy Evaluation 16
2.4 Policy Evaluation Methods 17
2.5 Policy Evaluation Challenges 18
2.6 Politics And Policy 18
2.7 Agriculture And Policy 19
2.8 Agricultural Sustainability And Public Policies 19

2.1 POLICY

Politics is everywhere. The policy outlines our socially accepted standards and practices to ensure some sort of predictability in scarce resource distribution so that we can all contribute to a social outcome. The overall policy can be defined as a course or philosophy of action that a state, party, corporation, or person has adopted or proposed. There is no specific policy category. Policies can usually be broken down into:

- Personal;
- Organizational; and
- Public.

That represents the jurisdictional territories to which they refer. Public policy will be the topic of this book. Each rule is special and requires to be perceived rather than to be listed strictly. Tobacco law is a perfect example of this. Tobacco policy has shown how a policy can change and how the policies of diverse position can be taken. The policy is not always easy and is also hard to classify. Policies have a number of elements leading to classifications. Several of the policy item classifications are as shown in Table 2.1.

Table 2.1. Policy Classification Based on Policy Elements

Policy Classification	Description of Element
Reactive and Proactive	Refers to the timetable for the implementation of the rule.
Substantive and Administrative	Functional refers to laws or services that influence the essential or functional dimensions of work in the community while the operational or administrative dimension (including monitoring and reporting) is administrative.
Vertical and Horizontal	Vertical refers to the traditional, formal policy-making model through which the traditional body (government) initiates, passes, and imposes policies. Horizontal integrates more entities into policy development (for example, PPPs).
Current and Future	When society changes the future, the policy becomes more and more relevant when aspects of our society require government involvement (e.g., file-sharing, and innovation over time that was not a conventional government priority). Current policy dimensions are fields that already have control over the governing bodies.

Lowi Classification: • Regulatory; • Distributive; • Redistributive; • Constituent.	**Regulatory:** Apparently, regulation is just one of several ways that governments seek to control society and individual behavior. There are some very clear goals best pursued through regulatory techniques, and reading every account of regulatory administration indicates a distinct set of moral and political implications associated with this form of governmental commitment. **Distributive:** Policies with many beneficiaries (such as farm subsidies) beyond those who "bid" for the system. **Redistributive:** Policies that reassign services (such as federal equalization payments) from one region to another. **Constituent:** While there is some controversy regarding Lowi's understanding of the concept of constituent, it may apply to the top-down system of elected officials and administrative agencies.
Public Policy vs. Social Policy	**Social Policy**: It will help the community improve in different aspects of like: • Quality of life; • Education; • Citizenship; • Culture. Social policy is part of public policy, but more than that, public policy is economic policy, industrial policy, social policy, etc. Definitive solutions to demand, deprivation, and inequality are likely to remain elusive, and as such, maintaining opportunities for dialogue, creativity, innovation, and learning in strategies to social development is important

Source: Lowi (1972).

Although classifying a policy may be a noteworthy thing, its value does not depend on its classification.

2.2 THE POLICY CYCLE

That legislation has the same basic guidelines that detail the period from conception to assessment, regardless of political structure, party in power, population, problem, or concept.

1. **(Definition of the issue) Agenda Setting:** A problem that can be addressed by the public policy is defined on the basis of some proof.
2. **Policy Formulation:** Politicians and bureaucrats evaluate possible policy options, the most efficient, and the most cost-effective.

3. **Decision-Making:** Vote and enact distracted driving laws by the legislative body.
4. **Implementation:** The enforcement agency complies with the law.
5. **Evaluation:** Regulation, regulation, and execution are expressed by the public. If there is an appetite for further improvement (too rough, not good enough, etc.) this is the basis for setting the agenda and beginning the process again.

2.3 POLICY EVALUATION

There are no two equivalent policies being developed. Significantly, minor policy differences can have profound impacts on everyday life. Policy analysis seeks to define both costs and benefits, whether direct/indirect, financial, cultural, political, or any other indicator. In implementing policy, rigorous assessment is crucial to reducing risk exposure and should not be hurried. To track legislation at a given timeframe, qualitative, and quantitative criteria are used. Using available data, the parameters are operationalized into indicators. Information is derived from estimates, other (secondary) or initial (primary) publicly available sources.

The following statistics characteristics should be observed:

- **Validity**, i.e., how precise the criterion of the predictor is.
- **Reliability**, i.e., how reliably to calculate the criterion.
- **Sensitivity**, i.e., the capacity to catch even the slightest deviations from the original state applicable to the selection criterion.
- The following areas are evaluated:
- **Specific policy areas –** (government's family policy).
- **Specific policy programs** – (government's policy statement).
- **Application of specific instruments** – (new tax).
- **Policy measures** – (gambling ban).
- **A specific quality of the policy process** – (quality of governance, anti-corruption effectiveness).
- **Performance of administrative units** (state, region, municipality, central government, ministry) in fulfilling a defined goal (quality of education, environmental protection).
- **Quality of service provision** (by organizations in health care, education, social services).

Assessment can be carried out at various stages of the policy process. Table 2.2 shows the assessment levels and styles.

Table 2.2. Policy Stages and Types of Evaluation Carried Out

Policy Process Stage	**Type of Evaluation**	**Evaluation Methods**
Policy formulation, decision making	Ex-ante evaluation	Ex-ante methods
Policy implementation	Interim/midterm evaluation	Ex-ante methods
Policy evaluation	Ex-post evaluation	Ex-post methods

Source: Drhová and Ochrana (2011).

2.4 POLICY EVALUATION METHODS

There are already a number of competing models, opposing strategies, alternative methods, and divergent techniques that can be applied to policies that differ in scope, exhaustiveness, and complexity. Therefore, the aim is to reconcile policy analysis with the purpose of the assessment initiative. Several methods for policy analysis are available here.

Cost-output methods (often collectively mistitled as cost-benefit analysis (CBA)):

1. **One-Criterion Analysis:** It includes:
   i. **Cost-Minimization Analysis (CMA):** Measurement of costs (e.g., total project price).
   ii. **Cost-Benefit Analysis (CBA):** Ratio of investment and production in monetary units.
   iii. **Cost-Effectiveness Analysis (CEA):** Ratio of investment and in-kind output.
   iv. **Cost-Utility Analysis (CUA):** Ratio of investment and degree of achievement/satisfaction of goals.
2. **Multi-Criteria Analysis:** It includes the following:

i. Multiple-Criteria Decision Analysis: Different weights are allocated to the individual parameters considered in accordance with their relative importance for defined goals. Experts describe the parameters and measure them. The alternatives are listed by summarizing the weighted criteria.

ii. Rational Choice Theory: Postulates that the actions of all actors and institutions (individual or aggregate) are a function of self-interest, utility maximization, subject to a given institutional framework. When weighing costs and benefits, people make decisions. The market is (subject to conditions) the most powerful regulator.

3. Additional Methods:

i. Comparative Analysis: For example, a comparison of the best example of policy-bench marking.

ii. Process Analysis: Staged process management sequence.

iii. Frame Reflection: In contrast to positivist approaches.

iv. Impact Assessment: Mostly used (not exclusively) in drafting or amending legislation or regulations as an ex-ante measure of their efficacy (EIA, SEA, RIA, etc.).

v. SWOT Analysis: Strengths, weaknesses, opportunities, and threats.

2.5 POLICY EVALUATION CHALLENGES

- Policy phases, actions of actors, or policy areas may overlap, feedback into, or interact with each other. They can change the social/economic/political context.
- The policy implementation process may involve new, unexpected events and actors.
- Public policy's usually long-term effects are difficult to predict, while most initiatives are analyzed immediately after implementation, or at least in significantly shorter time frames.
- It takes time and resources to assess. Decision-makers can never afford it, and even if they can, their reporting and procedures appear to be insufficiently comprehensive.

2.6 POLITICS AND POLICY

Often people associate the policy with politics. However, the policy is so much more than politics. Obviously, politics has a huge implication on policy development and is often the quickest way to get a formal policy in developing countries. Policy and politics are much more than partisan negotiations. Government policy has three main sources the political side, the bureaucratic side, and the judiciary. Political parties run elections on their respective political platforms that outline their general beliefs and policy options for their respective jurisdictions. When elected, parties enact their legislation choices thus forming the political side of the policy. Changes to regulation or even the introduction of new legislation can be promoted through civil servants. While this tends to be more time consuming, this also assures that legislation is constantly being monitored, evaluated, and amended regardless of political interest. That said, at the end of the day, new pieces of legislation require political acceptance.

2.7 AGRICULTURE AND POLICY

There are disputes like any other agricultural company. Conflicts can emerge because of actors 'unethical behavior. Unethical behavior can result in the cost of health, environmental costs and sometimes threaten human and animal rights. Certain industries or business activities, apart from the above, may have a negative or otherwise impact on the agricultural sector. Therefore, to monitor and control this, policies are formulated. Such interventions are likely directed at causal factors such as the basis of agricultural capital, agricultural production, demand for agricultural products, agricultural price and volatility levels, rural employment, and quality of food. Generally, they are enforced by mechanisms such as taxes and subsidies, direct government production and service delivery, and direct regulatory control.

2.8 AGRICULTURAL SUSTAINABILITY AND PUBLIC POLICIES

Sustainable agriculture can be characterized in several forms, but essentially, it aims to maintain farmers, resources, and communities by encouraging sustainable, environmentally safe, and community-friendly farming practices and techniques. Sustainable agriculture blends in with modern farming and complements it. This honors the producers' real values and their goods. Through organic farming, it derives and observes. This operates on large and small farms and ranches, utilizing emerging technologies and reinstating the past's good practices. In short, sustainable farming:

- **Economically Feasible:** It is not sustainable if it is not profitable.
- **Socially Supportive:** Standard of living is fundamental for farmers, farm families, and farming communities.
- **Ecologically Sound:** The resource base that supports us all must be preserved.

Many strategies were implemented to accomplish the above elements. Such measures take the form of public policies in most developing countries. Some of the public legislations that affect agriculture's sustainability are:

- **General Economic and Social Policies:** Designed to control overall economic growth, trade, price levels, employment, investment, and population, accomplished mainly through the use of monetary and fiscal techniques.
- **Policies Relating to Agricultural and Rural Development:** Such laws are typically designed to influence determinants such as agricultural resource base, agricultural production, agricultural product consumption, agricultural price, and variability levels, rural income, and food quality. Generally, they are enforced by mechanisms such as taxes and subsidies, direct government production and service provision, and direct regulatory control.
- **Policies Relating to Markets:** As well as the development of market structures and laws, as well as the restriction of ownership rights.
- **Policies Aimed at Establishing a Democratic and Participatory:** Process designed to involve all interested groups in decision making and implementing.

2.8.1 General Economic and Social Policies

This include:

1. Fiscal and monetary policies;
2. Trade and exchange rate policies;
3. Labor and employment policies;
4. Investment and foreign aid;
5. Population policies;
6. Incomes and equity policies.

2.8.1.1 Fiscal and Monetary Policies

Public expenditure, taxation, and subsidies are included in fiscal policies. Specific influences on agriculture derive from spending on issues like agricultural research and extension, and infrastructure. On the other end, taxes may be aimed to help manage the use of resources such as taxes at land lease or taxes on polluters. When laborers' net wages are to increase with overall economic growth, employers' labor costs need to rise more steadily to cover the additional tax. Companies will find it attractive to replace other less heavily taxed natural resources for labor in the face of a higher wage bill. Such a tax system would, of course, lead to unsustainable use of natural resources, sustainable or otherwise, in relation to labor. Further skewing the tax system towards resource taxes will help foster more sustainable development. In several of the developing countries whereby income taxes are not that omnipresent, the problem will be less the trade-off between income taxation and natural resource taxation than between the latter and other tax forms.

More broadly, reasonable governance is important for the development of agriculture in the short to medium term. The explanation is that economic uncertainty, which is highly probable to deter private investment, can be generated without it, and regular budget problems that interfere with the provision of important public services. In the long run, a rather large public sector, with high-income taxes and high government expenditure, may 'crowd out' private sector growth, of which agriculture is typically one. In the long run, the manner in which the government distributes spending between industries and operations, and the way in which taxes are levied differently on different sources of income, production, and property, also influences both the sectoral composition of GDP and the distribution of income. Policymakers that allocate resources primarily to urban areas and tax farming, directly or indirectly; will, therefore, discourage agricultural development, whether wisely or not (Markandya and Richardson 1994).

Inflation, interest rates, and credit supply can be influenced by monetary policies. Inflation's impact on agriculture is probable to be complicated and unpredictable. Interventions to reduce inflation, however, such as price controls on basic items such as food, would undoubtedly benefit the agricultural sector and are therefore likely to hinder the growth of agriculture. In addition, inflation causes economic fluctuations that, in the primary, are also likely to be incompatible with sustainable farming achievement. The common perception of the connection between interest rates and sustainable agriculture is that low rates are desirable in order to encourage landholders to invest in asset management initiatives that only produce long-term benefits. However, when low-interest rates are achieved through deliberately holding down prices, the effect may be "economic repression," which implies that the financial sector's growth will be hindered. Doing so will demotivate structured savings and thus restrict the credit funds that financial institutions can borrow. For the provision of financing by formal financial institutions, rural people who undertake agriculture are often 'at the end of the line.' As a result, the rural investment rate continues to be slowed down, with negative impacts on sustainable farming.

2.8.1.2 Trade and Exchange Rate Policies

This policy category includes import and export taxes and trade restrictions. These policies tend to lower domestic product export prices and accelerate domestic prices on imported goods. Such effects will have a significant effect on resources and markets, and it is impossible to say for sure what will be the impact on sustainable farming. Nevertheless, rural earnings would decline as far as export taxes are levied on agricultural products. The harm can occur explicitly and as producers shift away from export production through the impact on the prices of domestically produced food. Since sustainable agriculture is mainly about sustainable rural livelihoods, rural income-reducing initiatives also harm sustainability. Import duties on agricultural inputs or import restrictions are likely to have similar consequences, except for inputs such as agricultural chemicals that pose serious environmental and human health risks. In a world environment, a rather more flexible foreign trade system is usually considered better for sustainable development, with fewer taxes and limits on imports and exports. The argument for free trade is that it will encourage development to take place in accordance with the comparative advantage economic principle. It, in effect, would suggest that there would be reduced total capital and other inputs required to achieve a level of production that would be great for everyone and the world. Often, though free trade can, at least at first, have negative effects on capital, while obviously having the potential benefits on economic growth and productivity. The world can also struggle when, for instance, free trade encourages rich countries to sell to poor countries some of their pollution problems.

As far as the exchange rate policy is concerned, some countries worried about the impact on their global purchasing power of negative external balances have tried to maintain a high official exchange rate by limiting imports. History and economic logic also imply that in the longer term, these strategies are likely to fail. While they are in effect, however, they transform domestic trade terms against those economic sectors that produce tradable products, including agriculture. And the losses caused may be huge, far outweighing any benefits that might be provided to farmers like fertilizer bounties. These inequalities can obviously be disastrous for sustainable farming.

2.8.1.3 Labor and Employment Policies

Wage policies typically only encompass the part of the unionized labor force in the formal sector. The percentage of labor in such jobs is low in many developing countries, and wage policies have minimal impact on either aggregate wage levels or sustainable agriculture. (The same may not apply to industrialized countries.) Moreover, wage policies may influence labor allocation across sectors. Therefore, if huge differences between urban and rural incomes arise, they can lead to an undesirable escalation of rural-urban migration, with subsequent urban overcrowding and environmental contamination problems.

The problem of rural joblessness, whether open or concealed, which exists in some countries is also of interest. There is a severe threat to sustainable livelihoods in countries where social welfare programs are not well developed, underemployment, or unemployment among rural or urban workers. In the medium to longer-term, approaches can be found by promoting economic growth and workforce production. Programs for 'Food for Work' may provide an opportunity to incorporate poverty alleviation with labor-intensive public works. Such works can be used to preserve or improve the resource base, e.g., through forestry programs or public works to control soil erosion.

2.8.1.4 Investment and Foreign Aid

Since the sustainability policy objective is to pass the existing resource base corresponding to the next generation, investment policy is obviously essential. This is partially about building a 'secure' atmosphere for private investors. Very many obstacles to foreign investors' entry will dissuade international capital flows, as will overly stringent rules on income repatriation. Likewise, economic uncertainty and social upheaval will dissuade all investors, whether foreign or local. On the other extreme, investments in sustainable agriculture can be disastrous if stakeholders do not have to compensate for the negative externalities that they create (e.g., reservoirs that take water from upstream users, wells that lower the water table for everyone). Certainly, policies must be in a position either to avoid these negative externalities or to compensate for them by shareholders.

Since public funds are always, minimal, direct investment by the government should be directed to areas where the market failure results in underinvestment. These fields include human capital investments (i.e., in people). Creating sustainable human capital would likely require significant government spending in health services, education, and training. Likewise, public investment in freely accessible resources like many fisheries and some forests and in state-owned resources such as rural infrastructure may be required (for a description of the various types of resource ownership regimes, see Bromley and Cernea, 1989). For sustainable agriculture, an adequate percentage of such developments must be targeted to rural areas where these facilities are usually much lower than those in the cities.

Public property and open access properties that are critical for sustainable agriculture may include fishing, forests, and water supply. Many government properties, like public roads, also have attributes of open access. Since private individual investors are often able to capture all the benefits of investing in open access assets on their own, involvement is often required. Governments may need to take steps either to undertake certain socially productive but privately unprofitable investments or to establish institutional structures that internalize externalities to allow private investors to make an acceptable return on their capital. Definitions of the latter form of policy interference involve water supply system privatization and contracting for the installation and maintenance of toll roads.

Government investment choices must be predicated, as far as necessary, on a careful evaluation of each investment's social benefit. The methodologies used to undertake such project assessments are well known and have been lengthened in recent years in an attempt to take due account of environmental impacts (Edwards-Jones, 1996; World Bank, 1991). Nonetheless, as discussed above, quality metrics based on discounted cash flow may need to be used as part of a multi-criteria evaluation that also involves other factors such as equity between generations.

From less advanced countries, where government funds are commonly very highly restricted, foreign aid, including concessional loans, can be used to help address any shortcomings in the level of public investment required for sustainable agriculture.

2.8.1.5 Population Policies

The menace presented by prominent population growth to sustainable agriculture. It is evident that population increase should be reduced and likely reversed, at least in the long run, in order to achieve sustainability. For several developing countries, population growth introduces difficulties even in the shorter run. In order to strengthen food production as well as the service provision such as education and health, considerable investments are required in line with the growing numbers. Therefore, sustainable development in such situations is made more difficult. The problem is that in all cultures some of the more effective methods of birth control are not appropriate. It continues to complicate the entire debate of population policy for policymakers. However, there are other ways of approaching the topic than through a head-on confrontation with ethical values that are sometimes strongly held.

Policies that boost girls 'education and women's advancement, including employment opportunities for younger women, would typically lead to a decrease in fertility. However, as women's prominence increases, they are far more inclined to take care of their own fertility, no longer dependent on their male partners, local health workers, or religious leaders' decisions. Even specifically, birth rates tend to drop as child mortality declines, urbanization expands, and living standards increase. The policy initiatives aimed at promoting such results are rarely controversial and will slow population growth. This being said, it is considered by some to be a good policy to ensure that no woman is deprived access to resources of restricting the rate with which she conceives, irrespective of religious or other tabous considerations that determine which approaches are available to her for which reason.

Population policy also applies to policies affecting people's geographical distribution. Public authorities can affect the rate of migration to urban areas, mainly by exploiting really rural-urban income differentials, wisely or otherwise. Policies to focus government investment and provision of services in cities would speed up rural-urban migration, and vice versa. Likewise, policymakers may take policy efforts to try to change rural population distribution through, for instance, land settlement initiatives such as the Rwandan Land Defragmentation Program.

2.8.1.6 Incomes and Equity Policies

The value of taxation has already been mentioned above in shaping incentives for responsible use of capital. Nevertheless, a second possibility corresponds to the distribution of income and assets when setting taxes. Apparently, taxing the rich and denying them off some of their wealth to address the needs of this current generation poor, and investing in the future for the benefit of poor people, can be one way to achieve the aim of sustainable development. Sadly, on any large scale, it is never politically possible! Nevertheless, where prosperity or income is derived from economic rents resulting from public investment, such as increased value or productivity of land due to the development of public infrastructure, it can be more acceptable to tax at least a portion of those gains.

Policies that directly target the poor can also be introduced, such as programs for famine relief, food for work initiatives, or the provision of free or subsidized services. Many developed countries have comprehensive social welfare programs in place to help the needy, such as the elderly, the aged, or the unemployed. Because all these services are very costly, they are much more minimal or even completely absent in most developing countries. The line of reasoning for policies aimed at achieving a more proportionate income distribution is not that the poor are causing more resource degradation than the rich, and so their poverty must be helped. Of addition, the reverse is often the case, considering the much higher consumption rates of rich countries of products such as fossil fuels. Quite the opposite, the objective is to enable the poor of today to have a decent standard of living. They could then have the mechanism to provide their offspring with a more sustainable future by offering them with good nutrition, sound health care, and good education, for example.

2.8.2 Policies Relating to Agricultural and Rural Development

Though the above-mentioned overall economic and social policies may be very essential for sustainable agriculture, they predominantly fall outside the area of responsibility of agricultural professionals. On the other extreme, the policy areas addressed next correspond directly to the rural sector and will be within the expertise of agriculture ministries in many cases. These include:

1. Rural infrastructure;
2. Building human capital for the rural sector;
3. Agricultural research and technology development;
4. Agricultural prices;
5. Stabilization and risk in agriculture;
6. Direct government involvement;
7. Sustainable rural livelihoods;
8. Food and nutrition.

2.8.2.1 Rural Infrastructure

Advancements in rural development lead to sustainable agriculture by increasing the quality of utilities or other productivity-enhancing facilities. A main road that decreases traveling time and vehicle maintenance costs also decreases the marketing costs of agricultural products and reduces the costs of farm and household requirements produced. Additionally, an irrigation system increases farmland productive capacity while a telephone system decreases agricultural marketing transaction costs and increasing efficiency by providing producers better access to price information. Although public investment in rural infrastructure is significant for sustainable farming, the development of systems and funding to maintain existing infrastructure is also necessary. Rather than the latter, infrastructure investment may be unsustainable or less profitable than it should. The rapid degradation of all forms of infrastructure due to lack of maintenance was one of the most significant impacts of the situation in Africa in the 1980s on sustainable development.

Since infrastructure construction is generally expensive and because there are many incentives and limited funds, major policy questions arise as to which infrastructure projects should be given priority. The right investment assessment is important in such a situation. Apparently, such assessments should take account of the proposed project's environmental consequences. For example, careful consideration to alignment and layout features such as managing the storm-water run-off can add little to costs when planning a new path but can significantly reduce the environmental harm. Because the planning is well done, changes to infrastructure will encourage sustainable agriculture:

- Improving market conditions for producers in previously isolated areas.
- By allowing new or more extensive use of land or other resources that were previously too secluded, reducing pressure on other areas.
- By allowing previously economically deprived communities to enjoy better access to services such as health and education and extension of agriculture.

2.8.2.2 Building Human Capital for the Rural Sector

Advancement of human capital is an essential component of sustainable agriculture, which can be too often ignored in farmers' thought. Nevertheless, as mentioned earlier, human capital developments have been the driver of most of the recent increases in agricultural land and labor productivity. Because land borders have been crossed in most parts of the world and areas available for agriculture and forestry are likely to decrease, policies aimed at improving rural human capital need to be given high priority. Providing free education and health care in rural areas are two keyways to improve the human resource base for agriculture. None of these will normally be the accountability of the farm planners. Nevertheless, the education of farmers and the distribution of agricultural information to farmers and others is usually a matter for some responsibility in the ministries of agriculture.

Indeed, policy actions here concern the development and operation of training facilities and programs for expanding the education to rural villages. It is also necessary to consider the context, structure, and orientation of agricultural extension. It may not be the role of the current extension service to support sustainable agriculture. The staff's skills might need to be updated to give them a better understanding of sustainable methods of farming. Considering the growing awareness of the value of people's involvement in achieving sustainable agriculture, such extension programs used for a 'top-down' approach may need to undergo drastic reforms. Mass media's position in supporting sustainable agriculture should also be taken into consideration in the policy review. Rather sustainable farming techniques can be encouraged by means of media such as radio, which together with other marketing strategies can be a fairly cheap and effective way to change attitudes and values about the use of rural resources.

2.8.2.3 Agricultural Research and Technology Development

Advanced technology's contribution to sustainable agriculture has already been highlighted. Policy problems are related to how to promote the development of such enhanced and sustainable technologies. The level of support for agricultural research and the distribution of such funds among research organizations, products, disciplines, and projects will be at the concern in the public sector. It is necessary to evaluate the pros and cons of a methodology to farming systems versus a much more traditional disciplinary division of activity. Whichever technique is taken, there must be protocols in place to set research goals that are appropriate and sensitive to rural producers' needs and circumstances. The work carried out must also be periodically updated to guarantee that funds are being used appropriately and well and that progress is made towards the expected objectives.

The recruitment of R&D programs for sustainable agriculture often deserves to be given political attention. This suggests deciding the distribution of funds to universities' agricultural faculties and to colleges of agriculture. This also brings up the question of whether to include in-country study education in different sub-disciplines or to use universities abroad that might be better equipped for the mission. Due to the global mobility of good scientists, recruitment of qualified research staff may be a concern in many less developed countries (LDCs). For the suitable recruitment of research programs, initiatives such as bonds and incentive payments might need to be put in place. In contrast to R&D programs in the public sector, policy proposals should also be regarded to support efforts in the private sector. Tools typically involve potential government assistance for private or corporate research organizations, possibly by raising agricultural sales taxes. In order to offer innovators the opportunity to make money from their investments, interest must also be paid to property rights legislation, such as patent laws and plant variety rights. Another method of involvement that can produce social benefits and promote sustainable agriculture may be possible tax breaks for firms doing R&D.

2.8.2.4 Agricultural Prices

Policies aimed at increasing the prices charged for agricultural products can be enforced by regulating or taxing competitive imports, by reducing quotas or direct subsidies to production. Prices of producers can be lowered by limiting or taxing agricultural exports, by subsidizing imports, or by taxing sales directly. In the olden days, at least, in developing countries, governments had already normally pursued to drive down farm prices to keep food prices low. The objective was often to help urban dwellers and to curb urban wage growth. On the other extreme, policymakers in industrialized countries usually tried to raise farm prices to satisfy agricultural lobby groups. Lately, there has been that awareness that both forms of distortion cause resource misallocation and, thus, are not advantageous to sustainable farming.

Whereas any ineffectiveness in the allocation of resources may be harmful to sustainable agriculture, the distorted agricultural prices have some specific negative impacts. Minimal agricultural prices endanger sustainable agriculture by preventing the expansion of farm production and rendering sustainable livelihoods difficult for rural people. Under a low-price system, investment in agricultural capital, such as land enhancements, will be dampened. Inflated prices, on the other end, contribute to the uneconomic use of materials, some of which can harm the environment, such as chemicals. Inflated prices may cause marginal lands to be used too intensively. We may also cause economically unprofitable and wasteful yet private investment, such as unnecessary woodland and forest clearing or wetland drainage, for agricultural use.

2.8.2.5 Stabilization and Risk in Agriculture

There are two major areas of risk-related policy interference in agriculture. The first is to reduce the risk. Massive natural disasters including cyclones, extreme flooding, and fires can have major harmful effects on the resource base. The unexpected erosion, landslides or flooding can irreversibly destroy property. Likewise, property such as crops, trees, animals, and land-based improvements such as fences, terraces, irrigation works, roads, and villages can be damaged or destroyed across large areas. Legislators need to focus on legitimate measures to combat or limit the impact of disasters like this. Tools involve building protective functions such as levee banks or fire breaks, and setting up and maintaining disaster Global information and early warning systems (GIEWS). Another potential hazard that can be mitigated by proper quarantine initiatives and by having plans in place to control outbreaks before they spread is the invasion of agricultural systems by severe pests, diseases, or weeds. Man-made disasters, like wars and civil unrest, can cause serious damage on the same scale as many natural disasters at least. In these situations, it is obviously more difficult to both avoid and minimize the consequences.

After a catastrophe, whether natural or man-made, the second type of policy action is required. Governments (maybe even with international agencies) may need to adopt different forms of disaster relief to restore the damaged structures with minimal risk to sustainability. Emergency food supply, supply of crop replanting materials, supply of replacement breeding animals and help with reconstruction may be included in the relief measures adopted.

2.8.2.6 Direct Government Involvement

Public authorities often participate in rural resource management directly (normally via government entities established for this function), more often in forestry than in agriculture. They as well frequently take an active part in the supply of agricultural inputs, rural credit provision, and marketing of agricultural production. With particular reference to all such involvement, the policy question to be resolved is whether government agencies are as efficient and effective as a private enterprise would be in achieving sustainable agriculture. In the assumption that the explanation is in the negative, governments are gradually moving to privatize these types of functions. However, being too dogmatic about the issue is unwise. There may be situations where it may be beneficial to have public ownership. Administrations, for instance, may usually have access to capital at cheaper rates than private firms. Therefore, they are definitely better positioned to make the long-term investments required for sustainable production in, say, forestry than the private sector. Consequently, direct government involvement in agricultural production and marketing needs to be examined on a case-by-case basis and not evaluated in any doctrinaire way.

2.8.2.7 Sustainable Rural Livelihoods

Economically viable rural livelihoods, in many developing countries (and in some developed ones) policies are required now and, in the future, to address the recurrent rural poverty problem. Sadly, defining, and enforcing effective corrective actions is not straightforward-if it was, the poverty problem would have been addressed a long time ago.

Sustainable poverty reduction would certainly require a thorough and successful implementation of a wide range of policy initiatives under all or most of the headings in this chapter of the guidance. To explain what may be involved, the box below includes a suggested list of policies required to assist rural poor in achieving sustainable livelihoods.

Box 7. SUSTAINABLE RURAL LIVELIHOODS FOR THE 21ST CENTURY: POLICY IMPLICATIONS

Adapted from Chambers and Conway 1992, pp. 33-[illegible]

I. Enhancing capability

The provision of enabling infrastructure and services including

- education for livelihood-[illegible] capability
- health, both preventive and curative to prevent permanent disability
- bigger and better baskets of choices for agriculture, and support for farmers' experiments
- transport, communications and information services (about rights, markets, prices, skills ...)
- flexible credit for new small enterprises

II. Improving equity

Giving priority to the capabilities and access of the poorer, including minorities and women, via:

- redistribution of tangible assets, especially land, and land to the tiller
- secure rights to land, water, trees and other resources, and secure inheritance for children
- protection and management of common property resources and equitable rights of access for the poorer
- enhancing the intensity and productivity of resource use, and exploiting small-scale economic synergy
- rights and effective access to services, especially education, health and credit
- [illegible] restrictions which impoverish and weaken the poor

III. Increasing social sustainability

Reducing vulnerability so that the poor do not become poorer by:

- establishing peace and equitable law and order
- disaster prevention
- counter-seasonal strategies to provide food, income and work for the poorer at bad times of the year
- prompt support in bad years, and high prices for tangible assets people sell in distress
- health services that are accessible and effective in bad seasons, including treatment for accidents
- conditions for lowering fertility

2.8.2.8 Food and Nutrition

It is indistinguishable from sustainable agriculture to provide a sufficient diet and to meet nutritional needs for all. An increase in population and rising incomes would lead to significant increases in food demand. Therefore, it is important to increasingly reduce the number of poor people who often go hungry for sustainable development, to alleviate suffering and to provide them with better opportunities to lead good, productive, and fulfilled lives.

Food and nutrition policy objectives include food security, safe, and high-quality food, and balanced and healthy diets for all. Those objectives are largely consistent with the wider targets of sustainable agriculture. Sustainable agricultural production would result in increased supplies of food and increased opportunities to earn income, leading to poverty reduction and malnutrition. Nonetheless, specific measures may be required in some countries to strengthen the food security of the poor and malnourished. There, the necessary policy initiatives are the same as those referred to in reference to the issue of sustainable rural living.

Focusing on food safety also means addressing any disparity in the percentage of agricultural research and extending efforts aimed at food crops instead of manufacturing or commercial crops. In the past, in some countries, there has been a propensity to ignore roots, tubers, plantains, traditional legumes, oilseeds, vegetables, and fruits that are commonly eaten but are less frequently traded domestically and internationally. Encouraging some of these crops' increasing production could lead to improved human diets and more sustainable production systems. The explanation is that such crops can offer alternatives to the key staples or export crops being produced intensively. Post-harvest systems for all food crops that are affected by significant losses and deterioration of value may also need to be provided with more consideration.

Efforts to increase nutrition quality and safety directly affect health and nutritional status. These include setting up and enforcing food laws, encouraging consumer groups, and enhancing food quality, health, and preparation education. Measures are necessary to avoid food contamination with agro-chemicals, or by pests like micro-organisms, as are protocols for detecting such contamination in foods grown or imported locally. Wide food and diet education, provided through formal education and mass media, can encourage good eating habits and healthy lifestyles, thus increasing the occurrence of obesity-related diseases. Improvements in child nutrition are particularly important for sustainable agriculture to ensure that children grow up are able to fulfill useful roles in future society.

2.8.3 Business and Property Rights Policies

These include:

- Resource property rights;
- Institutional development.

2.8.3.1 Resource Property Rights

Sustainable agriculture's primary property rights are those related to land and water (such as freshwater and marine fisheries supplies). Most property is usually owned by private or community interest, fishing is owned by public or community ownership, or is open access, and most water resources are owned by the public. Policy options for these different types of property rights include:

- Policy on asset reallocation between state, collective, and private ownership;
- Policy on the allocation of private property between individuals;
- Policies regulating the use of open-access tools, state, and private property;
- Policies for creating and implementing resource efficiency and sustainability.

It is possible that all four categories of policy initiatives will focus on stability, performance, and equity. However, especially for the first two, where ownership shifts, it may be impossible to predict the full consequences of a policy and may not automatically be beneficial for all three criteria. Shifts in property rights are inclined to make many people better and others miserable by their very definition, which means, as noted earlier, that such reforms are often politically sensitive and divisive.

Changes in property rights may be justified if these rights lead to the degradation of an open access or common property resource by overuse. The intervention can range from assisting in creating or reinforcing a user organization that has the right to manage the resource, to privatizing or nationalizing the property. While the modern trend is more in favor of the former than the latter, consideration of likely implications is required on a case-by-case basis. Previously, forests in community ownership were nationalized in Burma and Nepal with the aim of limiting overuse. As the dispossessed communities no longer saw the forest as 'theirs,' the result was an increase in illegal timber cutting, and government enforcement of cutting restrictions was weak. In South Asia, the transfer of irrigation tanks to village councils or other democratic bodies at the time of independence from the control of local rulers generally resulted in a decline in maintenance standards. Land settlement schemes involve the transfer of property rights from the public to private ownership, although the settlers rarely have full freehold title to the land.

There may be very unequal access to resources when a few people own a resource's disproportionate share. These conditions may be incompatible with sustainable farming and may require ownership redistribution. Dispossessed owners may or may not be paid and may seek full or partial payment if they are compensated. A land reform under slogans such as 'farm to the tiller' is the most common example of such policies. Experience shows that, due to the power and prestige of the land-owning class, progressive land reform is difficult to implement. In fact, the results are often not as good as the expectation of the supporters, at least in the short to medium term. Nevertheless, if the current ownership structure is not sustainable, these are not grounds to do nothing.

Regulation for improving the efficiency of the use of public and open-access property services involves the implementation or modification of user charged rates or the enforcement of user quotas. For illustration, the freedom to use common pastureland, forests, or fishery resources may be limited in order to avoid overuse. In some cases, existing restrictions on common property use could have broken down due to challenges such as those arising from population growth and intensified advertising. As a direct consequence, policy measures may be necessary to reinforce or develop new former rationing institutions. For example, the number of fishing operators in a given fishery and the size and nature of the catch of each operator may be set limits.

Challenges of water policy correspond primarily to the private use of public, open access or community resources. There are vast differences in the constitutional and institutional structures governing such use. These arrangements have an impact on resource efficiency and sustainability, including contamination degradation of the resource. As metropolitan and manufacturing water utilization rises, water management for multiple uses (including reuse) will become increasingly important, as will the demand for new mechanisms to improve the efficiency of water allocation among users. Both practical water pricing and the implementation, where feasible, of 'polluter pays' water contamination charges appeal as 'win-win' policy reforms to many economists. They promote an even more sustainable use of a precious resource and accumulate financial resources that can be invested in sustainable development, such as water supply management or water catchment infrastructure maintenance. However, the distributional impacts of the new measures must be carefully considered in both cases. In addition, the near implausibility of instituting an effective pollution tax generated by many small-scale farmers limits the practicalities of applying the principle of polluter pays in agriculture. Similarly, most governments 'propensity to pay loggers less than the timber's maximum market value in national forests contributes to the public purse's forgiven revenue. Worse, it also causes resources use to be ineffective and unsustainable.

Property rights are likely to be a source of inefficiency if they fail to ensure the transfer of resources to those who are best able to use them. For example, selling outright land is prohibited in many countries, and renting land is illegal in other cases. Furthermore, the absence of a transferable title to land may inhibit users of that land from accessing formal credit. This will have negative effects on efficiency and, if the lack of equity capital prevents investment in land enhancement, possibly sustainability. Tenure reforms could be designed in such situations to be more consistent with sustainable agriculture. The security of that tenure may affect the care with which the land is preserved and used even in individual tenure. There may be no incentive for land-users to manage the resource with long-term productivity in mind if access is only for a limited time, as in some leasehold arrangements. The same may apply if the rules prohibit the owner's surviving spouse or children from inheriting the rights of ownership. Other forms of property such as common property rights or state-owned resources such as fishing and irrigation water can benefit from title security and transferability.

2.8.3.2 Institutional Development

Institutions' are described in this perspective as the laws, guidelines, and other components that shape the social interaction structural structure. We establish cooperative and competitive partnerships that are a community or, more importantly, an economic order. Under this concept, organizations are not the same as institutions, although an organization can form part of the institutional framework. Potentially important for sustainable agriculture are many different types of institutions. We can be split into institutions based on society and institutions based on the sector. There are different types of cooperative agreements and value systems within the former which influence agricultural production and the use of rural resources. These include informal structures such as family ties and obligations, rank, and social status systems, common values and beliefs, religious or other tabulations, and stress from peer groups. There is, of course, limited scope for government policy involvement in these regions, but not insignificant. Campaigns for education and media may lead to shifting attitudes and values. Government officials can 'cultivate change agents' such as community leaders to pass on information and ideas on sustainable development to others in their neighborhoods. Likewise, the government may encourage local entities such as religious institutions and women's groups to promote healthcare in local communities.

Governments can set up or leverage more formal organizations. For instance, laws and regulations governing the operation of cooperatives, political parties and lobby groups, land tenure structures, or regulations governing the operation of financial organizations such as banks and credit unions. Under other headings, many of these more formal institutions are listed. Market-related organizations are associated with agricultural commodity production, manufacturing, and marketing and management of agricultural resources. The classification also requires the provision of related services to entities that are ancillary to agriculture. In particular, policies to promote market growth will be compatible with sustainable agriculture, in line with the notion that command, and control systems generally do not work as well as market-based ones. Appropriate government action may include reinforcing many market-related institutions by eliminating regulations and constraints on business development and creating an economic environment in which business entrepreneurship can thrive. Fairtrade regulations may need to be strengthened, and the influence of monopolies may need to be curbed. Providing good market information systems (MISs) and other steps to encourage small business development in agricultural marketing would tend to benefit both farmers and food customers by lower marketing margins. Likewise, it may be necessary to create the required mechanism to promote financing for a growing rural business sector. In order to enable business owners to raise equity capital and spread business risks across the wider community, action may also be required to promote the development of a stock exchange if none exists. Despite the usual political sensitivity of such matters, if local resources are insufficient, consideration may be required to loosen restrictive rules regulating foreign investment to agricultural marketing and finance.

2.8.4 Policies to Create Democratic and Participatory Mechanisms

These include:

- Decentralization;
- People's participation and empowerment.

2.8.4.1 Decentralization

Promising agricultural conservation policymaking needs policymakers to have a clear understanding of the development and resource management processes they deal with. Usually, this means a need for strong acquaintance with farm and rural household structures-something that may not be easy for urban policymakers. Since it is the farmers, foresters, fishermen, and local people who eventually have to determine what to do in the sustainable management of rural resources, it is appropriate to include them in decision-making on agricultural sustainability as fully as possible. National leaders, research, and extension managers and the like cannot have enough extensive knowledge of all regional situations to make policymaking work. The more decisions that can be made and the more responsibilities that can be delegated to the local level, including local communities, the more the system is likely to succeed. Of course, delegating important policy decisions to the local level would be reckless if, at the same time, local people, organizations, and governments were not equipped with the education, services, and other help needed to fulfill such responsibilities.

Decentralization alone will not succeed unless the national government and local level create clear lines of communication. Data on local needs and conditions must be effectively communicated from the regional and provincial levels to the center in order to make sensible decisions on the overall allocation of resources. There must also be procedures in place to determine where gaps hinder development at the regional or provincial level, so that central authorities can take remedial action. It suggests that the significant policy decisions are to assess the impact to which it is practical and prudent to delegate responsibility and support to federal, district, and local bodies, including local community organizations. Such delegation may include the development of suitable ways to track these delegated activities and the creation and use of effective ways to communicate between the grades.

2.8.4.2 People's Participation and Empowerment

There is a wide and diverse literature on the role of citizens in agricultural sustainability, and here it is hard to do justice to everything. The involvement of people is an essential ingredient of any effective agricultural sustainability strategy for the reasons given above. Unfortunately, though, much of what is published about involvement is short on practical implementation recommendations, while long on rhetoric. The fundamental problem with a policy to encourage the participation of people is that many current agricultural institutions, such as universities, research organizations, extension bodies, and regulatory authorities, find it difficult to learn from and collaborate with farmers and rural people. It is because they are defined by a rigid hierarchy and centrally controlled hierarchical authority; their practitioners are experts and see only a narrow view of the world; and they have no systematic quality feedback systems "(Pretty, 1995, p. 202). Pretty, among others, advocated the need for a radical paradigm shift of new concepts, principles, and attitudes focused on the interpretation of new roles for development organizations and professionals. He does, however, agree that it will not be easy to achieve such a transformation.

A more realistic approach is taken here, considering the possible difficulty in implementing the proposed radical change of procedures for the complete and successful participation of people. This outlines a policy that is more evolutionary than groundbreaking. It has several components which, in turn, are discussed. First, a truly participatory approach requires a reasonable development of democratic processes, including respect for human rights, as well as concern for the status of women, children, and minorities. In addition, participation requires freedom from the ravages of war and civil disturbance, as well as reasonable law and order and security standards. Second, qualifications need to be established and mentalities and values need to be modified both in local communities and among farmers. There is a need for integration of sustainable agriculture issues at all levels of formal and informal education and training. In addition, there is a need to 'reshape the learning environment,' according to certain commentators, to transform rural organizations into 'learning organizations.' A hint can be obtained from Box below of what these commentators have in mind. Which policy steps are required to bring about such a transition, is less clear.

Third and connected to the institutional change just described, agricultural research, extension, and support structures need to be made more responsive to their customers' requirements and situations. Multiple scenarios were recommended for conducting research and extension, and some were tested predicated on a participatory approach. Whereas there are often bureaucratic and other obstacles to the successful application of such methodologies, it is often possible to move at least a little along the road. This needs a policy decision with the required reorientation of activities and strategies in favor of pursuing that path, then that decision to be enforced. The application must include providing adequate preparation and benefits for workers. Forging stronger ties between research and expansion will in many cases be a significant co-requirement for a more productive overall interaction with client farmers and rural people.

A TYPOLOGY OF PARTICIPATION IN DEVELOPMENT PROGRAMS AND PROJECTS

Adapted from Pretty 1995, p. 173

1.Passive participation People participate by being told what is going to happen or has already happened. It is a unilateral announcement by administration or project management without any listening to people's responses. The information being shared belongs only to external professional.

2.Participation in information giving. People participate in answering questions posed by investigators using questionnaire surveys or similar approaches. People do not have the opportunity to influence proceedings, as the findings are neither shared nor checked for accuracy.

3.Participation by consultation. People participate by being consulted and external agents listen to their views. These external agents define both problems and solutions but may modify these in the light of people's responses. Such a consultative process does not concede any share in decision making and professionals are under no obligation to accept people's views.

4.Participation for material incentives. People participate by providing resources, for example labour, in return for food, cash or other material incentives. Much on-fun research falls into this category, as farmers provide the fields but are not involved in experimentation or the process of learning. Although often called participation, people have no stake in prolonging activities when the incentives end.

5.Functional participation. People participate by forming groups to meet predetermined objectives through the development or promotion of externally initiated social organizations. Such involvement is seldom at early stages of project cycles or planning, but rather after major decisions have been made. These institutions tend to be dependent on external initiators and facilitators but may become self-dependent.

6.Interactive participation. People participate in joint analysis, which leads to action plans and the formation of new local institutions or the strengthening of existing ones. These groups take control over local decisions and so people have a stake in maintaining structures or practices.

7.Self-mobilization. People participate by taking initiatives to change systems, independent of external institutions. They develop contacts with external organizations for resources and technical advice they need but retain control over how resources are used. Such self-initiated collective action may or may not challenge existing inequitable distributions of wealth and power.

Fourth, a political decision to encourage and operate through local organizations, particularly NGOs, can overcome some of the challenges of transforming secret government organizations into people-sensitive entities. This is about delegating all roles and resources to these organizations and creating adequate mechanisms for collaboration and consultation, monitoring, and assessment.

Eventually, by making reasonable use of necessary communication and information technology, people's engagement can be increased. On the one hand, the two-way flow of information between rural people and local organizations and, on the other, policymakers and planners must be as efficient as possible. It means using a range of communication channels, from regional and district meetings and conferences, to using, where appropriate, modern electronic media. Considering innovative solutions to resource management problems can require access to important digital or other databases containing information of local significance by local people, directly or through intermediaries. These data can be collected from aerial photography or satellite imaging, or from the locals themselves. Information on prospective improved technologies for agriculture and resource management that have been tested in other similar environments is also relevant.

2.8.5 Policies Specifically Fixated on the Use of Natural Resources and Environmental Protection

Although many of the above policies will have significant implications on the use of rural resources and thc environment, there are a number of policy measures that focus specifically on these areas. These are included:

- Direct government action;
- Control instruments;
- Economic incentives.

2.8.5.1 Direct Government Action

During which rural resource depletion and environmental pollution can arise due to market failure, governments may act directly to try to correct these problems. Governments may, for example, support, and conduct work on land preservation and restoration. These projects will often be on public land, but may also be on private land, with or without the landholders' permission, depending on the externalities' perceived severity. Likewise, governments may choose to make more intensive use of unused land or underutilized land to alleviate the pressure on existing agricultural areas. This will likely require work to clear the land, maybe form it, and build the infrastructure necessary, such as highways, communications systems, irrigation facilities, and drainage systems. Many land settlement schemes are based on these kinds of public spending, and often include additional public support to enable settlers to establish themselves in the new environment.

Both land enhancement and land settlement schemes must be subject to careful prior assessment, including both environmental impact assessments and analysis of social cost-benefit. There are also questions on the extent of cost recovery from recipients (or polluters) for such works. If the beneficiaries are prosperous, there would appear to be no reason why they should not have to pay a large proportion of the cost. However, where the benefit of relatively poor smallholders may not be adequate to recover costs. In addition, it may not be feasible to formulate a cost-effective way to recover costs, especially when the beneficiaries are unknown or widely dispersed. For example, how are taxes to be collected on recipients of measures to ensure cleaner air?

Although nation-states that participate in rural production growth initiatives, they also generally invest in resource protection measures such as setting up and maintaining conservation areas and national parks. Actions to preserve the genetic diversity of useful and potentially useful genetic material are important for sustainable agriculture. For plants, genetic material can be preserved in forms such as tissue culture, seed banks, conservation plots for plant varieties, botanical gardens, or reserves for flora. It is harder to preserve animal genetic material. Nonetheless, on experimental farms or in conservation areas, parks or zoos, small herds or flocks of endangered races or species may be kept. For some time it may be possible to store frozen sperm, ova or fertilized embryo. Governments may also choose to pay farmers or other farmers to continue farming endangered plant or animal species, or to preserve reserves of flora or fauna on their property.

2.8.5.2 Control Instruments

There is a broad range of potential control tools that governments can consider using. This requires laws, restrictions, and bans on certain forms of energy and farming practices. For example, it may be forbidden or strictly controlled to use certain chemicals, such as unique toxic sprays. Farmers may be penalized for certain procedures that are considered to be harmful to the environment, such as crop residue burning. Instead, they may need to follow other practices, such as managing noxious insects or weeds, under the risk of a fine. Governments and government agencies can monitor the allocation of certain assets. For example, quotas for water which irrigators can draw from a public irrigation system, a river, or an underground source are generally allocated. The number and size of trees they can cut can be limited to users of a forest resource. Quotas on the size and composition of fish catches or on the fishing gear that can be used are gradually being implemented.

As mentioned above, the development of such rules and regulations by governments is one thing, but it is not always easy to enforce them. The private benefit to be gained by breaking or 'bending' the rules can be important for many individual resource users. There may be a significant level of non-compliance. There is also a risk that some resource users, particularly the more affluent, can bribe officials to disregard regulatory violations. If such bribery is prevalent, the whole system of organized government may even be compromised. In addition, controlling enforcement is likely to be very complicated and expensive due to the geographically dispersed nature of agriculture, forestry, and, in general, fishing. While it is easy for governments to devise rules and regulations to make more environmentally friendly use of rural and fishery resources, they may not always work as the policymaker's hope. Therefore, it may be best to look first at ways to promote sustainability using not so hard to implement economic incentives.

2.8.5.3 Economic Incentives

According to Markandya (1994, p. 19): there is indeed a vast array of policy instruments that can be used by governments to implement an environmental management approach to economic incentives. Some of them are more applicable to the management of natural resources, others to the protection of the environment. Others apply to both (pricing of products and inputs, taxes, bonds on performance, etc.). Both are based on the same concepts of "getting the right prices" and making the right to property clear, safe, and tradable. Some operate through existing markets (e.g., product pricing), while others mimic the market or attempt to create new markets (e.g., permits for tradable pollution). In several situations, such as forest policy and hazardous waste management, all sets of methods need to be used to produce cost-effective and efficient performance. A forest policy economic incentive program would include at least concession bidding, commodity pricing, resource taxes (royalties), likely performance bonds, and replanting investment opportunities. Instead, Markandya gives a list of the key instruments and a brief description of each instrument. Panayotou (1994a) offers another, rather more concise overview and related set of definitions. Some of the steps mentioned were specified in the above discussion, but others did not:

- **Tradable Resource Shares:** Assignment of a transferable right to a percentage share of an 'invisible' or 'uncertain' common property asset, such as fisheries.

- **Individual Tradable Quotas:** Allocation of the transferable quota for a fixed amount of the assets of common property.
- **Tradable Development Rights:** The grant of the right to develop a resource in another area in return for the concession of the right to develop a specific asset in a special conservation interest area.
- **Tradable Emission Permits:** Allows polluters to obtain air or water rights, such rights which are economically valuable because of the possibility of selling them to others. An example of this is the manure permits issued to Dutch farmers.
- **Environmental Taxes:** Taxes on goods that are harmful to the environment, such as petroleum products and pesticides, to limit their use.
- **Resource Taxes:** Establishing royalty, license fees, or other charges on government-owned or controlled assets at rates representing the true value of resources.
- **Effluent or Emission Taxes:** The popular 'polluter pays' rule, with charges best set in line with the true costs of the damage caused to the environment.
- **User Charges:** Setting charges for irrigation water, waste disposal or other services or inputs delivered by the public sector, primarily as a means of recovering costs, but also to reflect approximate actual costs.
- **Deposit Refund Schemes:** Presumptive charges on goods designed to shift blame to manufacturers or customers for regulating emissions. Sources include reimbursable deposits on pesticide bottles or batteries for automobiles.
- **Environmental Bonds:** Economic instruments that ensure adequate funds are available to repair damage to the environment, useful in mining or forestry, for example.
- **Subsidies:** Financial assistance to encourage sustainable behavior, such as promoting resource management investment.

Markandya maintains that all the methods he lists have been used in one country or another, and they should be familiar to policymakers concerned with sustainable agriculture. Not all of them are immediately relevant to the management of agricultural and rural resources, but there are many. For example, it is possible to make allocated water rights tradable. In addition, tradable rights could be conditional on a resource share in areas where water availability is unknown. On the other extreme, some of the proposed steps are hard to use. In developed countries, it has proven both difficult to implement environmental taxes to effectively control emissions and pricing government-owned property to represent their true values. Therefore, it is unclear whether such measures can be used in LDCs where administrative structures are less well defined.

3

ECONOMIC ANALYSIS OF PUBLIC POLICIES

CONTENTS

3.1 The Neoclassical View of Market Economies 46

3.2 Fundamental Economic Theorems of Welfare 48

3.3 Market Failures and Government Involvement Explanations 50

3.4 Intervention by The Government In The Economy 52

3.5 Welfare Economics 53

3.6 Demand Functions and Consumer Surplus 53

3.7 Correct Measures of Welfare Change: The Equivalent and Compensating Variations 55

3.8 The Relationship Between Change In Consumer Surplus, ΔCS, EV, and CV 58

3.9 Marginal Cost, Supply Function, And Producer's Surplus 59

3.10 Aggregation And The Difference Between Profits and Rents 61

3.11 Comparative Advantages And Gains From Trade 62

3.1 THE NEOCLASSICAL VIEW OF MARKET ECONOMIES

The extent of government intervention in agriculture may vary by creating incentives from direct control of the means of production, as in centrally planned economies, to indirect market intervention. Here we will analyze measures in the market economy as types of state intervention. What we mean by the need for many clarifications in the market economy. The "market" is a broad concept that includes the activities of purchasing and selling commodity transactions that together lead to price formation, so it does not have to be intended as the actual physical place where the transactions take place. Market economies are those where prices are the result of the decision of households and individuals to interact with production and consumption, rather than being set institutionally. Nonetheless, there are many ways the government can influence, and in some cases even in market economies effectively set the price levels. We would discuss some of them and see how many of those policies will likely have side effects, such as public spending or creating a difference between the price paid by consumers and the price earned by manufacturers.

Consider a very easy, two-person economy, say A and B. Each of them has a specified quantity of one of two products, X, and Y; so that X^A and Y^A are the endowments of individual A, and X^B and Y^B are the endowments of individual B. Therefore, the net wealth of this country is given by the quantities $X = X^A + X^B$ and $Y = Y^A + Y^B$. Let us assume also that the two individuals have preferences over the two goods, defined by the respective utility functions $U^A(X, Y)$ and $U^B(X, Y)$. How can we describe a possible equilibrium of this economy? In other words, if these people are left free to exchange their possessions, will they find an agreement on a rate at which to exchange, say, good X for good Y, (that is, a price for Y in terms of X) and how much will they actually trade?

Using the standard consumer behavior theory, the answer can be found using the Edge worth Box analytical tool. Imagine drawing a rectangular box of precisely X and Y dimensions. Then, the initial endowment can simply be represented by a point in the box where with coordinates X^A and Y^A (when measured from the lower-left corner) or X^B and Y^B (if measured from the upper right corner) (Figure 3.1).

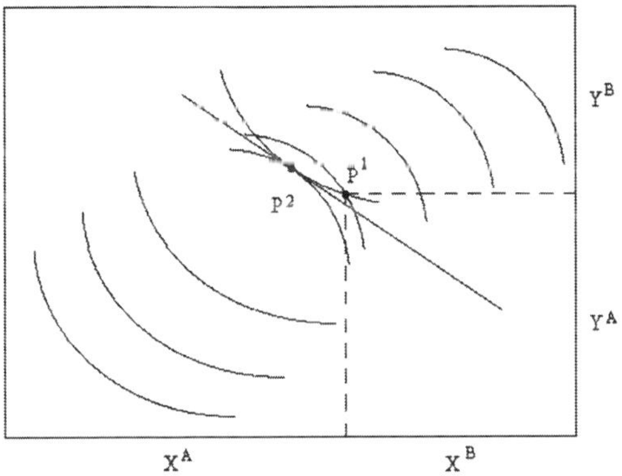

Figure 3.1. The Edgeworth box.

Source: Frank Ellis (2014).

When you look at the origin in the lower-left corner, the box can be viewed as the space for person A's consumption opportunities and you can draw the curves of indifference for A as you studied in the course of microeconomics. Instead, when the origin is located in the upper right corner, the curves of indifference for individual B can be interpreted as if they were "upside down," so going from right to left and upwards would mean the supply of goods for individual B and thus increasing it. With reference to Figure 3.1, the initial endowment for our simple economy is represented by point P^1. There will be indifference curves passing through point P^1 for both individual A and individual B. Imagine now moving along the indifference curve of individual A from point P^1 to pint P^2. What does it mean in terms of the re-allocation of the two goods? Well, it means that some of good X has been transferred from A to B in exchange for some of good Y. In fact, at point P^2, A will have more of Y and less of X. But notice that we are still on the same indifference curve for A, which means that A's level of utility is not changed. Individual A is as better off at point P^2 as he was at point P^1. However, point P^2 corresponds to a higher indifference curve for individual B than before. Moving from point P^1 to point P^2 has caused an increase in the utility level for B. This simple Example is meant to show that point P^1 was not an ideal resource allocation, as there are other points where the usefulness of one economy member could be increased without decreasing the usefulness of the other member.

Points such P^2 are called equilibriums of the economy, or also optimal allocation points. The attribute optimal corresponds exactly to what is defined as a "Pareto optimum" point, that is a point from where it is impossible to move without reducing the utility of at least one individual. At point P^2, the marginal rate of substitution of good X for good Y is the same for both A and B. In other words, the two members of our simple economy have found an agreement on a rate at The Edgeworth Box which to exchange X for Y, that is, they have found an equilibrium price.

According to neoclassical economics, the basic concept of a market economy is a situation for which all individuals in the economy are left free to trade anything they want to maximize their individual utility. If nothing prevents the exchanges from taking place, whenever two individuals would find it profitable to engage in an exchange (as it was for our individuals A and B in moving from point P^1 to point P^2) they will do so. Once there are no opportunities left for mutually beneficial exchanges, the economy would reach what is called a competitive equilibrium, which is optimal (according to the Pareto criterion) by definition.

3.2 FUNDAMENTAL ECONOMIC THEOREMS OF WELFARE

The theoretical model which we introduced in the previous section has been generalized to more complex cases where there are more than two persons in which production is allowed, in the sense that the original endowments of production factors (land, labor, natural resources) can be used for transformation into other products that are then used for consumption. In this more general case, a competitive equilibrium means that:

- The rate of transformation of any two factors of production is the same in all production activities.
- The marginal rate of substitution of any two consumption goods is the same for all consumption activities.
- The set of those rates of transformation and marginal rates of substitution constitutes the equilibrium set of competitive prices of the economy.

We are not going to go into the details of the analytical proofs of such statements, but the basic concept is the same that characterizes our simple example above: if nothing prevents individuals from engaging in exchange and production activities, they will do so until all opportunities for further mutually beneficial exchanges are exhausted. If this happens, a rational equilibrium has been achieved and, by implication, it will lead to an optimal allocation of resources in the economy by Pareto. This last definition is sometimes viewed as a "theorem" in economics texts. It is considered the first fundamental theorem of welfare economics and reads as follows: "Every competitive equilibrium is optimal for Pareto under a set of specific assumptions." Nonetheless, it should be clear that the correlation between competitive equilibrium and optimality of Pareto is supported by the competitive equilibrium and need not be proven as a real theorem would be necessary. More interesting is probably the second fundamental theorem of welfare economics, according to which: 'for any initial resource allocation, there is at least one competitive equilibrium, which means that it does not matter from where you start, in terms of initial resource allocation, the economy can always achieve a competitive equilibrium, which is an 'optimal' allocation of resources. I put the word optimal between quotes because I want to emphasize that it is a very specific type of optimality and something that may correspond to situations that none of us will probably regard as "optimal" in any way. As an example, let us return for a moment to our economy made of only two people, and consider an initial endowment of $X^A = X$, $X^B = 0$; $Y^A = Y$ and $Y^B = 0$. (In other words, A gets everything, and B gets nothing). This allocation would match the point in the Edgeworth box's upper right corner. It is easy to see that such a point is indeed a "competitive equilibrium," because it will never be in A's individual interest to move from there, given the total availability of resources. It would mean giving up one or both goods in exchange for nothing. In other words, without making A worse off, there is no way to move from such a point, and in this sense, the point is optimal for Pareto. I am sure, however, that none of us would regard such a situation as "optimal."

In practice, the principle of Pareto optimality refers to an economic efficiency theory: a condition that is not ideal for Pareto is definitely an inefficient system, in the sense that there are alternate distributions and resource uses that can lead to higher overall levels of aggregate utility for society as a whole. It is interested only with efficiency and cannot accommodate potential concerns about the distribution of utility among individuals, which is included in the equity concerns category. Nevertheless, some economists have repeatedly invoked the concept of economic efficiency as the fundamental justification for the laissez-faire view of state intervention in the economy, a view which dates back at least to the time when Adam Smith wrote his treaty on the nation's wealth. It has since been the flag of many politicians and economists, particularly those critics of the communist type's centrally planned economies. This view was opposed by a number of other politicians and economists and instead proposed an active role for the state in the economy. The next session will illustrate the arguments put forward to support such an alternative view of the state intervention's role.

3.3 MARKET FAILURES AND GOVERNMENT INVOLVEMENT EXPLANATIONS

It is a fact that the free market and laissez-faire forms of economic policies have often contributed to conditions deemed sub-optimal from many points of view, even from strictly efficient considerations. Therefore, by acknowledging fundamentally the theoretical argument found in the neoclassical theory of competitive equilibrium, many economists have tried to study in more detail the possible reasons why the theory of competitive equilibrium. The factors that were found to prevent the economy from settling on efficient, productive balances are called market failures, suggesting the presence of something that prevents economic agents from participating in all profitable trades. As a consequence, the economy will reach equilibriums that are not efficient and thus not potentially productive if any of these deficiencies occur. Some of the economic literature's documented market failures can be defined as:

- Lack of competition;
- Presence of externalities and incomplete property rights;
- Presence of public goods and common property resources;
- Incomplete and asymmetric information.

3.3.1 Non-Competitive Markets

If one side of the deal has market power, the resulting cost does not meet the total cost of production, which is necessary to achieve competitive performance. Part of the revenue from selling the commodity in a monopoly position will be pure rent rather than usual returns on production factors, thereby breaking down one of the necessary conditions for quality. As a result, less products are sold at a higher price.

3.3.2 Presence of Externalities and Incomplete Property Rights

An externality is an effect on other entities that are directly involved in the process of some production or consumption action. Typically, the external gain or costs associated with the externality are not known or borne by the participants involved in the transaction, and as such, their presence is not expressed in the equilibrium value, which does not capture external benefits and external costs, resulting in a socially inefficient allocation of resources. Ronald Coase related the issue of externalities to the issue of incomplete property rights by proposing that any inefficiency caused by the existence of externalities could be resolved by the sufficient interpretation of property rights, which would allow external effects to be internalized. The most common example is a factory whose activity releases air pollution that causes environmental harm. This is an externality if the company owner is not held liable for the harm caused by pollution to the general population. The wasteful consequence is that too much pollution will be generated because the producer doesn't pay the relative costs to society, and society can't force the corporation to reduce pollution because there is no property right to clean air.

3.3.3 Public Goods and Common Property Resources

When a good is characterized by non-exclusiveness, non-rivalism is defined as a public good rather than a private good. It is not possible to define private property rights to public goods, and therefore there are no opportunities to exchange them. When left to the private initiative, public services such as public defense, education, and universal health care (such as immunization programs), preservation of the natural environment, etc. will be under-provided. The explanation is that it will not be profitable for any private operator to provide a good that other people can enjoy without charging.

3.3.4 Incomplete and Asymmetric Information

Welfare economics theorems suggest that people are aware of all the trading incentives that exist in the economy in order to identify and leverage those mutually beneficial to each other. It is a very strong belief of the fact that is not accurate. For example, the production uncertainty we discussed yesterday which prevent producers from making the most efficient input usage decision. And that's all because of insufficient data about the likelihood of the bad weather occurring. Also, when the benefits of such commodities stretch over a long period of time (e.g., the exploitation of forestry or other natural resources such as oil reserves), ignorance of the possible future benefits of such resources that contributes to over-exploitation in the present. Such are all examples of insufficient data if the agents who have to determine are not fully aware of the advantages and costs of a given economic action. The existence of asymmetric information is often very common, including the fact that the two parties involved in the transaction may have different levels of awareness about the transaction's benefits and costs. Asymmetric data contributes to anomalies such as moral hazard and adverse selection that are extensively studied for contract development in particular, as well as insurance and labor contracts. The existence of asymmetric information causes additional costs associated with the need to track the insured or the worker's operation, which would not occur if the data was symmetrical.

3.4 INTERVENTION BY THE GOVERNMENT IN THE ECONOMY

To correct market failures and increase efficiency, government intervention may be justified. For example, the introduction of taxes on polluting practices may be intended to address externalities. Public provision of public goods can correct private operators for the supply of such goods. The emergence of asymmetric information can be resolved by public contracts and subsidized coverage, etc. One can think of a form of public intervention that could, in theory, compensate for the negative effect for any market failure. Please note, however, that the correction of market failures only makes it possible to achieve resource efficiency. These types of intervention do not address issues of unequal net benefit distribution—i.e., the equity concern. This leads to a whole range of other possible forms of public intervention whose objective is to redistribute income directly or indirectly to achieve a higher level of security in society. To sum up, it is very unlikely that the government's laissez-faire or non-intervention in market operation will achieve even the efficient economic use of resources, not to mention equity. For this reason, the extent of state involvement in the economy can be very high even in capitalist economies, as opposed to the traditional view that widespread state involvement in the economy is typical of socialist economies. In short, it may be necessary to involve the state in the economy:

- To correct for market failures;
- To achieve nonefficiency objectives.

Wide participation by the government, however, does not automatically mean improved performance or equity outcomes. The concept of the state that we assume throughout the discussion is very idealistic and abstract: we imagine the state as a benevolent, well-informed, and technically equipped agent able to correct market failures without inducing other forms of "failures." Actually, the government and state are made up of people who can suffer from the same knowledge problems that affect ordinary citizens. In other words, the state can be as inefficient as the private market because of many phenomena called "state failures" (Ellis, p. 10–13). The most widely discussed form of state failure when recent economic development literature is the so-called "rent-seeking" or directly unproductive profit-seeking (DUP) activities. In evaluating programs, we need to be aware of these issues. In other words, in the policy analysis, one should ask:

- Does the policy address equity objectives, efficiency objectives, or both?
- If it addresses efficiency, which form of market failure it tries to correct for?
- If the policy requires direct involvement of the state in the market, are there other less intrusive, more private means of achieving the same objective?
- If not, which potential forms of "state failure" might be involved and how can they be prevented?

3.5 WELFARE ECONOMICS

In the section above, we have seen many arguments on why the government should interfere in the economy. The next step will be to try and understand what happens to all the agents involved when the government takes action to change a certain market's natural outcome. The key question we're going to be dealing with is: "Who's winning? Who is losing? To how much is it?" The answer to this question is at the core of the study of the policy effect. Two welfare economics principles will be used mainly throughout this course to address the basic question and we will first explain them.

3.6 DEMAND FUNCTIONS AND CONSUMER SURPLUS

Referring to consumer behavior economic theory. The solution to the problem of utility maximization subject to budget constraint leads to the derivation of the demand function of an individual, i.e., a relationship between quantity consumed and price. Using general notation, the problem is:

max $U(x_1, x_2, x_3\ldots\ldots, x_N)$

Subject to:

$p_1x_1 + p_2x_2 + p_3x_3 \ldots\ldots, + p_Nx_N < y$

Leads to a solution in terms of the optimal quantity demanded of all goods:

$x_1^* = f_1(p_1, p_2 \ldots, p_N, y)$, $x_2^* = f_2(p_1, p_2 \ldots, p_N, y)$, $\ldots\ldots\ldots\ldots x_N^* = f_N(p_1, p_2 \ldots, p_N, y)$

which is a system of demand functions, where the quantity demanded of a certain good is expressed as a function of the price of that good, the prices of other goods, and the level of income.

Any demand function can be represented in a graph, and this graph can be used to determine what happens when one of the independent variables changes to the quantity requested. For example, with reference to Figure 3.2 which depicts the demand function for the good x_1 suppose that the consumer faces a price level p_1° Suppose also that the level of the only other good is p_2° and the income is y°.

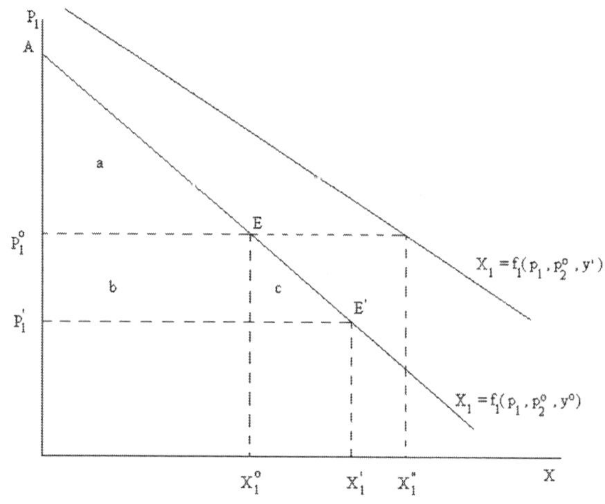

Figure 3.2. Demand function and consumer's surplus.

Source: Frank Ellis (2014).

Then, the quantity consumed will be $x_1^\circ = f_1(p_1^\circ, p_2^\circ, y)$, as indicated by point E in the graph. What happens if, for any reason, the price falls to a level p_1? Usually, what we would expect is that, given a lower price, the consumer will demand more of the good. The demand function tells us that he will demand a quantity $x_1' = f_1(p_1{}' \, p_2^\circ, y^\circ) > x_1^\circ$. How can we analyze the effect of a change in the level of income? We have to realize that an increase in income from, say y° to y,' will determine a shift of the demand function from $x_1 = f_1(p_1, p_2^\circ, y^\circ)$ to $x_1 = f_1(p_1, p_2^\circ, y')$. Thus, if the price of good x_1 remains p_1°, the new quantity demand will be;

$x_1'' = f_1(p_1^\circ, p_2^\circ, y') > x_1^\circ$

We could do the same exercise by changing the price of the other good, p_2 and predict what would be the change induced in the demand for x_1. In short, by understanding the demand function, we can forecast the increase in demand quantity induced by any price and/or income changes. Observing how the quantity required changes, however, does not tell us what happens in terms of usefulness, that is, if the user is better off, worse off, or has the same utility as before after the change. This is why economists have described the so-called consumer surplus that is intended as a monetary measure of the utility associated with a certain option of consumption.

Let us look again at the graph in Figure 3.2. If the price of good 1 is p_1° the consumer would buy x_1° and will spend a total of p_1° x_1°. However, if the price were higher, the consumer would have still bought some of the good, which means that the consumer was willing to pay more than p_1° or quantities of the good less than x_1°. This means also that, by buying all x_1° at the price p_1° the consumer is receiving a benefit equal to the area comprised between the demand function and the horizontal line passing through p_1°, which is indicated as an area 'a' in the graph. This area defines the consumer's surplus, which is a monetary measure of the utility associated with the purchase of a good at a fixed price. With this concept, we are now able to answer the question: what happens to the consumer's welfare when the price of good 1 changes from p_1° to p_1'?The effect of this change in price is an increase in consumer surplus from the area a to area a+ b+ c, that is a net increase of area b+ c. Notice that this increase in consumer's surplus can be seen as composed by two parts: area b, which is the surplus derived to the consumer because he can now buy the old amount x_1° at a lower price, and area c, which is generated because now the consumer will buy more of the good.

3.7 CORRECT MEASURES OF WELFARE CHANGE: THE EQUIVALENT AND COMPENSATING VARIATIONS

The surplus of the market is an appealing indicator of money-related welfare shift because it is easily determined when demand elasticity is known. His definition as the region below ordinary demand, however, poses some conceptual problems, and its use may decide some errors in assessing the actual monetary value of income changes. Luckily, economists have come up with two alternative social policy measures, called the comparable variation and the compensating variation. First, consider what a correct measure of welfare change should be for a consumer to describe them. It should measure the change in utility level caused by the policy to be evaluated. However, measuring the change in utility level as measured by the difference in utility function values would give an undetermined response, since utility function is an ordinary measure. In other words, utility functions serve only to rank possible choices, and even if they express utility levels on different scales, two different utility functions that generate the same ranking are perfectly equivalent. Suppose, for example, that there are only two products and you have two separate utility functions, defined as:

$U(x_1, x_2) = (x_1x_2)^2$

and

$V(x_1, x_2) = x_1x_2$

It is easy to prove that these two utility functions generate the same ranking of all possible consumption bundles (x,y). For example, consider the values reported in the Table 3.1.

Table 3.1. Ranking of All Possible Consumption Bundles of (x, y)

x_1	x_2	$U(x_1, x_2)$	$V(x_1, x_2)$	**Ranking**
1	2	4	2	3
3	1	9	3	2
2	2	16	4	1
1	1	1	1	4

As can be seen, the ranking of alternatives induced by the two utility functions is the same, even though the level of utility is measured by different numbers (Figure 3.3). If we were to measure the change inutility induced by adding one unit of good y to the bundle (1,1), we will have:

$U = U(1,2) - U(1,1) = 4 - 1 = 3$

$\Delta V = V(1,2) - V(1,1) = 2 - 1 = 1.$

That's why we can't just use the difference in the cost of the utility function as an indicator of the welfare shift. The corresponding variance and the compensating variation are two better measures. The equivalent variation of a certain policy (e.g., a change in price levels) is defined as the amount of money that will generate the same increase in utility caused by the policy when it is paid to the consumer. In Figure 3.3, its representation can be seen graphically.

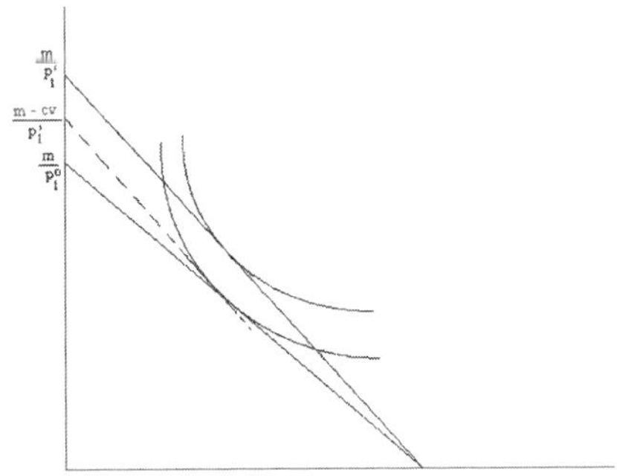

Figure 3.3. The compensating variation of a reduction in price.

Source: Frank Ellis (2014).

In the graph, we are considering a reduction of price from p1° to p1'. As a consequence, the budget line would rotate, and the consumer would reach a higher indifference curve. The equivalent variation, EV, is the quantity of money which, added to income while keeping the price constant to the original level, would bring the consumer to the same higher in difference curve (Figure 3.4).

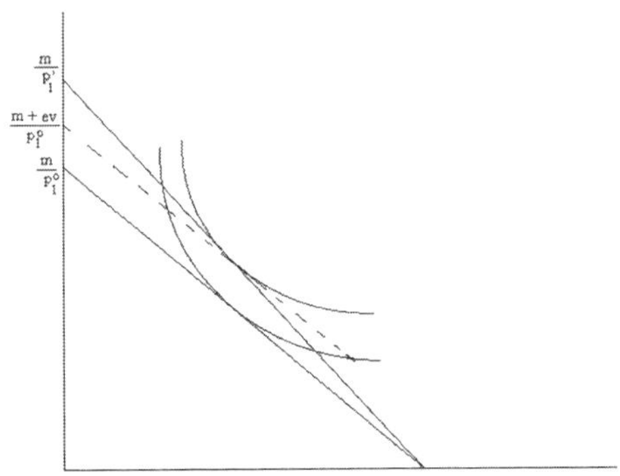

Figure 3.4. The equivalent variation for a reduction in price.

Source: Frank Ellis (2014).

Alternatively, the compensating variation of a certain policy is defined as the amount of money that would carry the consumer back to the old utility rate if taken away from the consumer after the policy implementation. The graph in Figure 3.4 illustrates the compensating variation for a reduction in price from $p_1°$ to p_1.' It can be shown that the EV (equivalent variation) and CV (compensating variation) can be measured as areas to the left of the compensated demand functions and included between the two price levels. The difference between EV and CV is in which of the utility level is taken as a reference: for EV. We consider the final utility level u,' while for CV we consider the initial utility level, u°.

3.8 THE RELATIONSHIP BETWEEN CHANGE IN CONSUMER SURPLUS, ΔCS, EV, AND CV

There is a reliable relationship between the product surplus shift, the corresponding variance, and the compensating variation that can be seen in the chart below. The increase in market surplus is often greater than the compensating variation, and smaller than the comparable variation, in order to minimize prices, which implies a positive impact on utility. On the other hand, it can be shown that the change in consumer surplus is larger than the equivalent variation for policies that determine a reduction in utility, and smaller than the compensating variation. In other words:

1. CV <Δ CS < EV, for policies that increase utility.
2. EV <Δ CS < CV, for policies that decrease utility.

The difference between the change in consumer surplus and the two correct measures of welfare change, EV, and CV, depends on the income effect: if the income effect is large, then approximating either the CV or the EV with the change in consumer surplus will determine a sensible error (Figure 3.5).

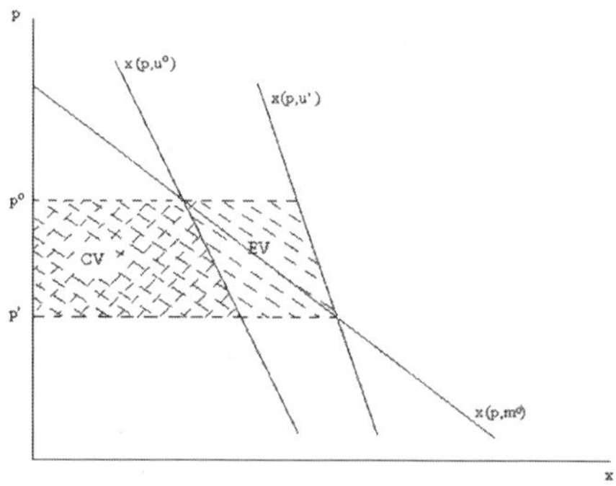

Figure 3.5. Change in consumer surplus Variation, equivalent Variation, and compensating variation.

Source: Frank Ellis (2014).

One other question is related to which one of the two measures, EV or CV, one wants to use. Recall that the difference between the two is the utility level taken as reference: the CV is calculated with reference to the initial utility level, u^0, the EV with reference to the new utility level, u.' Thus, using the CV as a measure of welfare change, implicitly amounts, if consumers have the right to the ante-policy situation and to the initial level of utility (Figure 3.6).

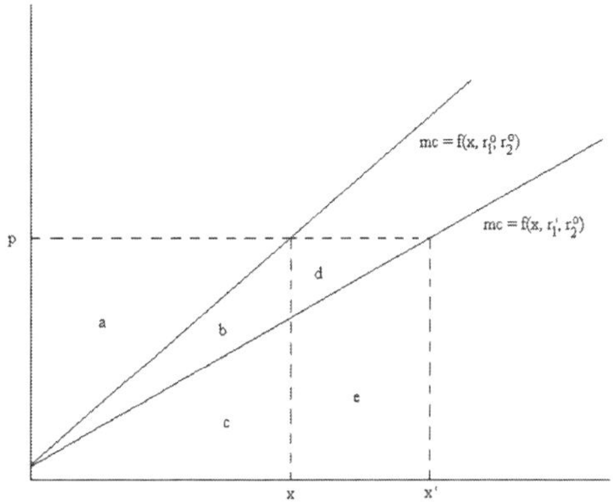

Figure 3.6. Marginal cost curves and producer's surplus.

Source: Frank Ellis (2014).

Using the EV, on the contrary, is equivalent to assume that consumers have the right to the post-policy, final level of utility. The one-point worth of attention in the context of a course on agricultural policies in developing countries is that, by using Δ CS instead of CV as a measure of welfare change, one overestimates the benefits and underestimates the costs of the policy to the consumers. And, as we have seen, the bias will be relevant whenever the income effect of the change is higher. For agricultural prices, for example, the bias will be higher for poor consumers which spend most of their income in agricultural products. In the rest of these notes, we will continue to use the change in consumer surplus to indicate the effects of policy on consumers. We must remember, however, that it could mean an imprecise assessment of the actual welfare effect in the cases noted above.

3.9 MARGINAL COST, SUPPLY FUNCTION, AND PRODUCER'S SURPLUS

Consumers' equivalent in the market is the firms. Each company will have a supply function in a competitive industry, that is, a relationship between the quantities offered for market sale and the price. With regard to the economics of production, the quantity offered by a profit-maximizing, competitive company is the quantity for which price is the marginal cost. This means that the supply function coincides with the company's marginal cost function, which is a function of the output level and the input prices in general: mc = f (x, r_1, r_2, r_3, ………, r_M). The graph in Figure 3.6 represents one such function, where, for simplicity, only two inputs are considered. Consider first the case when the prices of the two inputs are fixed at levels $r_1°$ and $r_2°$. When the price is p, the firm will supply an amount x: f(p, $r_1°$, $r_2°$) = p. The total revenues from this choice will be equal to the area a + b + c. However, area b + c corresponds to the total variable cost of producing an amount x, so that only the area a is actual benefits (more precisely, it includes profits and returns to the fixed factors of production, as land and fixed investments). Such an area can be used as a monetary measure of the benefits that the firm will receive by selling the amount x at price p (Figure 3.7).

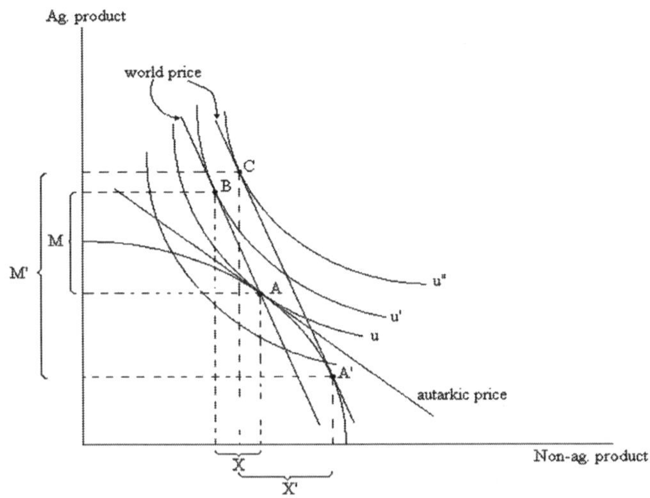

Figure 3.7. The transformation curve and the autarkic equilibrium.

Source: Frank Ellis (2014).

The area 'a' in the graph, that is the area comprised between the horizontal line passing through the price level and the marginal cost curve, defines the producer's surplus. With this definition, we can now try and calculate what happens if, for example, the price of one of the inputs falls, say from $r_1°$ to $r_2°$. The new marginal cost curve will now become mc = f(x,

r_1,' r_2°), the quantity offered for sale will increase up to x,' and the producer's surplus will increase by the area b + d. Notice that we can interpret this change in consumer's surplus as made of two components: the area b, which correspond to the reduction in costs to produce the old amount x, plus the area d, which is the additional surplus generated by the fact that now the firm will increase production up to x.'

3.10 AGGREGATION AND THE DIFFERENCE BETWEEN PROFITS AND RENTS

Throughout the previous discussion on the surplus of consumers and producers, we considered, respectively, an individual product and a single company. In fact, the theoretical basis for considering the surplus of the market as a monetary measure of utility is strictly true only for an individual demand. And, similarly, the supply function only corresponds to an individual, competitive firm's marginal cost. However, when we evaluate policies, we will always apply to the entire market: we will consider aggregate or economy demand and supply rather than the independent demand and supply function. It is then fair to question if the concepts of consumer and producer surpluses can still be used as the areas between the function of demand or price, and between value and marginal price as valid welfare reform measures. It turns out that under some restrictive assumptions, it is still legitimate to do so. Based on the assumption that all consumers are identical, a valid monetary measure of the sum of the utility of individuals is the area below the market demand function and above the price level. Generally speaking, we should remember that direct usefulness comparison is not legitimate, since usefulness is just an ordinary measure. Simply summarizing the surpluses of the individual consumer, as we implicitly do when we measure the aggregate consumer surplus as the area below market demand, we neglect the possibility that consumers may be different and that, for example, the same reduction in income may be more onerous for poor consumers than for rich consumers. In other words, we neglect potential equity issues by only measuring the aggregate consumer surplus.

Things are less troublesome for the aggregate supply function: if the manufacturing sector is efficient, the aggregate supply is essentially the horizontal sum of the individual supply functions, even if companies vary in the nature of their marginal costs. Nonetheless, another subject that deserves consideration is the difference between income and returns to fixed production factors, or what we can call rentals. In the long run, there will be no profits for a competitive industry, and the whole area above the marginal cost curve is merely rents representing returns to the fixed factors. If the businessman is also the owner of the fixed output variable (for example, if the farmers own the land they grow), then there is no practical difference between income and rents: The same person will be compensated by both. If, instead, the land is owned by a landlord who rents it to the farmer, and if the supply of land is inelastic, any change in the surplus of the producer would eventually be transferred entirely to the landlord. Once again, equity concerns may need to be addressed.

3.11 COMPARATIVE ADVANTAGES AND GAINS FROM TRADE

The concept of comparative advantages and gains from trade and specialization is one last element in welfare economics. Let's use the principles of product transition curve and curves of indifference in microeconomics to explain it. Assume that the economy has a fixed amount of two resources: land and labor. And also believe that it is possible to use the land we labor to manufacture agricultural and industrial goods. The conversion curve shown in the graph below reflects the productive combinations of agricultural and industrial output that can be achieved by using the fixed amount of land and labor available in the economy. If a set of indifference curves can represent the structure of the country's preferences, then the maximum social welfare will be achieved, in autarky, at a point corresponding to the highest possible curve of indifference that the country can reach, given the availability of resources and technology. Also, the common tangent to the curve of transformation and the curve of indifference is the autarkic price ratio of agricultural and non-agricultural goods.

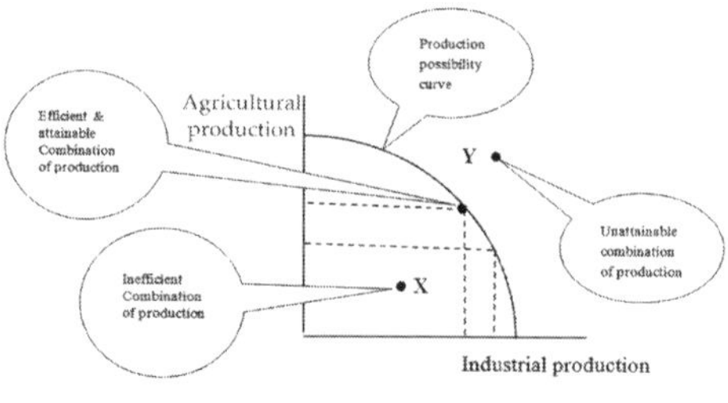

Figure 3.8. Production possibility frontier.

Source: Frank Ellis (2014).

Now, suppose the relative price of agricultural and non-agricultural products on the world market is different, as indicated by the lower dotted line, for example. This would mean that agricultural product on the world market is valued relatively less than it is valued on the domestic market, and that the country has a comparative advantage in producing non-agricultural products (Figure 3.8).If the country opens up to international trade, then exporting some of the non-agricultural products on the world market and importing some agricultural products would be easy. This trade, which corresponds to moving up demand, by exporting a certain quantity of non-agricultural products and by importing a certain quantity of agricultural products, which would allow social welfare to increase. This rise in welfare can be viewed as export benefits that can be made even if the country does not adjust its production schedule. However, there are additional gains with an open market (OM) that can be taken advantage of through specialization. If the country rearranges its production activities and moves along the transformation curve, exports, and imports can be increased with a further improvement in social welfare. These additional gains are due to production specialization in the activity for which the country has a comparative advantage. In an open economy, there are always gains from trade and specialization. If domestic prices are equal to world prices, the only condition under which such gains do not exist. Because of this, it is usually conceived that the opportunity cost in an economy for domestic resources is measured by the respective world market price. World prices are thus a benchmark, which is a point of reference, for assessing how much prices are distorted within a country (this is at the core of analyzes carried out using the policy analysis matrix (PAM)) (Figure 3.9).

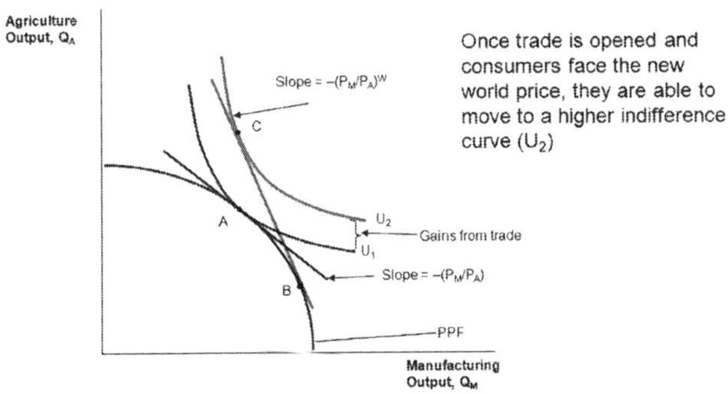

Figure 3.9. Production possibility frontier with trade.

Source: Frank Ellis (2014).

4

PROCESS OF POLICY ANALYSIS

CONTENTS

4.1 Policy Analysis 66
4.2 Alternative Frameworks For Policy Analysis 66
4.3 Phases of Policy Analysis 68
4.4 The Policy Analysis Matrix (PAM) 73

4.1 POLICY ANALYSIS

Policy analysis can be defined as the technical and economic research that considers, assesses, and compares alternative policy instruments in terms of net benefits and evaluates the effect of the policy chosen at a later stage and offers lessons from its implementation for the future. It is, therefore, the responsibility of policy analysts, who are not actually responsible for the possible implementation of the policy, to direct the decision-making process which policymakers can accomplish. Proper policy analysis requires a sound understanding as to the general conditions of the economy of the conditions of the sector for which the policy is intended. A sound knowledge of the technological and natural processes involved in the manufacturing processes is also an important advantage in helping to evaluate the physical effects of public intervention along with the monetary ones. In determining the overall effects of a price policy, the agronomic, economic, and social aspects of the sector are involved. No single book like this can provide all the information needed for a comprehensive policy analysis to be carried out. What we aim to achieve is to formulate a structured way of thinking on agricultural policies, a framework that can be used as a reference when needed to carry out all the phases of the analysis.

4.2 ALTERNATIVE FRAMEWORKS FOR POLICY ANALYSIS

Among those based on economic theory, there are different possible structures for policy analysis. The most popular model is the timetable-based supply and demand. To follow this method, an analyst first defines the appropriate market (such as the domestic maize consumption market, the local agricultural aggregate output market, or the labor market in a rural community, etc.). Then he must identify the functions of demand and supply. This is probably the analyses most demanding task. In theory, demand, and supply functions can be calculated using observed data on past market outcomes (time series data), using data on different economic units (cross-sectional data), or both (panel data). Estimating supply and demand schedules in accordance with economic theory, however, poses many problems and requires ample data. In reality, it usually takes time the analyst may not have. Of this purpose, analysts typically rely on second-hand sources of measurements of elasticity from various other sources. The manual by Elisabeth Sadoulet and Alain de Janvry (1995) entitled: "Quantitative Development Analysis" provides an excellent detailed explanation of this framework, focused on the microeconomic analysis of individual behavior. In the book, the authors start from analyzing the actions of the sector's individual agents (farmers, consumers, government) to create the necessary aggregate relationships that require the required level of analysis (market, sector, or national).

An alternative model for policy analysis, the so-called policy analysis matrix (PAM), developed by Monke and Pearson (1991), eliminates the need to estimate microeconomic relationships that form the basis of the timetable for market supply and demand. Rather, the model is based on building representative production systems, the quality of which is evaluated through budget analysis. The concentration in PAM studies is on a commodity-based basis. The production, storage, and marketing activities bring the commodity to the final consumers can characterize that commodity. The quality of the entire system can be calculated by the profit-related result it produces, which is the difference between income and price. Revenues are merely the result of the consumer good's quantity and quality, as stated on the final market. Costs are the sum of the volume and price of the products used throughout the supply chain, from the field to the manufacturing sector, to the sales process. The primary intuition in using the PAM to test policy is that the overall effect of policies and other market distortions affecting a given commodity system can be measured by the induced price difference.

In the section on comparative advantages and gains from trade, in a situation of liberalized trade, producing where the marginal rate of production is equal to the ratio of world prices and then exporting goods at such prices on the world market would allow maximizing the country's overall welfare. The statement is subject to many false assumptions, the most important of which is the absence of transaction costs on both domestic and international markets. Nevertheless, it suggests that the existence of a disparity between the country's prevailing prices and world prices implies a possible deviation from the most effective resource allocation. Analysts can measure the impact of the whole set of policies and all other distortions that affect the market for a commodity by evaluating the relevant quantities in the budgets of a PAM first at private prices (that is at the prices actually faced by the agents) and then at their opportunity cost (which is often directly linked to the world price). In the overall policy discussion, PAM is extremely useful. Second, because it's very clear conceptually and easy to understand. Furthermore, and most importantly, because the researcher is expected to carefully examine many different technological and social aspects of the successful processes being analyzed in the process of building and evaluating the outcome of a PAM study.

4.3 PHASES OF POLICY ANALYSIS

Following Colman and Young, as Ellis points out, one of the potential features of the phases of the policy analysis cycle is as follows:

- Assessment of price effects, which means not only own price effects in a single market, but also the influence on closely related markets.
- Production effects, including the quantities of outputs and inputs.
- Consumption effects, meaning the demand impact of the policy in affected markets.
- Results of trade and balance of payments, including results on imports, exports, foreign reserves, and exchange rates.
- Budget effects, meaning the impact on government tax receipts and public expenditure.
- Income distribution effects, meaning the impact of policies on equity.
- Effects of social welfare, which means recognizing the winners and the losers of policy initiatives, and assessing the overall impact on social welfare.

As can be seen, the job is quite complex, which is why we sometimes need to make some simplifying assumptions that make it possible for the analytical dimensions. The key simplifications normally considered when performing economic policy research are as follows:

- Performing a partial equilibrium rather than a general study of equilibrium.
- Performing a comparative static evaluation rather than a dynamic analysis.
- Performing a commodity-oriented analysis instead of a sector analysis.
- Analyzing the impact of a single policy viewed in isolation from all other policies in place at a given time, rather than the cumulative effects of all policies affecting a particular product chain, a region, or the country's entire agricultural sector.

4.3.1 Partial vs. General Equilibrium Analysis

A partial analysis of the equilibrium would limit the scope of the analysis to a single market, or at most to a limited set of closely linked markets. For example, when considering the effects of a policy which raises the price of maize, a general equilibrium study must take into account all the effects that such a policy will have on:

- Farmers' production of maize;
- Maize consumption by end consumers;
- Certain grain industry that can replace maize consumption;
- The market for maize from livestock operations using maize as animal feed;
- Market of other feed crops which may replace maize in the production of animals;
- Development of alternative crops for agricultural land that may compete with maize and so on. The list may be very long in order to make the research very difficult.

In some cases, it may be enough to limit the analysis to just the first two elements: maize supply and consumption, as opposed to the direct effects, the other effect may be negligible. This may improve the viability of the study, but we must bear in mind that simplification often requires some information loss, and we must be careful to determine when the information we lose will not change the overall policy decision. From an economic point of view, from the demand side, from the production side, or from both, different markets can be associated. The related relationships from the consumer side are those of complementarity and replaceability. Recall from the market theory that if the cross-price elasticity is negative, two products are comparable, implying that if one good's price increases, the second good's demand decreases. Alternatively, if the cross-price elasticity is positive, two goods are said to be substitutes, that is when the consumption of one good increases after the value of the other good increases. From the point of view of production, output markets are related to the input markets used in the process of production. Nonetheless, the generated demand for inputs is directly dependent on the price of production. Of fact, different products may be jointly produced, and therefore any change in the production of one output would necessarily affect the production of the other. Lastly, different products can be related together as their output is competing for the use of a common factor, such as property. All of these relations also require that the study of the consequences of a given policy be generalized to several markets, thereby heading towards a general analysis of equilibrium. An important point to note is that the research in any of the markets will deliver a valid measure of overall benefits if markets are only vertically linked. Nonetheless, the distribution of profits can only be understood by the study of all markets.

The following summary is considered from Figure 4.1. Suppose a farm product is generated using soil, labor, and other farm inputs. This material is then used in conjunction with other promotional inputs to provide consumers on the retail market with a final commodity. If the equilibrium on the retail market is evaluated, the area identified as the consumer's surplus (e) rises for consumers, whereas the area identified as the producer's surplus contains surpluses that accumulate different functions in the production chain, i.e., surplus for,

- farm labor holders;
- land;
- other farm inputs; and
- to providers of marketing inputs.

Consider the selling of the commodity on the retail market to trigger a derived demand for farm production and marketing inputs to see why it is so. If one analyzes the agricultural product's wholesale market, then the consumer's surplus estimated under the marketing firms' demand will include the consumer's final consumer surplus plus the selling input suppliers' surplus.

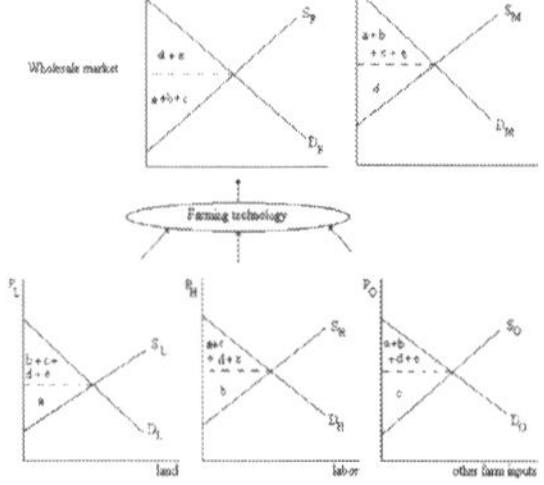

Figure 4.1. Distribution of welfare in a multi-market model.

Source: Frank Ellis (2014).

On the other hand, if one focuses on the derived marketing product demand, then the region below the derived marketing input demand feature will include profits to final consumers and all input manufacturers in the agricultural system. The research of agricultural inputs could also be carried out at the market level. The area identified as the surplus of the manufacturer will refer to the net returns of the specific input to the suppliers in each of those regions, while the area defined as the surplus of the buyer will include the benefits to all others.

The subject almost seeks to highlight the difference between personal incidence and functional incidence or benefits distribution. We typically perform functional incidence analysis in economics. That is, we calculate the welfare that the manufacturers, buyers, taxpayers, and holders of fixed assets accrue to individuals in their economic activities, not as specific individuals. Buyers are also always taxpayers, for instance, while peasant farmers are both producers and consumers of the better at the same time. For example, this means that if we were to examine the personal welfare impact of a subsidy on agricultural products on such farmers, we would include the benefits that accrue to them as producers and subtract the loss of welfare to be attributed to them as consumers. Basically, the private event is what would really matter from a social point of view. Nonetheless, a detailed description of ownership of production factors is required to determine personal occurrence, something that is rarely available.

4.3.2 Comparative Static vs. Dynamic Analysis

We have held discussions so far, and we believe a static structure for some of those we will carry. For example, we assumed a fixed supply role because describing the definition of change in the producer's surplus due to a price subsidy. However, under such modeling choice, there is a specific restrictive assumption of supply dynamics, namely that the supply function does not shift due to the subsidy being present. This can only be so when there are restrictions on the availability of equipment or resources that impede the increase for agricultural supply. For all other cases, we would expect the subsidy's existence to draw more capital in the sector by moving the supply function to the right. At the same time, other factors such as new technology growth may help to increase efficiency and demand. This means that the supply elasticity is either zero or very low due to technological and resource constraints), otherwise, if the analysis is carried out at a level where no such constraints are in effect, the elasticity will be positive and will increase over time. Recognition of this reality has very important consequences for evaluating the welfare effects of policies, especially those that are obviously aimed at improving the conditions of agricultural producers, as we will address next. Suppose we want to analyze the impact on the agricultural product of a price subsidy. If the supply elasticity is zero due to the presence of a limited resource, such as a fixed amount of land, the surplus of any producer will end up paying only for land rents. The explanation is that the higher price would lead to a higher demand for land extracted from it. In addition, faced with a perfectly inelastic supply, the higher demand for land would result in a higher land price. The added cost of land would erode all the incentives of a higher output value, and they are farmers who really profit from the subsidy. When properly understood, this debate has interesting implications for the effects of eliminating a subsidy for farming, which is becoming increasingly common under World Trade Organization (WTO) regulations. As a result, where there is an effective land market, young farmers who bought the land when the subsidy program was in effect had already charged the capitalized cost of the benefits due to the program in terms of the higher land price. We experience a real loss when the system is discontinued in terms of depreciation of their land resources.

The other case is when the supply elasticity is positive and grows over time. In the short run, as we move to a longer run, the supply elasticity may be small to raise. To carry out a fixed analysis of the distribution of benefits, therefore, explicitly leads to set a run time. Consider the potential advantages of a fixed price aid per unit. The distribution of benefits should change depending on the elasticity of the supply. A greater proportion would go to customers the higher the supply elasticity. All the benefits will go to customers in the extreme case of a fully elastic supply function. Combining the outcomes of these two situations, the image one can draw is that in the long run, any support for agricultural production will end up either paying rents to the owner of the fixed assets or being enjoyed by customers through lower prices for agricultural products. The theories that contributed to a conclusion of this kind are not as strong as one might think. The reason for this finding can be found by considering that labor, the other development variable of which the agricultural sector is particularly rich in developing countries, cannot adequately benefit from sector aid in the long term due to its very existence. The argument I would like to make with the whole debate on the dynamics of supply response and the occurrence of agricultural policies is that, by performing only comparative static analyzes, there is a risk of overestimating the benefits in terms of labor returns and underestimating the benefits in terms of returns to land and other fixed factors or returns to consumers from a policy.On the other hand, the same form of myopic approach could have underestimated the costs of policies to tax agriculture to fund industry and consumers in urban areas, which have been so prevalent in many developing countries in recent decades.

4.4 THE POLICY ANALYSIS MATRIX (PAM)

A PAM can be viewed as a way for representative consumer frameworks to coordinate budget data. The way data is collected, analyzed, and arranged makes it possible to assess the impact of the collection of all policies and fluctuations of the market on a given representative product system. Collecting and adding PAM's for multiple product systems can then expand the study to a region's or country's entire agricultural sector. Therefore, the focus is on a commodity-by-commodity basis, and the main requirement is that only a few representative structures can be correctly identified. There are typically three rows and four columns in the PAM for a representative system. The first row contains actual values of revenues (A) and costs, divided into payments to tradable inputs (B) and to domestic factors (C). Actual values mean that the values are obtained by direct collection of current data on quantities and prices as they manifest themselves in the economy. The differences between revenues and costs measures private profits (D = A – B – C). Remember that costs are divided into only two categories: tradable commodities (i.e., items that can theoretically be traded on international markets) and domestic non-tradable factors (i.e., property, capital, and labor). Intermediate goods that are not explicitly tradable must be disaggregated into their basic components so that any element of value can be identified either as a result of tradable input (oil, fertilizers, chemicals, etc.) or domestic factors. Thus, the value in D measures the total private productivity under the study of the commodity system. The key idea behind the PAM analysis is that this observed profitability can either be the "real" outcome of the economy's fundamental economic forces or an "artificial" outcome caused by political transfers. The second row of the matrix is intended to represent the optimal, most productive rate of productivity of the commodity system in order to determine the degree to which private profitability is due to market forces. It is based on so-called social prices by measuring the budgets. Social prices are described as those expressing in an undistorted economy the opportunity cost of the goods or services. Creating the PAM's second-row then amounts to define social prices and predict how quantities under those prices will change (Table 4.1).

Table 4.1. The Policy Analysis Matrix (PAM)

	Revenues	**Costs**		**Profits**
		Tradable Inputs	**Domestic Factors**	
Private prices	A	B	C	D
Social prices	E	F	G	H
Effects of divergences and efficient policy	I	J	K	L

The values in the second-row express revenues (E), costs for tradable goods (F) and costs for domestic factors (G) all evaluated as if social prices prevailed. The difference between revenues and costs yields social profitability (H = E – F – G) and expresses the ideal potential level of profits that the commodity system could generate. By comparing the private with social profitability, then, the analyst can judge whether the commodity system under analysis is subsidized or penalized under the prevailing set of policies. To this aim, the third row of the PAM contains the differences between the values in the first and in the second row. The values in this row express the overall effect of policy and other distortion that affect the production of the commodity. The difference between private and social values can be considered as transfers. We can distinguish between revenue transfers (I = A – E), tradable cost transfers (J = B – F), domestic factor transfers (K = C – G), and total transfers (L = I – J – K = D – H). For example, a positive value for L means that private profits in the commodity system being examined (D) are higher than what they would be if the economy where at its efficient equilibrium (H). In other words, the sector is subsidized as a result of these policies being in place. The overall effect, L, is also equal to the difference between the level of output transfers minus the sum of input and factor transfers (L = I – J – K), so that one can identify whether the distortion is due to revenue transfers, tradable cost transfers, and/or factor transfers.

As a result, the analysis of a commodity system through the PAM can highlight the relative position of the system in terms of implicit taxation of subsidization. But nothing can be said on the non-efficiency effects of such transfers. In other words, the PAM can tell that a given set of policies will induce inefficiencies in the economy and can quantify those inefficiencies, also by pointing to the main sources of inefficiencies (whether they are mainly due to revenues, tradable costs, or domestic transfers), but tells nothing on how to eliminate such inefficiencies without compromising the non-efficiency objectives of the policy. One way in which the PAM could be used, in principle, to suggest ways of improving the conditions of the economy is through simulations. If one is able to imagine an alternative set of policies, one can build simulated budgets under these hypothetical conditions, and observe how the level of distortions might change. However, the simulation results are strongly dependent on the ability of forecasting how the entries in the first row of the PAM would change under the set of hypothetical policies, an exercise that usually has a high degree of imprecision. To conclude the PAM approach for policy analysis can:

- Measure the efficiency cost of existing policies and market failures.
- Compare the relative position of different commodity systems in terms of net transfers.
- Help to highlight the efficiency cost of policies that may have equity objectives.

Nevertheless, it cannot identify the causes of inefficiency directly, so that an informed decision on how to adjust the policies in place requires additional data that can only be gained through a more detailed study of the benefits and costs of each policy, such as conventional partial equilibrium analysis of individual policies.

1. Identifying the representative systems;
2. Constructing the baseline budgets, under private prices;
3. Determining the social prices for goods and factors;
4. Constructing the budgets under social prices;
5. Evaluating the results.

4.4.1 Identification of Representative Systems

As we have seen, the PAM is better structured in terms of commodity systems, which are identified as the vertically integrated production chains ranging from farm production to the consumer retail market, including any processing, and marketing activities that may occur between them. The work can be national in scope, but it is usually carried out at a local or sub-regional level (different regional analyzes may then be aggregated to yield results on larger territorial aggregates). The next step is to determine a representative farm production, processing, and marketing operation to be evaluated once the area of interest has been defined. The product network will usually consist of many fields, a few processing plants and a few marketing firms (including wholesale supply, transportation, and retail). Farms may vary in size (small, medium, or large farms); type of management (farms, cooperatives, corporate farms, etc.) and level of resource endowment (irrigated or not, mechanized or not, etc.). That type of farm will have to be reflected in the process if the element of farm output is to be completely accounted for. Usually, one representative farm per type is described, and then the representative farms' results are aggregated with weights corresponding to the relative production share due to each type. If they exist, one can rely on available statistical data (such as data on the agricultural census) to identify the representative farms. If statistical data are not available, experts with sound knowledge of the farming sector understudy can be relied on, likely by supplementing the information provided with ad hoc surveys. The goal is to attempt to find the smallest number of representative farms that can account for the region's highest share of agricultural production. In terms of their technical and economic structure, manufacturing, and advertising practices are typically more homogeneous and easier to explain.

4.4.2 Construction of the Baseline Budgets

The baseline budgets are an account of the economic results of the production activities of the system. The accounting equation defines profits as the difference between revenues and costs.

Profit = Revenues – Costs

Revenues, in turn, are the sum of the products between prices and quantities of all the final outputs $p_i^p q_i^p$, where the superscript p is used to indicate that these are private values. Analogously, costs are the sum of products between prices and quantities of inputs. Inputs are divided into tradable and non-tradable (i.e., domestic factors of production), so that the accounting equation can be written as:

$$\text{Profit} = \Sigma p_i^p q_i^p - \Sigma\, s_j^p q_j^p - \Sigma\, r_k^p q_k^p$$

where s_j^p are the private prices of tradable inputs, and r_k^p are the private prices of domestic factors of production. Basically, to construct a budget means to provide a detailed account of all inputs used in the production process and of the outputs produced. For agricultural productions, it may be convenient to organize the data according to the various operations that are performed during the production cycle of a crop. In this way, it is usually easier to correctly account for labor and machinery use. Many details need to be considered in accounting for the costs at the farm level, such as for example how to calculate annual costs for fixed inputs, or how to impute a cost for live animals. We will not go into the detail of describing these costs, because it could cover an entire book. In general, this is a demanding task and the overall quality of the results depends on how carefully this step of the analysis is performed.

4.4.3 Social Evaluation of Tradable Goods

Once the results of the baseline have been achieved, the analyst will construct the second row of the PAM, which involves quantifying market prices and adjusting the appropriate amounts according to the potential rewards defined by the social price system. The purpose of social prices is to express the goods' opportunity cost. The cost of opportunity for a good is what the good could receive in the next best alternative usage. The opportunity cost can be called the effective world price for tradable products and inputs as determined by the border price and adjusted for future costs required to move the good from the site of production or use to the nearest commercial border. The rationale for such a definition of opportunity cost is that under free trade, efficiency would be reached by trading the commodities at the prevailing world price. The world price is usually available as the cost, insurance, and freight (C.I.F.) price for imports, or as free-on-board (F.O.B.) price for exports. The difference between the two prices is insurance and handling needed at the entry/exit point:

C.I.F. = F.O.B. + Insurance + Freight

To express the effective opportunity cost of the good, these prices need to be adjusted to consider marketing costs. Marketing costs are the costs that are needed to bring the commodity from the point where it is produced or made available through imports, to the point where it is consumed or sold as export. To understand the adjustments needed to express the effective world price, consider Figure 4.2.

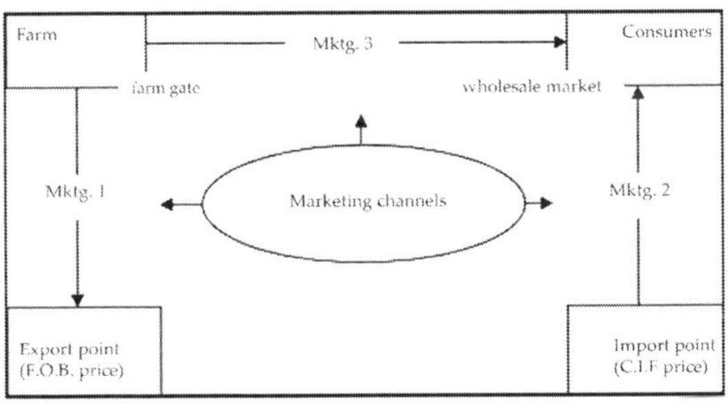

Figure 4.2. The marketing channels.

To be competitive on the world market and to be exported, the marginal cost of the product at the farm gate must be lower than the export price net of all marketing costs needed to take it from the farm gate to the border (mktg. 1). Under these conditions, the goods will be exported. On the other hand, goods for domestic consumption are imported when the marginal cost of production, inclusive of the marketing costs from the farm to the wholesale market (mktg. 3), is higher than the import price plus the marketing costs from the border to the wholesale market (mktg. 2). The relative magnitude of the marginal cost of production, marketing cost, and border prices determine whether a product is traded or not. Conditions for a good to be traded:

Exports:

F.O.B. – Mktg. 1 > mg. cost

Imports:

C.I.F. + mktg. 2 – mktg. 3 < mg. cost

When:

C.I.F. + mktg.2-mktg.3 > mg. cost > F.O.B-mktg.1

The good is non-traded.

The effective C.I.F. and F.O.B. prices can also be altered by Government intervention, through the direct imposition of levies or payment of subsidies. For example, a subsidy on exports will increase the C.I.F. price, whereas a tax on imports will increase the F.O.B. price. Also, the government may indirectly alter the effective border price by the exchange rate. For example, a devaluation of the local currency would have the same effect of a tax on imports and a subsidy on exports. A good which is potentially tradable, may become non-traded because of:

- High production costs;
- High marketing costs;
- Government intervention.

Usually, C.I.F. and F.O.B. prices are expressed in foreign exchange (usually, in U.S. dollars). To compare them with domestic production and marketing costs, they must be converted to local currency. Which exchange rate to use is a critical point in the determination of social prices. Under the free market for the foreign currency, the exchange rate should express the relative scarcity of foreign exchange needed to buy imports. Demand for foreign exchange is expressed by importers, whereas the supply of foreign exchange is generated by exports. The correct exchange rate is the one that balances demand and supply of foreign exchange, as for example would be a rate of 50:1 (that is, 50 units of the local currency are required for 1 US dollar) in Figure 4.3.

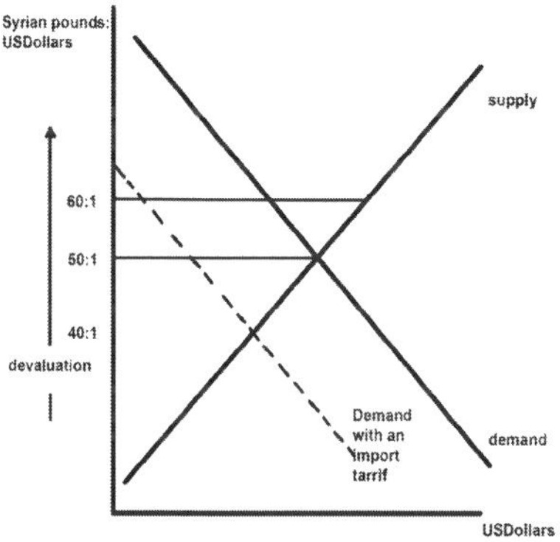

Figure 4.3. The exchange rate market.

For example, suppose the government sets the official exchange rate at 40:1 (i.e., the Syrian Pound is overvalued against its free-market level). As a result, there will be an excess demand for US dollars: citizens who need foreign exchange to buy imports would be willing to pay more than the official rate, but there will be a shortage of current exchange because those who export goods receive only the official rate. Governments need to engage in other practices to maintain such a rate, such as rationing, which is directly regulating foreign exchange supply or indirectly altering foreign exchange supply and demand by engaging in trade price policies. The government might, for instance, enforce a tariff on imports to reduce the opportunities for imports and demand for foreign exchange moves to the left. Whenever the official rate is set very far from the true equilibrium, informal markets that grow, for example by supplying foreign currency at a higher price, which would compensate for the rationing. Consequently, the existence of unregulated foreign exchange markets is an indicator that the official rate is not a good indication of the domestic currency's actual value compared to the foreign currency. If the official rates surpass the domestic currency, it would be equivalent to undervaluing imports and exports at the official rates. The official exchange rate should never be used for all these purposes to convert domestic currency CIF and FOB rates. If available, the market exchange rate must be used. If a market rate is not available, the exchange rate values of neighboring countries might instead be used. As we said, the prevailing market exchange rate in a country may be influenced by importation or export policy restrictions. Nonetheless, if one is only interested in comparing various sectors' long-term productivity, it may be reasonable to use such exchange rates. In all other situations (for example, if the analyst is interested in the short-run policy effects), it may not be acceptable to use a skewed market exchange rate.

4.4.4 Social Evaluation of Domestic Factors and Non-Tradable Commodities and Services

Since world prices cannot be used as a guide, it is more difficult to evaluate the correct social price. Regarding non-tradable products and services, such as energy, food, marketing, legal services, etc., any action that shifts their demand can distort the domestic, private valuation of these goods and services. Their cost should, therefore, be decomposed into their tradable and factor components so that one can use the previous section's shadow values for the tradable element and the second component's shadow price of factors. In theory, by applying general principles of equilibrium, the social analysis of domestic factors of production (land, capital, and labor) could be carried out. When competition in factor markets removes any excess profit, the cost of production in any sector must be equal to the weighted total of the input factors used in those sectors, with weights equal to the factors' efficient prices.

For example, in an economy with two outputs, Q_1 and Q_2, which uses labor, L, and capital, K, the following identities will hold:

$$wL_1 + rK_1 = P_1Q_1$$

$$wL_2 + rK_2 = P_2Q_2$$

From which:

$$wL_1/Q_1 + rK_1/Q_1 = P_1$$

$$wL_2/Q_2 + rK_2/Q_2 = P_2$$

If constant returns to scale can be assumed, the ratios L_1/Q_1, K_1/Q_1, L_2/Q_2, and K_2/Q_2 are constant input/output coefficient and we can indicate them as l_1 (i.e., the amount of labor needed to produce one unit of output in the first sector), k_1, l_2, and k_2, respectively:

$$wl_1 + rk_1 = P_1$$

$$wl_2 + rk_2 = P_2$$

Then the equilibrium factor prices can be calculated as:

$$w = (P_1k_2 - P_2k_1)/ (l_1k_2 - l_2k_1)$$

$$r = (P_2l_1 - P_1l_2)/ (l_1k_2 - l_2k_1)$$

You can generalize the basic general equilibrium model to any degree of detail. Nonetheless, estimating the general model of equilibrium usually requires a large amount of data and is usually impossible for many realistic studies of policy. An alternative approach is to consider specifically the variations known to affect the prices of variables. First, uncertainty in the factor markets may be present. Includes a possible list:

- Proportional taxes and subsidies (as for example social security taxes).
- Direct regulation of factor prices (such as minimum wage, rent control, etc.).
- Market failures (such as market segmentation and transaction costs).

Second, fluctuations in commodity markets can have an effect on variable prices: for example, when labor-intensive industries are subsidized compared to assets-intensive industries, total labor demand can increase while capital demand will decrease. Consequently, wage rates may increase, while interest rates may decline. Nonetheless, in particular, given the different levels of support for different industries and the differing degree of labor intensity, the effects from different sectors using the same factor can balance one another and have limited effects on the factor markets' equilibrium prices. Finally, the interest rate may be influenced by macroeconomic policy, thus increasing the price of land and labor relative to capital. How this would impact the price of these two other factors depends on the pattern of factors being complemented and substituted.

Overall, we can conclude by quoting Monke and Pearson, who says: "The most difficult aspect of social cost accounting is the social valuation of domestic factors. The crucial first step in estimating factors' social prices is to develop a consistent context in which divergences can be established. The quantification exercise becomes a sequence of systematic changes to the prices of the private market variable to identify the effects of discrepancies in the commodity market and the indirect effects of macroeconomic fluctuations and substitution of inputs. As with all shadow pricing approaches, to obtain accurate estimates of social values, full awareness of the product system response to price changes is required. Empirical estimates of social factor prices are therefore approximations and the analyst will be forced to make arbitrary judgments as to what constitutes major and minor changes" (Monke and Pearson, 1989). This remark makes it clear that the wage rates and interest rates used in the second row of the PAM equation are very important aspects of the overall analysis. Unfortunately, the findings may be heavily dependent on these prices, and thus the incorrect choice of these prices that mislead the overall study. However, one advantage of the PAM framework is that once the budgets are determined in all other quantities, it allows easy recalculation of budgets in terms of wage and interest rates under different scenarios, so that a sensitivity analysis of the results can be carried out.

5

AGRICULTURAL POLICY

CONTENTS

5.1 Agricultural Policy ... 84
5.2 Sectoral Focus ... 84
5.3 Other Sectoral Policies ... 84
5.4 Economy-Wide Policies ... 85
5.5 Delivery Method ... 85
5.6 Agricultural Policy Rationale and The State's Role in The Economy ... 97
5.7 The New-Institutional View of Agricultural Policy ... 97
5.8 Efficiency Vs. Equity ... 98
5.9 The State's Function In The Market Economy ... 99
5.10 The Importance of Economics In Agricultural Policy ... 100
5.11 Agricultural Policy of Economic Goals ... 100

5.1 AGRICULTURAL POLICY

Agricultural policy defines a collection of domestic farming laws and international agricultural products imports. Governments typically adopt agricultural policies in order to achieve a specific outcome on the markets for domestic agricultural products. Governments (and other actors) have available a variety of approaches, processes, and methods for facilitating change in behavior. These are called instruments of policy collectively. Government tools can be classified in multiple ways conceptually (Table 5.1).

Table 5.1. Classification of Policy Instruments Affecting the Agricultural Sector

	Primary Sectoral Focus of Policy		
Mechanism of Delivery	**Agriculture Sector Specific**	**Other Sectors**	**Economy Wide**
Regulatory instruments			
Voluntary instruments			
Economic instruments			
Public investments			

Source: FAO1987.

5.2 SECTORAL FOCUS

Specific policies in the agricultural sector that affect similar agricultural inputs (e.g., subsidies for fertilizers) or products (e.g., maize or cotton). We can include:

- Domestic price policies such as crop subsidies and taxes on agricultural-related commodities.
- Tariffs and other non-tariff barriers to international trade.
- Regulations such as price controls and environmental restrictions.

5.3 OTHER SECTORAL POLICIES

For example, other sectoral policies such as health, transport, education, business, labor, water, and sanitation policies can affect agriculture and trade, such as health and education policies can affect the productivity of labor in agriculture, and transport policies can affect the costs of agricultural marketing.

5.4 ECONOMY-WIDE POLICIES

These are defined nationally (usually by or similar to the Ministry of Finance) and affect all sectors, including agriculture. We could include:

- Fiscal policies such as spending limits on sector budgets.
- Monetary policies such as inflation targets or national bank interest rates.
- Exchange rate policies.
- Policies on tenure and use of land and natural resources such as water.
- Labor policies, such as a minimum wage.

5.5 DELIVERY METHOD

1. **Regulatory Instruments:** There are those who use the legal system that the government or its representatives are enforcing. These may include, for example, setting compulsory requirements (e.g., food quality), outlawing other activities (e.g., dumping obsolete pesticides in the nearest river) or setting minimum and maximum commodity prices (also known as floor and ceiling).
2. **Voluntary Instruments:** Are cooperative agreements between private sector players (egg producers and supermarkets) as proposed and, more specifically, between government and private sector players. These are often ad hoc and informal: for example, when international food prices soared in 2008, governments in some West African countries called on major grain traders to agree to keep their prices down for a limited period of time (Wiggins et al., 2010). Formal voluntary agreements are often used in higher-income countries in the environmental field, for example by introducing appropriate technology; formal agreements can be made between a government and a group of farmers to reduce greenhouse gas emissions (OECD, 2013).
3. **Economic Instruments:** These are the ones that provide economic incentives for behavioral change. For agriculture, taxes, tariffs, and subsidies and the allocation of property and resources to use

(e.g., land, and water) are the most widely used economic tools by the government.

- Market-based strategies are a type of economic tools in which the government sets the conditions for fostering policy solutions for the private sector. For example, rather than setting a commodity's floor and ceiling rates, a government may encourage the development of market futures trading in the private sector.

4. **Public Investment Policies:** Agriculture and Commerce, for example in roads and education, can be influenced by a wide range of industries. Lack of ministry-to-minister coordination will result in investment choices that do not favor agriculture.

The factors to consider when choosing a policy framework over the other are often dynamic, and the choice of method depends on the specific policy objective. Implementation challenges and costs (e.g., data collection, audit, and enforcement) are major concerns. Voluntary agreements are most likely to succeed with a large and/or well-organized group that has some incentive to follow the agreement on its own. The divisions above are not hard and fast, and it may overlap with some instruments. That makes agriculture, which is also what makes it so interesting, one of the most complex and difficult policy areas. Many things make agricultural policy complex, some of them may seem simplistic or simple, but they have important policy implications. This can be the case;

5.5.1 Agriculture Is Economically and Politically Important

Agriculture is our main food source. Food is not merely a commodity that is culturally important and highly sensitive politically. In theory, the majority of its food could be imported by an urbanized country, and some do. For example, about 40% of its food is imported by the UK (DEFRA, 2006). Many countries, however, are reluctant to rely too much on imported food. For other purposes, imports require foreign exchange. In addition, there is a risk that failures in harvesting, war/civil conflict, or other factors may restrict and/or increase food imports. As in many countries as world food prices rose in 2007–2008 (Arezki and Brückner, 2011), if this occurs immediately, it can cause major political upheavals. For the poor, who need to spend a large proportion of their income on food, food prices are particularly important. Most governments are therefore keeping a close eye on domestic food production and many are implementing policies to promote it. For example, fibers such as cotton and jute, industrial inputs such as starch, and biopharmaceuticals are also the origin of some important non-food commodities. Traditionally, non-food crops (often referred to as industrial crops) have formed a small part of agricultural production and trade, but this is changing as biofuels and bioplastics expand. For low-income countries, the main source of jobs and economic activity is agriculture and related businesses (trade, storage, and food preparation). Agriculture provides more people worldwide with a livelihood than any other industry. The sector employs 1.3 billion employees for developing countries, representing approximately 50% of total employment "(Cheong et al., 2013, p. 1, citing FAO, 2011a). Agriculture has traditionally been a major driver of economic growth and poverty reduction (Johnston and Mellor, 1961; De Janvry and Sadoulet, 2009). In some countries, agriculture is also a major source of foreign earnings.

Lastly, the wider society appreciates many cultural and traditional aspects of agriculture, such as organic fruit varieties, a farm cheese, or the beauty of a landscape created by a patchwork of small farms. Even in high-income countries where agriculture contributes relatively small amounts to the economy, it gives farmers political influence. A case in point is France, where in 2010 agriculture contributed less than 2% of GDP (FAO, 2013a), but where farmers have a strong political presence.

5.5.2 Local Farmers Are Very Diverse

Compare agriculture with manufacturing, nutrition, education, or highways, and it becomes immediately evident that agriculture is a much more complex field. Agricultural policy should deal with everything from small irrigated rice plots to intensive rearing of livestock. For example, a farm may produce both vegetables and sheep with different needs within a single farm, there may be a number of farm enterprises. A blanket agricultural policy (such as a general crop subsidy) is a 'blunt tool' that needs to be thought through very carefully if it is not to have unintended effects on some farmers or farms, or to help some farmers much more than others.

5.5.3 The Agricultural Sector's Borders Are Fuzzy

Agriculture is closely linked to agribusiness and other rural interests such as fisheries and forest management. In addition, many industries usually control some factors affecting agricultural production (e.g., transport). Roads and transport, energy, communications, education, health, social services, economy, trade, and foreign affairs. Almost all sectors have some knock-on impact on agriculture or on nutrition. Many of these ministries have their own (different) policy goals, and Agriculture ministries may be at odds with their political colleagues (this is called lack of policy coherence). Coordination between sectors is, therefore, a major challenge.

5.5.4 Agricultural Output Relies on a Vast Number of Farmers' Individual Decisions

Highly decentralized agriculture. Individual farmers make day-to-day decisions that affect production and sales—for example, what crops to grow and how many hectares, what inputs to use and when to apply them, when to harvest, store, and market. This means that agricultural policy needs to be designed to influence many different people's decisions. In the following quote, which was written at a time when central government agricultural planning was, or had been, the dominant paradigm in several countries, the importance of this point was placed very clearly.

Agriculture is truly unique in that literally millions of people and households make their own decisions [so] influencing agricultural production decisions to increase food output is a completely different process from changing decisions on how much steel or cement they produce. In [.] many countries, a dozen or so individuals may take direct action, leading to an increase in steel production of about 10% in a year. A different small group of individuals, not even in [state-planned economies], may decide to increase food production by 10%. To be sure [.] the president and the cabinet may agree that they want a 10% increase in food production. We can tell the food logistics department, agriculture ministry, magazines, and farm extension agents that they want 10% increase in food production. But on their own, they cannot increase food production by 10%. They also need to convince their country's millions of farmers to want to increase food production by 10% and make it do so in their self-interest (Timmer et al., 1983, p. 4).

5.5.5 Farms Are Geographically Dispersed and Rural

Since land and water are important inputs into agricultural production, the majority of farms are in rural areas where land is cheaper. Compared to industry, farms are much dispersed geographically. Very few farmers in the world are entirely self-sufficient producers of subsistence many farmers sell at least some of their goods or purchase most of their inputs. Therefore, the agricultural market system plays a crucial role in getting inputs such as seeds, fertilizers, and veterinary medicinal products into farms, and in getting outputs (agricultural products) from farms to where they are needed, such as processing factories or directly to consumers in urban areas. This can be challenging and expensive, especially with scattered small farms in low-density countries. In addition to reducing the share of profits going to the farmer and 'driving a wedge' between the farmer's gate and consumer prices, high transport costs may also decrease competition among traders or lead to a complete absence of markets (De Janvry et al., 1991; Suzuki and Sexton, 2005) (Figures 5.1 and 5.2).

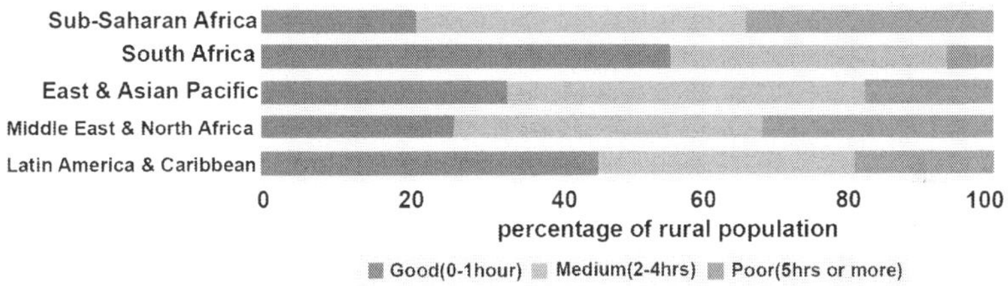

Figure 5.1. Time required reaching the market.

Source: World Bank (2007).

Figure 5.2. For many farmers, transporting inputs and outputs is a major issue.

Source: Google Pictures, 2019.

The transaction fees of distributed farms (cost of doing business with) are often high. Knowledge restrictions may prohibit the private sector from offering such products, such as individual farm insurance for crop failure. Because, it is too costly for the insurance company to go to the fields of farmers to check the status of crops and farmers may cheat (moral hazard) or may be tempted to take additional risks, such as not taking preventive measures to confront them. The issue of knowledge may be serious in low-income, low-density countries. A farmer, for instance, might sell her maize to a passing trader at a low price, and may not be aware that only a few villages away she could get a much higher price on the market. (Remember that neoclassical economic models assume that price information is ideal for both producers and consumers.) However, developments in communications, especially mobile phones, are slowly overcoming the barrier of information. A longer-term consequence of a rural location is that people in urban areas have more restricted day-to-day options and opportunities. Almost all agricultural jobs are hard and low-paid, and in the countryside, there are fewer alternative professions than in cities. In rural areas, shopping, education, and health services, transport, and communications, as well as cultural diversity prefer to be more minimal. For these reasons, many people, especially young people in all parts of the world, tend to move to towns when they get the opportunity, and away from farming. Although the pleasures of farming and rural life are deliberately chosen and enjoyed by a minority of people in all countries, the step around the world is towards urbanization, and towards smaller and older rural populations. The push toward urbanization has long-term agricultural policy consequences (Satterthwaite et al., 2010).

5.5.6 Agriculture Is Biological and Ecological Dependent

Agriculture relies on the growth and interaction between living plants or animals and their climate. A farmer usually has much less influence over his / her levels of production than a factory owner for this reason. While in some situations it is possible, for example, to exert a degree of control over agricultural production, think of heated glasshouses or chickens raised in a highly controlled environment, the vast majority of farming is greatly affected by external conditions, including interactions with soil, water, competing species (weeds), pests, and diseases. This has many consequences, including seasonality, time, and hazard tolerance, and natural environment impacts.

5.5.7 Agriculture Is Time-Sensitive and Seasonal

Agricultural production can be constant throughout the year, like a crop, in a few cases. Most of the world's agriculture is dependent on natural temperature and rainfall cycles, especially in developing countries, and there are 'ordinary' seasons for planting, growing, and harvesting in a particular area. Seasonality has a number of significant implications:

- Synchronization of planting and harvest results in (semi-) predictable volatility in the availability and price of an area crop. (In general, prices are at their lowest after harvest and their highest just before the next harvest, as you would expect.).
- In connection with this, it may be as important to store agricultural products as output. The harvest period for maize, for example, could only last for about a month, while buyers and processors will need maize all year round. This void is filled by processing. Price pressures, including those triggered by agricultural policy and other factors, can have an enormous impact on farmer and trader decisions about what to store and how long. At the same time, storage decisions can have a major impact on supply and demand. Timmer offered an extreme example, estimating that a decision by millions of consumers to buy extra rice to keep in the kitchen cupboard was sufficient to explain the enormous short-term spikes in world rice prices (Timmer, 2009).
- Supply of inputs can be crucial in time. A 2-week delay in delivering a key input in a factory can result in a production delay of 2 weeks. A 2-week delay in seed delivery in rain-fed agriculture may mean the loss of a whole year's harvest in the worst-case scenario. Fostering productive supply chains is one of the issues of agricultural policy.
- For many farms, labor requirements vary dramatically over the year. The preparation/planting, weeding, harvesting, and processing of land requires relatively high labor over a limited period of time. This provides the poorest people with (low) income, but a headache for farm managers who need to recruit and manage temporary work. This is an important economic reason why family farms have remained the predominant form of farm organization, even in wealthy countries such as the United States of America (Allen and Lueck, 1998; Eastwood et al., 2010). The divergent effects on farm owners/managers and farm labor must also be considered in agricultural policy. A policy of subsidizing tractors is likely to be popular with farm managers to take a simple example, but it can put farmworkers out of work. It is also common for farmers to take off-farm employment in a variety of businesses to maintain year-round income, meaning that links are important between agricultural and other labor markets.

5.5.8 Agriculture Is Extremely Risky

Farmers throughout the world are mainly talking about two topics, weather, and prices. These two variables drive the incentives for the effort in agriculture throughout the year (Timmer et al., 1983).

The annual variability in crop yields due to weather can be tremendous, particularly in rainfed agriculture, which accounts for about 80% of world agriculture (FAO, 2011b). These enormous swings can hurt both producers and consumers if the agricultural policy is not able to stabilize markets crucially, including trade. Malawi experienced famines in 1992, 2002, and 2005 and received substantial food aid; the country had a bumper harvest and exported maize in 2007, on the other hand. The political story is complex, and the weather has not been Malawi's only influence on yields and prices.

1. **Pests and Diseases:** Many crops and farm animals are also a major risk. An attack on an animal disease such as foot and mouth (cattle) or Newcastle disease (chickens) or the loss of an ox that is needed for plowing can potentially bankrupt a smallholder if insurance is not provided. Most farmers also face enormous price uncertainty. In economic terminology, the majority of farmers are price-takers—that is, they are too small to influence the market price they receive for their products. There may also be unpredictable variations in the prices of agricultural inputs and labor. Many agricultural products are faced with inelastic demand, which means that a fall in price does not result in an equivalent increase in demand. This means that, in the absence of any external policy intervention, a good year with a bumper harvest (very large harvest) can lead to a price crash and the farmer's lower income than a poor year. In addition, in a progressively globalized world, both input and output prices can be affected by factors beyond the awareness and experience of any individual farmer, such as a sudden increase in the global oil price, a shift in domestic subsidies paid to farmers in a major production region such as the European Union, a bumper harvest of the same crop in a far-off country, or a rise in the country. Finally, there are a variety of other external threats and uncertainties that can impact agricultural production and markets.

   Certain climate and non-price threats and shocks may include:

   - On family farms in all parts of the world, nutrition is one of the main threats. It may result in the loss of labor (both the sick person and their careers) at a key moment in the cropping season, as well as health care spending that would otherwise have been used to invest in the farm. For example, IFPRI discussion paper by Asenso-Okyere et al.,(2009) show that malaria, and or HIV Aids can cause major losses in some areas of agricultural production.

- Fire.
- Floods.
- Wildlife breakdowns and damage-both on the farm itself and on key infrastructure (such as a washed-out bridge).
- Theft of animals, stores or tools, for example.
- Social commitments to family members and friends (such as a funeral) may also deplete money and time, although this may later be reciprocated.
- The government itself may be a source of shocks in some countries, through grabbing land, forced labor, unexpected taxes, etc.

Bad weather, low prices and (often) pests and diseases are considered covariate threats, which means they appear to affect most or all of the farms in an area at about the same time. Threats are labeled idiosyncratic risks for individual farms and households like disease.

2. **Decision-Making in the Face of Uncertainty:** Farmers have to make investment and management decisions based on their perceptions of prices, costs, and risks, what crops, how much and when to plant, what resources to use, how much to sell and store. Many farmers are risk-averse and therefore invest less to maximize production and profits than would be optimal. For example, because of fear of drought risk (when fertilizer will be wasted), a farmer can fail to apply fertilizer. The aggregate effect of all these individual farmer decisions—as well as the risks themselves—can have enormous implications for the food supply, economic growth, and balance of payments of a nation, and consequently, for the survival of the powerful government. Reducing confusion for farmers is therefore often a high priority activity for national policymakers.

5.5.9 Agriculture Is Connected to the Natural Environment in Two Ways

Clearly, there are significant two-way links between agriculture and the natural environment that policymakers should recognize. It is estimated that agriculture accounts for almost 40% of land use and 70% of freshwater use around the world (FAO, 2013a). Agricultural production can contribute to climate change, as can climate change (Nelson et al., 2009; Hertel, 2013). The economic concept of externalities refers to benefits or losses incurred by the wider society or environment which are not reflected directly in private financial costs or profits. For instance, pouring into the river old pesticides can not affect the income of a farmer, but it will cost others (a negative externality). One of the challenges facing agricultural policymakers is to design policies that align market signals (economic incentives) for farms and agribusiness to promote positive externalities and minimize negative externalities.

Agriculture can have a harmful effect, if not well controlled, through:

- Increasing land and water use, increasing the world's amount of forest and wildland and ecosystem services.
- Air pollution and emissions of greenhouse gases, for example, methane from livestock digestion and nitrous oxide from burning and deforestation.
- Development of pests and diseases resistant to pesticides and antibiotics.
- Reduction in biodiversity.
- Soil erosion and loss of topsoil from poor soil management.
- Salinization (increasing salt levels in soil), e.g., from poor irrigation management.
- Pollution of soil and water from manures and slurries, fertilizers, and pesticides that harm habitats and human health.
- Disease transmission, either from animals (e.g., brucellosis) or by creating conditions that benefit vectors of disease (e.g., malarial mosquitoes).
- Use of non-renewable fossil fuels.
- Supporting rising populations of people with other detrimental environmental effects (e.g., through urbanization).

Steinfeld et al. (2006) address the major environmental challenges posed by increased livestock production, including the use of marginal land, emissions of carbon dioxide and methane, and water pollution.

5.5.10 Gender and Social Issues in Agriculture Are Relevant

Farming is not just a job, but a way of life that often includes the entire family (even in wealthy countries), and it typically provides both a home and a workplace. Economists sometimes treat the farming household as a single business enterprise (the unitary household model). There is ample evidence, however (e.g., Udry, 1996), that men and women often control different assets and make decisions about different parts of farming work. Women account for about half of the agricultural labor force in Africa, East, and South-East Asia and over one-third in South Asia (FAO, 2011a). Agricultural and trade policies should take into account differences in gender roles and unequal impacts on men and women. Women also face additional farming constraints, including lower access to resources, agricultural inputs, education, and data, compared to male farmers. In many cultures, women are historically primarily responsible for tasks such as food processing and preparation, child-rearing and fuel and water collection, all activities that are important to the rural household economy, although they are often not classified in national accounts as 'economically active jobs' (FAO, 2011a). Women make trade-offs in time between these activities and agriculture, which means that time-saving investments in other sectors (e.g., water supply, childcare) may have pay-offs in agricultural production. Another significant aspect of family farming is that households can consume or store a great deal of their own production, and several factors can influence their decision to store or sell the surplus. A fine line may exist between a household being a net producer (selling more food than buying) and a net consumer (buying more food than selling) (Aksoy and Isik-Dikmelik, 2008). The poorest farmers may need to sell for immediate needs, such as school fees for their children, immediately after harvest. On the other hand, farmers with a surplus can hold on to their output in order to get better prices later in the year. This can make forecasting rates of marketed output challenging for national policymakers. Eventually, it is differentiated by the social nature of agriculture from many other industries. The land is not just an economic input, for instance, but may have a major social and cultural significance, as well as providing family members with a place to live and a fallback job if other jobs fail.

5.5.11 Much of Agriculture Is Outside the Formal Economy in Low-Income Countries

Lastly, most small-scale farms (and small-scale farm traders) operate outside the formal economy, meaning that they are not registered, taxed, and poor quality when there is any information available about their production, trade, and use of inputs like labor. It is estimated that more than 60% of the world's agricultural workforce is employed informally (Bacchetta et al., 2009). Most trade transactions (such as sales or hiring labor) go unrecorded in poor rural areas; in addition, there are many deals outside the money system.

A note on terminology: historically, global reports on the informal economy have not included small-scale farms and people working on them, although this may change (Chen, 2007), so it may be easier to use the less accurate term 'outside the formal economy' in relation to farming.

This has two major implications for the architects of the agricultural policy:

- First of all, policy measures targeted at the formal agricultural economy may have little or no impact on those outside it. For example, it has been argued that South Africa's trade liberalization has not reduced poverty among the unskilled and rural poor, partially because 'the poor are largely isolated from the formal sector' (Sandrey et al., 2011, p. 6).
- Second, policymakers base their decisions on information (ideally, at least). With a few exceptions (for example, India, according to Mishra and Shankar (2013, p. 19), there is little or no data available in many government systems on small-scale farmers and agricultural traders, and the scattered and remote existence of farms makes data collection costly. This means that policy planners and economic modelers may work in a 'data vacuum' compared to some other industries, such as growth, sales, and labor data.

5.5.12 Unique Market and Market Concentration

From the farm to the market (in the same or different countries) exchange will take place at all rates. The structure of the agricultural market illustrates many of the farming characteristics mentioned above. The considerations below hinder policymaking:

1. The size, dispersion, and complexity of market chains and high marketing margins mean that changes in consumer prices or wholesale input prices are not reflected in changes in prices paid to and by farmers (i.e., weak price transmission). A rise in maize prices in the capital city, for example, could take a long time to

cause an increase in maize prices in a remote farm (if ever). This is one of the (many) reasons why the response of supply to a price increase is often poor and slow (Rao, 1989).

2. For example, concentration in key parts of value chains, the supply of inputs or wholesaling may mean small and uncompetitive markets. If agricultural policies are not well-designed, then other actors in the market chain will capture their benefits rather than the farmers as expected. For example, if a subsidy of fertilizers is not well-designed, then a few big traders may reap most of the benefits, and the farmer may not see much of a price difference.
3. In order to encourage higher productivity to agriculture; governments also invest in research and expansion. In many cases, however, technological change includes new inputs (such as seed varieties) that rely on the process of the input market to reach the farmer.

5.6 AGRICULTURAL POLICY RATIONALE AND THE STATE'S ROLE IN THE ECONOMY

Traditionally, in both developing and developed countries, agriculture is characterized by heavy government intervention. But the question is fair: why are we having agricultural policies? Why can the government decide to take action to alter the market's natural functioning? There have been proposed many explanations. Some of them have to do with the theory of economic efficiency and the supposed supremacy of competitive equilibrium. Therefore, the task of economic policy should be to eliminate all barriers that prevent markets from achieving a competitive balance. Some reasons are based on concerns regarding equality, which are concerns about equal wealth distribution among all people.

5.7 THE NEW-INSTITUTIONAL VIEW OF AGRICULTURAL POLICY

Markets are exchange-enabling economic structures. At the beginning of a country's economic growth, government action may be required to promote the creation of non-existent markets. A simple precondition for a market to exist, for instance, is that property rights are well defined and implemented. It is natural to understand that property rights must be clearly defined in order to trade it. Typically, granting, and implementing property rights is the responsibility of the government. For example, land reform policies are still a very important task for many developing countries' governments. Even though markets are well developed, government intervention may be necessary to achieve the efficiency expected by the classical theory of general equilibrium. In contrast, the presence of transaction costs that prohibit the occurrence of some of the most beneficial trades. Transaction costs are a very general concept that can be used to characterize a wide range of phenomena, including asymmetric information, strategic behavior, geographic distances, and lack of infrastructure. Transaction costs are all charges that have to be paid in the course of a transaction. These include transportation, administrative costs, storage of information, etc. Economic policy's current institutional view sees institutions as the economy's response to transaction costs. The corresponding view of the state's role in the economy is, therefore, to encourage the growth and functioning of all institutions (including markets among them). According to the transaction cost analysis of market failures, the role of the government should be that of reducing or eliminating transaction costs. Institutions are sets of rules and agreements governing economic activity.

5.8 EFFICIENCY VS. EQUITY

Efficiency should not be the public officials' only concern. Another justification for state economic intervention is to ensure equal distribution of resources among the population. For example, by raising higher proportional taxes to the highest income levels, progressive tax systems have the explicit goal of reducing the differences in disposable income. In addition, the main objective of reducing income disparities is to provide essential social services such as education and health services at a reduced cost to part of the population. Agricultural policies can also have effects on distribution. For example, low food prices have a greater benefit for poor consumers than they do for rich consumers. Unfortunately, there are trade-offs between efficiency and equity goals: for example, by keeping agricultural prices low, investment is discouraged and the sector's growth is compromised in the long run.

5.9 THE STATE'S FUNCTION IN THE MARKET ECONOMY

Governments have been heavily involved in the agricultural sector throughout the world over the past few years, both in developing and developed countries. Most of the operation consisted of direct market control and resource utilization. There were several institutions in place for governments to:

- regulate domestic prices of agricultural products and inputs (through taxes, subsidies, centralized procurement, buffer stocks, etc.).
- control the use and the price of factors.
- limit imports or exports, either directly or indirectly through the exchange rate.

Although in many countries these steps are still in effect, experience has shown that such a strong intervention can be unsustainable in the long run. The criteria to be satisfied by a successful sector management approach are (Norton, 2001):

- **Economic Sustainability:** The plan must be economically beneficial. A strategy that cannot be proven to be related to any clearly identifiable economic advantage for the country will not be accepted for a long time.
- **Sustainabilityin Social and Political Terms:** The advantages must be borne by a large part of the population that refers to the poorest part of the population in the less developed countries (LDCs). Any strategy can be continued for a long time in the absence of broad consensus, other than the threat of social unrest and revolts.
- **Fiscal Sustainability:** Most programs have an implied cost of the budget. Policies whose funding source is not clearly identified should not be enforced fiscal sustainability Most programs have an implied cost of the budget. Policies whose funding source is not clearly identified should not be enforced.
- **Sustainability of the Institutions:** To sustain them, most initiatives need the institution's growth and operation. The effectiveness of the policy is severely undermined when the organizational capacity to implement the policies is weak.
- **Environmental Preservation:** Last but not least, all economic

policies should also be evaluated in terms of their long-term environmental impact. Water reserves, fish stocks, forests, and soil should be protected from over-exploitation by resisting policies that do not create the right opportunities for natural environment conservation.

The definition of sustainability refers to a collection of action's long-term viability. Many observers believe that a modern view of the state's position in the economy should not be that of heavy, direct, price-and regulatory intervention. Rather, it is expected to be:

- Track market operation to identify potential anomalies and potential lack of competition.
- Provision of power, communications, and transport services where the demand is not sufficiently large to warrant the private provision of such services.
- Reducing transaction costs.
- Redistributing income across different sectors of the population (for example from urban to rural, from rich to poor, from the coastal areas to the interior, etc.).

In other words, the government must assist and encourage the functioning of the private sector by providing the infrastructural and institutional framework within which the private economy can operate at its best, and should constantly monitor this functioning by preventing the accumulation of economic power in the hands of a few large private agents.

5.10 THE IMPORTANCE OF ECONOMICS IN AGRICULTURAL POLICY

Agriculture is very open to opportunities from the economy. Agricultural economists have contributed to the development of agricultural programs and policies to tackle the different economic situations.

5.11 AGRICULTURAL POLICY OF ECONOMIC GOALS

The main goal of government intervention in free markets from an economic perspective is to mitigate market failure and encourage productivity. Market failure occurs when there is no effective and/or productive (at least cost) distribution of scarce resources by the free market to achieve full social welfare. Other economic goals may include:

- **Equity:** A 'fair' distribution of income among regions or types of people.
- **Stability:** Minimizing unexpected changes for farmers, businesses, and consumers, along with the costs of adjusting to changes.
- Other specific food security, health/nutrition, social, and environmental aims.

It depends on society and decision-makers how maximum social welfare is defined in practice. There are often trade-offs between different social priorities, such as the goal of maximizing farmers' incomes and the goal of reducing urban market food prices. Economists themselves do not agree on the goals and trade-offs to be made—this is the role of politicians in general. Economists, however, can estimate the potential size of costs and benefits of different policy choices for different groups in society, look at the effect of assigning different weights to different policy goals, and ultimately help decision-makers make better choices.

6

ECONOMICS OF AGRICULTURAL POLICY

CONTENTS

6.1 Development of The Economics of Agricultural Policy 104

6.2 The Farm Problem 104

6.3 The Economic Consequences of Aid For Markets And Related Policies 107

6.4 Political Economy Models 112

6.5 Economics of Quota And Price Discrimination Programs 113

6.6 The Economics of Government-Run Price Stabilization And Buffer Stock Schemes 115

6.7 The Economics of Government Policy For Subsidized Crop Insurance 118

6.8 The Economics of Agricultural R&D Policy 120

6.1 DEVELOPMENT OF THE ECONOMICS OF AGRICULTURAL POLICY

Agriculture has been the main part of the economy for most of human history. It was therefore natural that the economics of agricultural policy should be a core part of government activity's economics.

6.2 THE FARM PROBLEM

Almost all of the early study of the agricultural policy was focused on specific agricultural relationships that required broad government interventions on agricultural commodity markets. The central finding, dating back to the 1920s, was that agriculture suffered from low returns on human and other resources, low income for farm families, and excessive volatility (and particularly downside shocks) on returns and income from the investment. Economic experts participated in designing and promoting progressive food policies aimed at solving the perceived farm issue that market forces alone clearly could not address. TheodoreW. Schultz coined the iconic declaration of the farm question for subsequent generations in 1945 (Gardner, 1992; Brandow, 1977). Schultz conceived of the farm problem as being primarily guided from outside agriculture but exacerbated within a predominantly non-agricultural economy by the conditions inherent in agriculture. Combined with a lack of resources in agriculture, accounts of severe poverty and suffering suggested to Schultz, as to Davis, that migration from agriculture was inevitable. Schultz characterized the lack of stability to include natural variability in supply and demand for farm commodities as well as other factors resulting in highly volatile but generally decreasing relative prices of farm commodities and rapid reductions in labor used on farms. Davis (1947) questioned some interpretations of "instability" in the historical record in his long review Agriculture in an Unstable Economy, but mostly disagreed with Schultz and his colleagues' recommendations for active market interventions.

In recommendations for forward prices, sponsored by the government, among other things, D.Gale Johnson (1947) emphasized that farmers made investment and output decisions before they could recognize the market conditions they would face later and thus often made what, ex-post, turned out to be mistaken with uncertainty. Johnson, Schultz, and contemporaries encouraged the use of forward prices guaranteed by the government to direct good agricultural decisions. Earlier, putting aside the claims of variability,

Houthakker (1967) wrote, "The farm problem, it will be argued here, is primarily an economic growth problem. To put it briefly: the demand for agricultural products is increasing more slowly than demand for non-farm products; thus, economic growth requires a steady transfer of labor and other resources from agriculture to other sectors. Because there is resistance to this change, farming usually involves too many people and as a result, farm income per capita is depressed." Bruce Gardner (1992) drew Houthakker's link back to an informative paper by Simon (1947), who showed how agriculture develops with a steady outflow of labor in a two-sector system under economic growth. Glenn Johnson's book The U.S. Overproduction Trap was directed. "Some people would agree that the U.S. has a 'farm crisis'" (Johnson and Quance 1972, p. 1). Building on Johnson (1950), the rest of the book presented his "asset fixity" model, arising from adjustment costs that delay resource movements from farm industries, and marshaled proof that such adjustment costs are important. Cochrane (1958) pointed out that rapid marginal cost reductions by the implementation of the technology would lower prevailing farm prices and disadvantage lagging adopters and further use this as a justification for government supply management programs.

Agriculture faced several challenges, most of which were used for farm policies as a rationale (or sometimes rationalizations) (Benedict, 1953; Johnson, 1958; Hathaway, 1963; Tweeten, 1971). But the farm problem's economics per se centered on low and volatile farm prices and incomes. Among many others, Schultz (1945) pointed out several significant stylized facts regarding agriculture in modern society:

1. The aggregate functions of supply and demand for agricultural products are intermediate inelastic;
2. Technical adjustment shifts the supply curve faster than the increase in income shifts the demand curve;
3. The demand elasticity of income for many agricultural commodities is high. Johnson (1950) found that input prices dropped in the Great Depression together with production prices.

Functions of agricultural supply were more robust than could be indicated by direct observations or approximate estimates. Nevertheless, a relatively inelastic supply remained a stylized fact accepted. Political economists have long recognized that the more inelastic the demand function for domestic farm production, the higher the price variability resulting from a given amount of supply variability, and the greater the potential for domestic supply control to raise prices for agricultural products. Among others, Davis (1935) recognized that accounting for international export markets was essential for assessing the causes of declining agricultural prices and evaluating the New Deal policy. Together with trade barriers, early supply management strategies were designed to protect domestic markets from imports. With commodities such as wheat, exports were significant, and economists recognized that programs that caused high domestic prices would reduce or eliminate commercial exports (i.e., a fairly flexible market with exports). Therefore, the plans included inventory management and government policies on export dumping to move production out of the domestic market. Some economists had rejected their previous notions by the 1940s and particularly in the 1950s that core economic features of agriculture needed permanent supply control and price support. Nonetheless, Galbraith (1954) overemphasized the case when he argued that economists in agricultural policy were largely unanimous in strongly rejecting the political consensus that farming required farm subsidy programs to perform adequately in the post-war economy. Clearly, influential economists like Willard Cochrane continued to favor price support and programs for supply control. Galbraith himself argued that adequate data and relevant economic theory still showed that without a heavy New Deal government role, agriculture could not achieve efficiency or income goals, and that those who oppose price supports and supply controls had deliberately misread relevant evidence. For example, referring to the claim that demand for farm commodities might be elastic, Galbraith (1954), citing econometric studies by Karl Fox and George Mehren and a review of estimates by Schultz (1953), claimed that "the statement on price elasticity of demand [of supply control skeptics] is in flat conflict with the evidence." The differentiation between the farm policy's productivity and income targets was illustrated frequently—for example, by Schultz (1941). While extreme poverty on farms prompted support programs in the 1920s and 1930s, many economists recognized that support for prices benefited the majority of larger farms and did relatively little to alleviate rural poverty. Johnson (1944) re-emphasized the common distinction between cost and price control allocation and delivery functions. He also noted that farm prices may be significant for poverty alleviation in some cases and stressed, citing Marshall, that crippling poverty has long-term consequences for individuals, especially children, and the nation's future economic success. A major shift in the 1950s was the emergence of more comprehensive and systematic applications of explicit mathematical modeling of agricultural policy issues. For instance, Howell (1954) developed an explicit indifference curve method in an overlooked article in the Quarterly Journal of Economics to compare the welfare implications of price incentives and direct payment systems, concluding in favor of direct payments. Brandow and others have also begun to develop better statistical evidence on essential parameters and to use parameter estimates for modeling policy simulation (Schulze, 1971).

Experiencing data showing low income and low returns (ex-post), economists-built models where costly and time-consuming economic changes are needed. Economic development involved asset changes from agriculture, and this meant relatively low returns and extreme poverty in some cases during the transition. But the farming sector is relative to the rest of the economy in rich countries, the big adjustments are now complete, and farmers who make their living on the farm tend to earn normal returns and relatively high incomes. In addition, with convergence between farm and non-farm economies and markets available to deal with price risk, annual price volatility is less a variable in income or consumption variance on farms (Gardner, 2002). Despite the absence of sufficient evidence or analytical methods, the best early economists demonstrated that close observation of business dynamics, thorough application of economic intuition, and fairly simple models could provide deep insights into policy consequences.

6.3 THE ECONOMIC CONSEQUENCES OF AID FOR MARKETS AND RELATED POLICIES

By the 1980s, many economists had rejected the use of the farm issue as a basis for policy recommendations, including many who had previously supported subsidy programs. Nonetheless, the "farm problem" claim has remained popular among farm subsidy proponents in one form or another, and the New Deal programs focused on the "farm problem" principle still dominate agricultural commodity policies. How farm programs impact the size distribution of farms and related structural steps have been a longstanding issue. Postwar publications through 1985 did not include rigorous quantitative testing of the impacts of policies on farm size, and economic modeling was often unconvincing about significant effects, although various authors provided economic reasoning indicating that farm programs might increase or decrease farm size. Sumner (1985) found in his analysis of the relevant literature that farm price and income support systems as implemented in the United States had indirect and mostly minor or offsetting effects on distributions of farm size.

6.3.1 The Economic Welfare Impacts of Agricultural Policies

The study of the economic effects of agricultural policies, along with the policies themselves, has developed significantly over the past 100 years. Early research was often prescriptive and based on farm prices and profits (e.g., see the award-winning agricultural policy essays summarized by Nicholls and Johnson (1946) and the Jesness (1949) edited reading collection). The analysis of policies has gradually shifted to a more analytical approach, seeking to understand the choices made by policy instruments and their environments in relation to their disaggregated health consequences. It is now popular for agricultural economists to view the economic effects of policies in terms of cost and profit distribution between different interest groups, defined in terms of their positions as consumers, taxpayers or producers (or suppliers of production factors), and the net effects on society as a whole (the sum of the effects on producers and others). It wasn't always like that. As noted above, statistical system effects forecasts concentrated in the early days on the impact of aggregates such as output volumes, imports, number of farms, farm prices, consumer prices, land prices, and farm income as calculated in national accounts. Of example, in terms of these results, realistic analysis of the policy outcomes and many simulation model outcomes continues to be discussed rather than product or consumer surplus or theoretical constructs.

Deliberations of the systematic study of agricultural policy's welfare implications always begin with Wallace (1962). In a free market system for a non-traded commodity, Wallace (1962) compared the outcomes of two stylized policies: a price limit and a minimum cost or loss payment scheme. Such two policies were designed in Wallace (1962) to achieve a defined value for producers above the market-clearing price, but the quota policy benefits producers at the expense of consumers, with no impact on taxpayers, while the subsidy policy benefits both consumers and producers, all at the expense of taxpayers. Under the subsidy, the producers' gains are significantly higher. Based on the relative sizes of supply elasticity and demand elasticity, the net social cost or deadweight loss from the quota may be higher or lower than that for the subsidy. A disadvantage of this study is that it may not be appropriate to keep the price impact of the product constant when comparing the instruments. The papers by Nerlove (1958), Dardis (1967), and Josling (1969) are rooted in a more practical framework of contrasting policies. Instead of measuring social costs for a given price or gross income rise, strategies are measured in terms of redistribution efficiency or transfer efficiency. Export performance metrics provide a way to equate producers' gains with the total costs to consumers, taxpayers, and society. Gardner (1983), who used surplus transformation curves (STCs), traditionally credited to Josling (1974), popularized the concept of contrasting policies in terms of their marginal and average export performance. He showed how the option between subsidies and quotas depends on elasticity, the scale of the transfer from consumers-cum-taxpayers to producers, and the marginal cost of government funds for social opportunities. Such graphic representations allow us to compare policy implications, recommend more effective policies, and understand policy choices. Subsequently, other studies have expanded the study of Gardner to account for different policy mechanisms, interest groups, and business conditions, including cases with market power in trade. Alston and Hurd (1990) found that transfers from taxpayers to suppliers could be made without any inequalities in output or consumption if the policies are not mutually exclusive and can be mixed efficiently. In several papers, the concept that combining instruments could maximize transfer efficiency was formalized and expanded, moving beyond two interest groups and two policies. A synthesis and analysis of these and related studies were proposed by Bullock, Salhofer, and Kola (1999).

6.3.2 Multimarket Models

Though strong, the modern model of supply and demand for products on the Single Market has some shortcomings. Commodity market contributors are classified as either producers or consumers, and thus their welfare is consolidated. In order to address an interest in disaggregated welfare implications or provide other information, it is essential to use models that disaggregate horizontally across domestic and foreign producers and consumers and vertically between different suppliers of production factors and end consumers. In terms of different products and spatial aggregates, the correct extent of explanation of the vertical structure and factor markets and the horizontal structure can depend on the intent of the analysis. Modeling multiple connected markets allows us to take into account cross-market effects, which may be valuable to precisely measure the prevalence of the commodity in question on the market as well as to study the effects on the commodity market in question.

6.3.3 Capitalization of Program Benefits Into Land Values

Regarding Floyd (1965), agricultural commodity markets' two-factor, one-output models were used to investigate the incidence of agricultural policy among factor markets (see also Muth, 1964). Agricultural economists generally say that the benefits of agricultural subsidies are essentially largely, if not completely, capitalized into the land as the fixed factor. Nonetheless, as Alston and James (2002) demonstrate using a version of Floyd's model, this view relies on the use of severe and possibly incorrect assumptions for most applications. Analysis of such models shows that an absolutely decoupled fee attached to property should be fully expressed in cash rentals and fully capitalized into the land. The same would be true for an output subsidy on land use under unreasonable conditions (such as a fixed supply of land). More broadly, however, even land subsidies will have some impact on combinations of inputs and production, thereby moving the incidence to non-land product suppliers and consumers in part. It is expected that a subsidy on output will have even less of its impact on land, but it will still have a disproportionate impact on landowners as suppliers of the least elastic production factor. Econometric studies have generally found a surprisingly small proportion of landowners 'subsidy benefits (e.g., Kirwan, 2009). One reasonable interpretation is that the authors estimate an intermediate run effect that is less than the long-run effect due to the fixity associated with contracts or roles played by expectations or other dynamics.

Through time, the emphasis switched from examining policy effects on economies to focusing on the incidence of government economic welfare. Deadweight losses from farm product programs are generally small compared to the distributional impacts between various variable producers, intermediaries, taxpayers, and consumers. Further work is needed to align recent econometric results with theoretical model projections, but landowners do not get all or even most of the benefits from farm subsidies.

6.3.4 Practical Policy Models

When computational power grew in the 1960s, policy analysis undertaken to test government programs to implement statistical models using specifications of applicable supply and demand functions in production and input markets quickly became commonplace. Schultze (1971) analyzed Brandow and USDA-ERS early model findings to test farm income and other effects of alternative farm policies, including supply limits and price aid. By the late 1960s and early 1970s, these attempts were institutionalized with large multi-market models integrating multiple formulas to understand relations between crop and livestock markets. The USDA also regularly issued quantitative assessments of policy effects on a number of economic factors, including rates, farm income, and government budget costs. Usually, models did not report any effects on welfare indicators such as producer or product surplus. The Food and Agricultural Policy Research Institute (FAPRI) issued forecasts to Congress beginning in the 1980s. These models were also commonly used by organizations such as the World Bank (WB), which built on the work of Tyers and Anderson (1992), to analyze trade policy options.

Modeling developments included introducing more complex commodities, countries, and linkages, as well as integrating stochastic elements in simulations. The power of these broad models is their multi-market relations awareness. Nevertheless, a downside is that policies have traditionally been more complicated than the requirements of the model permit, so that even detailed models still start with rough approximations of how policies affect incentives. Policies are viewed as uniform ad valorem subsidy equivalents in many models, whereas the actual policies that include voluntary involvement choices, side conditions or other elements of multiple instruments, other nonlinearities, or other features that make an ad valorem subsidy equivalent far from being equivalent in specific respects. Voluntary production and input-based supply management policies along with market supports and direct payment systems, as implemented in the U.S., have been difficult to successfully describe in models that attempt to cover many goods and many countries. Commodity coverage limitations mean that few, if any, large multi-commodity models deal with fruits, vegetables, tree nuts, and other essential crops covering relatively few acres. Nevertheless, aggregation means that models often overlook, for example, market differentiation by wheat class or rice type, which is often vital to understanding a market or a policy that applies to it. As discussed in Josling et al. (this issue), these issues are more evident for computable general equilibrium (CGE) models of the kind which started to be widely implemented in the 1980s but became popular with the spread of the GTAP (Global Trade Analysis Project) method and data sets in the 1990s (Hertel, 1997) for modeling global agricultural policy.

A wide range of simulation methods have become available to applied researchers who are faced with the task of balancing the modeling context with the complexity of their study or policy problem and correcting the relevant details. Wide general models have many advantages, but they may not be versatile enough to address some specific policy questions. All empirical models require parameters, and parameter values are incorporated in many general-purpose systems, such as those associated with FAPRI or GTAP. The challenge for the user of these models is to understand how the model's parameters fit the research question in terms of run length, consistent prices, policy expectations, and other characteristics. In addition to modeling advances, policy research was supported by new data on subsidies and subsidy initiatives.

The producer subsidy equivalent (PSE) initiated by Josling in 1973 (FAO, 1973), discussed by Josling et al. and Hertel (1989), was one of the most positive moves. To contribute to a better understanding of specific policy issues and solutions, research needs to carefully identify the policies addressed and the most important aspects of market relationships. Multi-purpose multi-market models often offer reliability and wide reach, but this is often at the cost of inconsistent representations of policy instruments and parameters so that model outcomes do not accurately reflect policy offsets.

Realistic approaches to policy analysis require careful adjustment to policy measures and business nuances of design specifications. For big, complex general-purpose models, this is particularly challenging.

6.4 POLITICAL ECONOMY MODELS

Political scientists conducted frequent analyzes of agricultural policy in the JFE in the 1940s and 1950s. These consisted of economic concepts and facts, but in the way that emerged a few decades later, they did not apply economics to agricultural policy. In the 1970s and early 1980s, public-choice economics was widely throughout vogue, with numerous rent-seeking studies and other government-policy interest group models published by prominent economists including Annie Krueger, Gary Becker, Richard Posner, Gordon Tullock, and James Buchanan. Agricultural economists are able to grab the insights and apply them to examine the factors along with the effects of agricultural policies. Problems described in the literature include the causative factors of the choice of policy instruments and their settings (partly related to the literature on transfer efficiency) that define the pattern of benefits and costs and how those choices vary between countries and commodities, and why. Several researchers suggested and developed models of political preference to measure the parameters of public choice. Rausser and Freebairn (1974) were among the first to deduce implicit government benefit weights. Many applications have not always been as formal. Sieper's (1982) Rationalizing Rustic Regulation is a tour de force treatment which, when it first appeared as a conference paper in 1979, revolutionized economic perspectives on Australia's farm policy past. At about the same time, Rausser (1982, 1992) addressed U.S. strategy in terms of "positive" and "predatory," while Anderson and Hayami (1986) illustrated global disparities in support levels for farm producers. Gardner (1987a) tried to econometrically account for the pattern of aid to U.S. farmers, and Bullock (1995) explored the foundations of successful agricultural policy redistribution. De Gorter and Swinnen (2002) recognize these and other important contributions.

Political economy models have given some insight into the consequences of agricultural policy, but the clear and parsimonious models used do not capture much of the policy process well. Further work is needed to understand the various patterns of changes in agricultural policies between goods, nations, and over time.

6.5 ECONOMICS OF QUOTA AND PRICE DISCRIMINATION PROGRAMS

Most of the agricultural commodity policy's economic discussion centered on price support and related grain, oilseed, and cotton programs. Influential economists such as Cochrane (1959) were proposing production quotas schemes for all major program products, which became the basis for Wallace's (1962) and later Innes and Rausser's (1989) welfare correlations in a more general framework. But while land set-asides have been implemented for many years, the main field crops or livestock products have not been consistently applied to such allocation or quota system. Many major U.S. program crops such as cotton, peanuts, and dairy policy literature have focused on the effects of allocation and quotas, and price discrimination schemes. These commodities were considered separately, starting with the New Deal, because their markets and conditions of supply were distinct. This section first considers quota programs and then considers price discrimination schemes, in particular, to distinguish for different commodities between domestic and international markets. Major problems with quotas of input and output include:

- Measurement of price and quantity impact, including exchange;
- Welfare incidence;
- Costs of transfer restrictions;
- Program operation given yield and demand variability;
- Capitalization of benefits.

Each one of them has its very own literature that we can only concentrate on here. Current criticism of U.S. quota systems began with the review of Burley cigarette programs by Glenn Johnson (1952). His detailed consideration of the cost, income, and other impacts of input quotas has been considered an excellent model of policy analysis applied. Paul Johnson (1965) used a more direct graphical analysis in an important article to demonstrate the economic impact of production quotas and then extended this model with detailed empirical calculations to calculate the producer and consumer surplus welfare effects as demonstrated by Wallace (1962). Rucker, Thurman, and Sumner (1995) expanded the model to approximate supply parameters and found that quota transfers constraints imposed relatively small aggregate losses of deadweight but transferred large amounts of income between interest groups. Quota and allocation schemes have provided easy cases where rentals to government-created property and rent capitalization of asset values can be examined. Innovative econometric calculations of the capital value of tobacco allocations were presented by Seagraves (1969) to show that the rates of return to allocation ownership were quite high. Subsequent research (e.g., Barichello, 1995) has reported quota ownership return rates of 20% or more, suggesting that quota prices have been depressed by political risk (Johnson, 1991). In many countries and for many products, but particularly dairy, marketing quotas were used to enforce price discrimination. Through Australian dairy policy studies in the 1960s, Ross Parish and Alan Lloyd made early contributions to this literature. Rucker and Thurman (1990) thoroughly measured the welfare and other effects of a complex marketing quota policy for U.S. peanuts and price discrimination. In other countries, price discrimination and pooling policies were used more extensively (e.g., in Australia and Canada for dairy, wheat, sugar, and eggs), usually to keep domestic prices above international prices, and attracted a number of studies (e.g., Parish, 1962), some of which were published in AJAE. Sieper (1982) presented a comprehensive review and analysis of both the causes and consequences of these and other Australian agricultural price policies. Milk marketing orders have been the most prominent example of price discrimination and pooling rule in the United States.

Kessel (1967) originally examined the welfare economics and other implications of these programs and established them more fully through Ippolito and Masson (1978) with a model that was broadly applied and extended. Examples include work by Cox and Chavas (1991) and others who developed comprehensive simulation models for milk policy and Balagtas, Smith, and Sumner (2007), who found that incentives for individual farms to participate in the pool resulted in excess milk quality and consequent dissipation of rent. Like other policies, supply control details and price discrimination policies are important for loss of deadweight and distributional impacts. The quantitative effects of programs hinge on quota transfers and ownership limitations, and whether quotas apply to inputs or outputs. Return to quota ownership rates was generally high, likely due to political uncertainty and the expectation that the strategy might be short-lived. Usually, however, once services were discontinued, significant compensation payments were made to quota holders. Price discrimination policies may favor producers on the high price market at the expense of customers, but the effectiveness depends on the policy's supply response. In some cases, rentals are dissipated by increased output and by the expense of meeting the high entry criteria.

Supply management systems and price discrimination strategies have, primarily at the expense of consumers, favored manufacturers, and quota holders. Comprehensive impacts are heavily dependent on policy details. Specific program features such as restrictions on quota ownership and policy uncertainty have influenced the extent and distribution of quota benefits, and inadequate entry barriers have undermined price discrimination and pooling programs.

6.6 THE ECONOMICS OF GOVERNMENT-RUN PRICE STABILIZATION AND BUFFER STOCK SCHEMES

The concern in the impact of government policies on food storage and price stability dates at least as far back as Joseph's Old Testament account, which told the Pharaoh to store grain during times of abundance to avoid drought shortages (Genesis 41:53–57). As early as the first century BCE (Chen, 1974), government grain storage systems were introduced in China. Henry A. Wallace championed the creation of an "ever ordinary granary" as an agricultural secretary in the 1930s to smooth out demand and stabilize prices. Nevertheless, when these proposals were introduced in the 1938 Agricultural Adjustment Act, little was known about how buyers and farmers were influenced by public and private processing. Since then, there has been significant progress in understanding the economics of price stability and the function of processing.

6.6.1 Ever-Normal Granary

Wallace (1937) defined the ever-normal granary as a 'definite scheme whereby supplies would be sufficiently large to take care of the consumer after years of drought or other major calamities, but whereby the farmer would not be unduly penalized in years of favorable weather.' Under the scheme, if crops were high, the government would support prices by providing guaranteed rates of com to farmers. If prices were high enough at the time of the loan maturity, farmers would be able to repay the loans; but, if prices were low, producers would lose the collateral (i.e., the crop) to the government, essentially offering a floor below market prices in years of bumper crops. If prices were high due to short supplies, the government would release stocks on the market, thus dampening price hikes.

Economic experts were not all admirers. Davis (1938) was an early analyst who illustrated the challenges of handling buffer inventory systems, including:

1. Troubles with marketing help in relation to market prices without significant surpluses;
2. High possibility of processing, particularly in back-to-back droughts;
3. The high costs of the public storage to taxpayers;
4. The negative impact of buffer stock systems on trade.

Considered assumptions are that the ever-normal granary program, whatever its real intention, is simply a scheme for far-reaching control of farm production and marketing, at great expense to taxpayers and possibly customers. It would fail to achieve its main stated goals. Sometimes it would seem effective in service, sometimes a great debacle. Perhaps it would trigger more crises than it would pre-empt. It would do less good than crying "(Davis, 1938, p. 20). The welfare consequences of price stability are now long and rich literature. In this topic, Myers, Sexton, and Tomek provide a summary. A key limitation of the literature on early market stabilization (e.g., Waugh, 1944; Oi, 1961; Massel, 1969) was that the models had to be unduly simplistic in order to achieve tractable empirical results: stabilization policies were assumed to be costless, production decisions were assumed to be based on absolute foresight, and trade and private storage were usually removed from consideration. As researchers tried to create more realistic models, producing algebraic results that could be easily interpreted became increasingly difficult.

6.6.2 Storage Models

The shock of world grain prices in the early 1970s triggered a wide range of government research and multilateral carry out initiatives and the role of private storage in government activities. A key feature of this literature was the belief that the processing decisions were logical and forward-looking. Robert Gustafson (1958a, 1958b) was the first to use dynamic programming in the research funded and published by USDA to create optimal storage rules that considered potential supply variations. The further implementation of Gustafson's work was postponed until the studies by Johnson (1975), Johnson, and Sumner (1976), and Gardner (1979) were widely considered methodologically path-breaking and appreciated in this sense. Helmberger and Weaver (1977) and Newbery and Stiglitz (1981) contributed significantly to the design of forward-looking storage designs. Wright and Williams (1982, 1984) developed solutions for storage models with responsive supply and rational price expectations based on this earlier work. Their book of 1991 remains one of the storage model's clearest formulations (Williams and Wright, 1991). In the presence of private stockholders, Miranda, and Helmberger (1988) and Wright and Williams (1988) extended the storage model to include buffer stock schemes, and Miranda and Glauber (1995) extended the model further to include trade. These conceptual developments supported practical applications in contexts where government buffer stocks and other schemes for public storage had been implemented and generally failed, as Davis had predicted many years earlier. A relatively recent and spectacular example was the failure of Bardsley's (1994) analysis of the Australian wool reserve price scheme. The value of storage models for policy analysis is that in the case of forward-looking companies and private equity holders, researchers have been able to examine government price-stabilizing mechanisms. Although results rely on the requirements of parameters, numerically-based storage models provided additional insights into welfare issues and inventory management policies.

Governments have very limited potential to use transportation systems to balance markets in ways that are important to producers or customers without creating even more severe problems. The increase in food prices in 2007–2009 again raised issues such as global grain stocks linked to food security and commodity price stabilization schemes. Significantly, the majority of proposals included setting up strategic humanitarian reserves in poor countries rather than the large buffer stock schemes of the kind envisaged in the 1970s. The latest processing and stabilization policy debate echoed the economics literature's key findings. Analysts and officials acknowledged that attempts to stabilize prices through physical buffer stocks or "digital stocks" schemes involving short speculative positions on futures and options markets are likely to be expensive, unsuccessful, and short-lived (Wright, 2009). In fact, private stockholders are now recognized as key contributors to price stability, traditionally ignored or mistrusted in policy discussions.

6.7 THE ECONOMICS OF GOVERNMENT POLICY FOR SUBSIDIZED CROP INSURANCE

Economic studies on crop insurance can be traced back at least as far as the private insurance markets report by Valgren (1922). With the launch of the federal crop insurance system in 1938, several policy analyses, and some research are published in the JFE and USDA publications. This research was mostly descriptive in nature, but the issues facing crop insurance were discussed extensively, including what would later be known as adverse selection and moral hazard issues (Rowe and Smith, 1940). With the passage of the 1980 Federal Crop Insurance Act, economists began to pay serious attention to government programs to subsidize crop insurance. The 1980 Act (and subsequent legislation in 1994 and 2000) transformed the crop insurance plan from a small pilot project with minimal participation to a national scheme covering most of the major crops in most major growing regions. The amount of crop insurance research has increased dramatically, especially since 1994, parallel to program growth and actuarial data availability.

6.7.1 Economic Evaluation of Government Programs for Crop Insurance and Disaster Assistance

It was largely favored by early writings on the crop insurance program. Even now, some critics still say that under restricted and cautious testing by the state, the system is permitted. Some researchers have concluded, in some analysis of the crop insurance program that premiums would have to be subsidized up to 50% in order to attain 50% participation. Goodwin and Smith's (1995) comprehensive review of crop insurance showed why few, if any, private crop insurance markets existed and concluded that the cost of properly addressing adverse selection and moral hazard issues made crop insurance premiums prohibitively expensive without subsidies. Glauber (2004) pointed out that the overall performance of the program as measured by allowances paid to producers as a percentage of premiums collected were unchanged over the twenty-five years, even as increased subsidies brought more participants into the program.

The design of successful government crop insurance schemes (Chambers, 1989, 2002) concentrated on moral hazard and adverse selection problems. Botts and Boles (1958) developed numerical methods to determine crop yield risks on the basis of crop yield distributions and improved early informative research with better individual farm data (Skees and Reed, 1986; Knight and Coble, 1999; Babcock, Hart, and Hayes, 2004). The use of cumulative or weighted risks rather than individual risks offers another approach to addressing adverse problems of selection and moral hazard. Halcrow (1949) demonstrates that insurance contracts focused on zone yields could provide producers with substantial protection while avoiding adverse selection and moral hazard issues. Miranda (1991) recast the theory of Halcrow using a theoretical approach based on the capital asset pricing model based on financial economics. Several articles analyzed region yields and indexed insurance contracts after Miranda. The design of optimum area yield contracts was explored by Bourgeon and Chambers (2003).

6.7.2 The Effects of Subsidized Crop Insurance on Production Decisions

To the extent that production choices are influenced by subsidies or risk reduction, producer, and consumer welfare are likely to be affected. Nelson and Loehman (1987) recognized the potential for crop insurance to increase output. Empirical insurance work focused on its effects on the area planted and the use of inputs. Wu (1999) came to the conclusion that farms purchasing insurance were more likely to produce soybeans and less likely to produce forage crops. Goodwin, Vandeveer, and Deal (2004) found that crop premium costs had small effects on crop mix. Cross-commodity effects are likely to be mitigated by the fact that subsidized insurance for numerous crop alternatives is now available in the United States. Although no researches have directly examined the effects of crop insurance on yield, a great deal of research has been done on the effects of crop insurance on input use (see Glauber, 2004 review). Babcock and Hennesey (1996) and Smith and Goodwin (1996) concluded that the effects of crop insurance on input consumption are negative; suggesting that the resulting yield effect is likely to be negative. It remains an open question whether this effect is sufficiently large to offset any positive effect on crop acreage.

Developing and implementing government crop insurance that does not involve large premiums and possible losses of production is very difficult. The extreme complexity of developing agricultural insurance schemes that cater to farmers without large premium subsidies has been identified by models and empirical research. Moral hazard and adverse choice combine to make high and low break-even premiums. In addition, the unavoidable political demand to use insurance schemes as subsidy modes, particularly for regions with low or variable productivity, leads to costly and distorting government-sponsored insurance programs.

6.8 THE ECONOMICS OF AGRICULTURAL R&D POLICY

Agricultural studies work has changed agriculture, thus leading to the transformation of entire economies. Economic and policy issues arise because agricultural research is subject to a variety of market failures, because the resulting innovations and technological changes have significant economic implications for net income and distribution among individuals and production factors, and the consequences are difficult to discern. These problems were discussed and reported in a literature on agricultural R&D economics that started as such with T's work in the 1950s. W. Schultz and so on. Over the next half-century or so, economists have built analyzes, models, and calculations of the economic consequences of agricultural R&D and related policies in publications relating to a wide range of literature, drawing on and sometimes adding to the full range of economic subfields. Late foundations led to sub-literatures on:

1. Incorporate information and engineering positions in production models (e.g., Schultz, 1956; Griliches, 1964; Evenson and Kislev, 1973);
2. The adoption of innovations (e.g., Griliches, 1957; Evenson, 1967), (c) studies of research policies (e.g., Ruttan, 1982);
3. Modeling and measuring research impacts (e.g., Griliches, 1958; Petersen, 1967).

6.8.1 Studies of Research Institutions and Investments

A substantial portion of the economic literature on agricultural R&D policy involves studies identifying, recording, and quantifying the organizations that finance, oversee, and perform agricultural research, and the investments they make (e.g., Ruttan, 1982; Huffman and Evenson, 1993; Alston and Pardey, 1996; Alston et al., 2010). Such "descriptive" studies are of interest, but for econometric and other modeling studies, they also provide an organizational frame of reference including information. Agricultural R&D policies debated in this literature have highlighted responses to market failures that otherwise contributed to the private sector's underinvestment compared to the social optimum in certain forms of R&D (and farmers' education and extension). These replies included:

1. Enhanced intellectual property rights for invention;
2. Prizes, subsidies, or other incentives;
3. Government production of R&D in public institutions, the main instrument, and the subject of most of the work.

Many other policies of government have a direct impact on agricultural development, including:

1. Various kinds of technological regulation (e.g., animal welfare regulations, pesticide regulations, varietal restrictions, including those applied to biotech crop varieties);
2. Other environmental policies;
3. Certain types of farm commodity policies, such as quotas. Each of these has its own literature.

6.8.2 Models of the Size and Distribution of Research Benefits

Agricultural economic experts have used commodity market supply and demand models to represent the impact of agricultural research. Research in a standard research benefit model causes the supply curve of commodities to shift back and forth against a stationary demand curve, resulting in an increase in the quantity produced and consumed, and a lower price. The advantages were measured using Marshallian estimates of research-induced changes in consumer surplus to benefit consumers and research-induced changes in producer surplus to benefit producers. Several literature issues relate to the methods used to calculate the time-varying research-induced reduction in the production cost of the industry-wide system. The scale and composition of the sector to which the change factor belongs are other important factors.

Most of the documentation is about the determinants of agricultural R&D policy's incidence in spreading taxpayer-funded R&D benefits (and costs). The distribution of benefits between producers and consumers depends on the relative elasticity of supply and demand, the essence of the supply shift caused by study, and, less significantly, the operational types of supply and demand (Alston, Norton, and Pardey, 1995). Producers must benefit from a vertically parallel supply shift, but if demand is inelastic (e.g., Lindner and Jarrett, 1978), they will lose from a pivotal supply shift. The existence of the supply shift caused by research was controversial because it is critical for outcomes and not easy to observe. The possibility of losses to aggregate producers is often discounted on the grounds that either demand is relatively elastic or that a parallel shift in supply induced by research is relatively likely, but concrete empirical evidence has been elusive on this issue. Another problem is the allocation between producers of product benefits. But if we can be confident that producers will prosper, those who don't adopt the new technology won't gain and could even get worse if others' adoption leads to price cuts. Besides issues concerning the distribution of benefits and costs between adopters and non-adopters, there may be other distributional issues related to how the "producer surplus" is distributed among factor suppliers— do landowners benefit at the expense of farm labor suppliers, including farm operators, or vice versa? The standard model views R&D as being given free of charge by the government and the resulting innovation.

Moschini and Lapan (1997) have expanded the basic model to deal with proprietary work in an important contribution. The basic model also assumes market competition for goods and the lack of any other inequalities of the economy. Work benefits models have been extended to include different types of market distortions, including those arising from:

1. Government policies such as agricultural product programs or barriers to trade, including failure to enforce sufficient export taxes in the case of large countries;
2. The exercise of market power by middlemen;
3. Environmental externalities.

A typical finding is that in most situations the primary effect of a market distortion in this sense is to adjust the distribution of research benefits, with relatively small effects on the overall benefits (e.g., for information see Alston, Norton, and Pardey, 1995). Agricultural research models in a skewed market setting were used to draw inferences about the effect of market distortions on investment rates in agricultural research and the pace and direction of technological change (e.g., Hayami and Ruttan, 1971; Schultz, 1978; Mellor and Johnston, 1984, as reviewed by Alston, Norton, and Pardey, 1995). Several studies have used models of political economy or interest groups where the inequalities themselves are endogenous and are calculated in accordance with the research investment (e.g., de Gorter and Zilberman, 1990; Swinnen and de Gorter, 1998).

6.8.3 Models and Measures of Research Impacts

Several studies have modeled agricultural production or productivity as a function of agricultural research and expansion, often to estimate the rate of return on the study. Alston et al. (2000) provide a comprehensive summary of this literature (see also Schuh and Tollini, 1979; Evenson, 2002; Alston et al., 2010). Alston et al. (2000) performed a meta-analysis of 292 studies that recorded return estimates for agricultural research and development. A prevailing and consistent finding throughout the studies was that the return rate was quite high. The main mass of internal rates of return distribution reported in the literature ranges from 20% to 80% per annum. Many research reports may not have approached the same studies in the same way but have come to different general conclusions (see, for example, Evenson, 2002). Modeling of R&D lags and spillovers is correlated with key issues identified in these reviews. The distributions of lags used in R&D influence models have evolved. It was prevalent until recently to limit the length of the lag to less than twenty years. In earlier studies, available time series were short and lag lengths were presumed to be very short, but the more recent research usually tends to use much longer lags, as supported by Pardey and Craig's (1989) and Huffman and Evenson's (1993) work. A relatively long lag has implications for econometric estimates of the productivity effects of research and typically implies a lower rate of research return. Griliches (1957) analysis of hybrid-corn technology generation and dissemination across the United States was a seminal study of diffusion economics as well as the spatial spillover of agricultural technology. This research influenced others to incorporate individual innovations, many involving spatial spillovers. Many studies have attempted to determine, using regression-based approaches, the overall effects of R&D on total agricultural productivity, including spillover effects (e.g., Huffman and Evenson, 1993; Alston et al., 2010).

Agricultural productivity outcomes and experimental benefits have shown very high return rates. Despite substantial government intervention, these returns represent major and persistent underinvestment in agricultural R&D. Distributional effect measurements are less accurate and delicate. We still have no convincing, clear econometric evidence to demonstrate that farmers have actually benefited from technological change.

7

SPECIFIC AGRICULTURAL POLICY ANALYSIS

CONTENTS

7.1 Specific Agricultural Policy Review 126
7.2 Trade Policies 129
7.3 Exchange Rate Policy 133
7.4 Sectoral Policies 135
7.5 Policies That Promote Access To Resources 141
7.6 Credit Policies For Agriculture And Rural Areas 146
7.7 Water Utilization And Irrigation Policy 151

7.1 SPECIFIC AGRICULTURAL POLICY REVIEW

As discussed earlier on policy classification. Agricultural policies can also be classified in several ways, depending on their goals, the tools used, the commodity system that results from preagricultural productivity, and the experimental benefits showed very high yields. These returns represent a major and ongoing underinvestment in agricultural R&D, despite significant government intervention. Estimates of distributional effects are less reliable and more sensitive. There is still no compelling, consistent econometric evidence to demonstrate that farmers have actually benefited from the centered technological change, etc. The agricultural policy can be defined as follows in Norton (2002):

- Policies that affect producer's incentives, which include:

o Output price policies.

- Trade and exchange rate policies;
- Other policies that influence incentives;
- Policies that grant producers access to resources, among which we can identify:

o Food policy and food security.

- Land tenure policies;
- Water access policies and irrigation;
- Agricultural technology policies;
- Policies that influence access to factors' markets, most importantly:

o Labor market.

- Credit market.

Such a distinction is more in line with the modern view of agricultural sector government intervention as defined in previous sections and emphasizes the institutional position of policy.

7.1.1 Policies Have an Impact on Producer Incentives

Prices direct economic activities. For this reason, one of the most vital approaches to attempting and having an effect on economic activity is by changing expenditure, and policies aimed at enhancing incentives for producers can be described as rate policies. What are the costs of farmers? Any company's end result is measured using profit, which depends on the prices of each output and input. So, what absolutely things are the relative style of output versus entering prices for incentives for farmers, as a substitute for the absolute price of output and input prices. In other words, there is an expansion in profits only if output expenses rise proportionally extra than the prices of inputs. For example, when we discuss the consequences of higher input spending on a diagram with a constant grant function, we implicitly count on the rate remaining unchanged for those inputs. Only if all different prices are saved constant, an expand in output charge skill an enlarge in the relative phrases of trade between outputs and inputs. To focus on the distinction among absolute and relative prices, we call real prices the ones expressed in relative terms. Usually, real prices are obtained by dividing the absolute or nominal price levels by an index of all prices. Changing the real price of agricultural products ensures that farm prices change according to the overall level of the economy's values. We need to understand what determines them in order to discuss possible policies to change real agricultural prices. We need to understand how prices are shaped, in other words.

7.1.1.1 The Agricultural Price Determinants

The most obvious determinant of markets is the demand and supply equilibrium. Although there is no perfect explanation of the processes by which demand and supply converge, it is a fact that the overall price rate is the product of the demand and supply experience. Although there may be a difference between supply and demand in short periods of time, in the long run, excess supply and excess demand are not sustainable. Consequently, if there is, for example, an increase in demand for agricultural products, this will ultimately create the impetus for price increases. However, and very important for agriculture, a shortage of supply (such as low harvests) for a commodity that is primarily focused on domestic markets would eventually lead to price increases. The impact of supply and demand changes on price levels depend largely on the relative size of supply and demand elasticity. The rise in demand for agricultural products, for example, would lead to a higher price increase and lower supply elasticity. A drop-in supply will also have a higher price impact, the more inelastic demand is. Increases in supply and demand due to seasonal and climate changes usually determine short-run fluxes that impact income stability. Terms of trade: it is a measure of the relative price of one sector of production. It is calculated as the ratio between an index of average price for the sector one is concerned, and an index of the average price of the rest of the economy.

More important for the level of income is the long-run price trend. It is a known fact that the relative price of agricultural products continues to decrease over the long term. The explanation for such a phenomenon is to be found in food product sales elasticity, which is almost always less than one. Norton reports that the income elasticity of food demand, on average across countries tends to be consistent with values of 0.6 to 0.7. This means, for example, that aggregate real income growth in the economy of 5% in one year will result in an increase in food demand of only 3 to 3.5% per year. The effect on prices depends on how fast the growth of agricultural production is, and on whether import can compensate for the higher demand. If the productivity of agriculture grows by more than 3–3.5%, the result will be that of declining agricultural prices. Population growth is the most essential factors of increasing demand for basic agricultural products, while technological progress is the force driving productivity growth. On a global scale, especially up to the eighteenth century at least, advances in agriculture allowed population growth to be closely linked. With the industrial revolution and agricultural mechanization, agricultural productivity began to grow faster than agricultural demand, resulting in falling real prices known as the farming crisis that has plagued many of the developing countries that are now.

The discussion above centered on an international, global perspective. Focusing more on the individual country level, the real price of agricultural products is closely linked to global market growth. In short, mostly when a country is 'small' as compared to the world market, domestic dynamics of production and demand may only have a small impact, mainly based on global prices, on the evolution of agricultural terms and conditions. This is important for the developing countries, where the high rates of increase in food demand, driven by population growth, which could have sustained stable relative prices for agriculture, have failed to do so because of the increases in imports. International trade avoided an increased food demand from the domestic agricultural sector. The relentless decrease of global price has forced the agricultural sector in an independent cycle of falling prices and rising agricultural imports to accept lower real precious items of what the closed economy could have accomplished. The drop in relative agricultural prices on the world market was exacerbated by the high subsidies granted to their farmers by large developed economies (in particular the USA and the European Community). A developing country which is open to international trade, thus, is highly dependent on imports and lacks domestic agricultural opportunities.

7.1.1.2 Objectives of Price Policies

In principle, price policies could be aimed at:

- increasing prices;
- decrease prices; and
- stabilize prices.

The aims are always related to more general economic and income allocation expectations, which can be reached on different markets through a variety of instruments.

7.1.1.3 Instruments of Agricultural Price Policies

Because most farm commodities can be exported, when trade or other policies are not limited, prices of agricultural products are dictated by global demand rates, which are to be called exogenous for a small country. The market policy objectives should, therefore, be achieved through the attempts to change farmers' and consumers' successful prices, which are the true opportunities. The main tools to adjust prices encountered by suppliers and consumers' value are:

- trade policies;
- exchange rate policy;
- sectoral policies;
- price controls;
- farm support prices;
- public storage; and
- input markets.

However, overall economic policies such as fiscal policies and macro-economic policies can have a significant impact on reward rates.

7.2 TRADE POLICIES

We specify the set of public interventions aimed at changing import and/or export volumes with the term trade policies. Such policies essentially bring a rift between domestic prices and world prices by affecting the scale of international trade. In the previous section, we defined the basic theory of trade profits, and stated that when a nation opens up to trade, the world price becomes the price to which both producers and consumers are reacting. Now, we will study the impact of trade policies in more depth and discover that limits on international trade can sometimes be advantageous to a state, revising the overall conclusion of international trade theory. We will see that some form of trade regulation may be needed to compensate for the negative effects of falling world agricultural prices. It should be remembered that during the last 70 years, all kinds of trade restrictions have been at the center of intense debate. The new WTO that has arisen has put strict limits, at least in principle, to the degree of trade rights granted to member states (Figure 7.1).

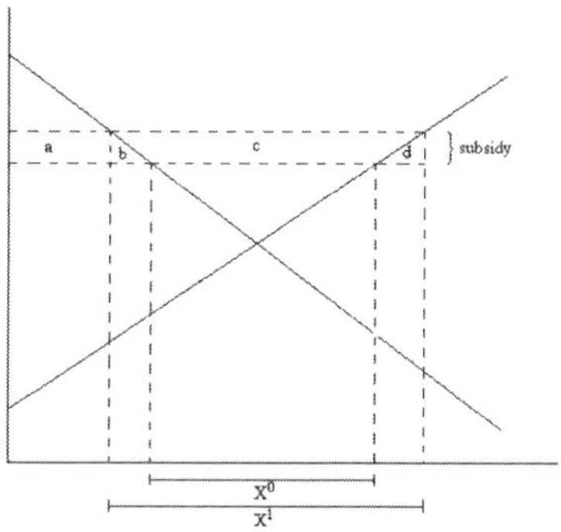

Figure 7.1. The effects of subsidies on exports.

Source: Frank Ellis (2014).

Trade barriers are, in theory, negative in the long term because they shield producers at a high cost. By contrast, to suppliers from around the world facing lower prices, protected markets appear to be less competitive on the world market. Nonetheless, developing countries may need some form of protection to offset the effect on exports of subsidies paid by rich economies which help maintain artificial low world prices. Low food prices (for example, rice, or wheat) have a particularly negative impact on rural poor families, who make up the bulk of their revenue for food production. The obstacle that the developing countries have to face is that they provide sufficient opportunities for the domestic agriculture sector by means of mutual involvement in international trade agreements. "Without falling into these self-defeating trap of protectionism" (Norton, 2002). The first way to do this could be to smartly merge import tariffs and export incentives, which were designed and implemented with mechanisms to provide the advantages that the nation has a specific competitive advantage to the producers of farm products.

7.2.1 Tariffs

Tariffs are import taxes so that the average domestic price equals the global price. The result of a tariff is usually that domestic production is shielded economically, as it makes imported goods to domestic markets more costly. The graph above shows the effects of tariff enforcement on imports. The effective domestic price will rise by the amount of the tariff above the world price. As a result: domestic production will increase, domestic consumption will decrease, and the level of imports will reduce from M_0 to M_1. (When a tariff is larger than the difference between autarkic price and world price, it is said a prohibitive tariff, and have the effect of eliminating all imports.) (Figure 7.2)

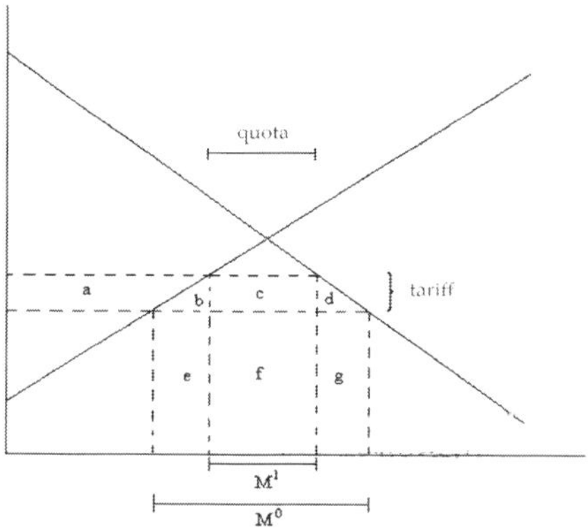

Figure 7.2. The effects of a tariff and of an equivalent quota on imports.

Source: Frank Ellis (2014).

Producers of import substitutes will gain (a), and the consumer will lose (a + b + c + d) when compared with the free trade situation. Also, the government will earn revenues from the tariff equal to the area (c) in the graph and the net efficiency loss is equal to area (b + d). We can have generalized or uniform tariffs, which would cover all tradable goods by the same percentage (i.e., all import price are raised by 5%), or specific tariffs, differentiated by product or sector (for example, agricultural products have a tariff of 3% while industrial products of 6%). A generalized tariff scheme can be easier to implement, and it should cause less distortion. In fact, a uniform tariff on all tradable goods will not change the relative prices of those goods, and the comparative advantages in the production of some products will be saved. Specific tariffs, instead, can be used to alter the relative profitability of some products and sectors against others. While such diversified tariffs could be beneficial in the short run to protect specific sectors, in the long run, they have the potentially negative effect of reducing the competitiveness of the protected sector. In fact, the least competitive sector is the one, which will have the stronger interest to obtain a preferential tariff (Norton, 2002) Tariffs are thus a powerful mechanism to protect sectors that produce import substitutes, and are justified whenever world price level is objectively too low to warrant the right incentives to the agricultural production. In general, however, a Country should not fall in the trap of raising prohibitive tariffs and go back to extreme protectionisms. Norton suggests that three principles should guide the setting of tariffs:

1. Tariff rates should not be high in general, and if they are, a program should be put in place to scale them downward over time.
2. Their rates should be relatively uniform over sectors and products.
3. The tariff system should be relatively stable over time, except for the downward adjustments planned years in advance.

7.2.2 Quotas and Other Non-Tariff Trade Restrictions

An alternative type of trade intervention is to limit import or export volumes by means of quotas. The effect of a quota on imports is the same as an equivalent tariff, as is illustrated in Figure 7.2. The only obvious difference is that the government is not going to raise tax revenue. However, if the quota is enforced by licensing, rents will be generated by the license holders that are quantitatively equivalent to the area(c). Apart from explicit quotas, there are many other forms of restrictions on trade.

7.2.3 Export Incentives

Instead of increasing imports, another set of trade policies that can be used to increase agricultural opportunities is aimed at improving exports. Export subsidies have the effect of increasing the effective price for producers and consumers, as shown in the above chapter on tariffs. The level of exports will increase from X^0 to X^1, the benefits for producers will be (a + b + c + d), whereas consumers will sustain a loss of (-a-b). The government expenditure will amount at an area equal to (-a-b-c-d), so that the overall, net effect of the policy will be a loss of welfare equal to area (-b-d). As can be seen, direct export subsidies are very costly for the government's budget. Generally, they cannot be used widely unless they are supported by an equivalent amount of import tariffs. Therefore, given that export subsidies are usually paid to exporters, the benefits will not reach the farmers whenever there is a concentration in the distribution sector (i.e., monopsony control on the part of exporters). Therefore, if the government really wants to target the farmers, the right to subsidy should be given directly to the producers, e.g., through a transferable permit system (See Norton, 2002).

Ultimately, a system of differential exchange rates was the main policy affecting agricultural trade, the operation of which will be studied. The intricate system of exchange rates is also undergoing a cycle of reform. It can be said, however, that it still dominates other policies.

7.3 EXCHANGE RATE POLICY

Exchange rate is the price of foreign currency. It is usually expressed as the amount of domestic currency required to purchase a foreign currency unit. Like any price, the supply and demand equilibrium should form its efficient level. Foreign currency supply is provided by exporters who sell their products abroad and are paid with foreign currency, while demand is created by importers who need foreign currency to pay on the world market for their purchases. An increase in the nominal value of the so-called exchange rate is called a devaluation or depreciation. In contrast, a decline in the nominal exchange rate price is a domestic currency appreciation or valuation. An exchange rate value above its efficient level is a domestic currency undervaluation, whereas an exchange rate below its efficient level implies overvaluation. There is a particular correlation in the country and abroad between the exchange rate and the overall price level. The purchasing power parity (PPP) rule states that the exchange rate should be balanced to retain the PPP. Consider the example below to understand how it works. A kilo of bread is worth 50 shillings (SH) and 1 dollar in the US at a given time. An exchange rate of 50 SH / US$ ensures the PPP as buying one kilo of bread in both Country A and the US would take the same amount of SH. Suppose Country A is now experiencing 10% inflation, while US prices are rising by only 5%. Today, in Syria, one kilo of bread would cost 55 SH and in the US $1.05. The exchange rate must depreciate to 55/1.05 = 52.4 SH / US$ in order to maintain PPP.

High domestic inflation, as the example shows, will push for depreciation (i.e., the more domestic currency for one foreign currency unit). Consequently, if the government tries to maintain a fixed exchange rate while there is a difference in inflation, the outcome is an overvaluation. The dynamics of imports and exports must ensure a balance of purchasing power in a free trade system. There are natural economic causes, however, why this balance may not be attained. For example, if a nation discovers reliable oil or gas reserves that unexpectedly raise export rates, this foreign exchange "excess supply" may help the exchange rate by preventing its depreciation. This occurrence is known as the "Dutch disease" and can be caused by different forms of foreign currency excess supply, such as emigrant remittances or subsidized exports. Maintaining the exchange rate at an overvalued rate leads to a bias against exporting sectors that are becoming less competitive in world markets, while imported goods are becoming more expensive.

7.3.1 Exchange Rate Regimes and Policies for Changing the Exchange Rate

We may have different regimes depending on how the exchange rate is set in the economy:

- **Market Exchange Rate:** Free fluctuation of the market exchange rate. In principle, it should oscillate to keep PPP. Nevertheless, it can be indirectly modified by changing the levels of supply and demand for foreign currency or by changing the interest rate and modifying the flows of capital.
- **Official Exchange Rate:** The level is set by government decree. A reduction of the nominal rate is an appreciation; an increase in the nominal rate is depreciation or devaluation. Then the official exchange rate can be pegged to some foreign currency.

Appreciation is negative for agriculture in most developing countries, whereas depreciation can be beneficial (e.g., India in the 1990s or the CFA (Financial Cooperation in Central Africa) devaluation of 1994 for African countries such as Côte d'Ivoire, Senegal, and Mali). In the long run, however, real growth cannot be achieved by continually devaluing the domestic currency. According to Norton, "The rate of exchange is the most powerful influence on relative prices in the economy, and its implications on real agricultural prices usually far outweigh the effects of other forms of price interventions." Because "agriculture is typically a sector which is most exposed to the influence of foreign trade: almost all its products are either exported or importable, or they are close substitutes in production or consumption with products which are importable or exportable. Agricultural prices are therefore largely determined by those of international markets and by the medium, that transmits them to the domestic economy, the exchange rate. The infrastructure and service sectors, on the other hand, generate mostly inputs that are neither imported nor exported, so that their domestic prices will rise with inflation, while those of agriculture are down with external influences and an appreciating exchange rate" (Norton, 2002). As a result, a smart policy should be carefully coordinating exchange rate policies with all other policies on price control and trade.

7.4 SECTORAL POLICIES

The trade and exchange rate strategies that we discussed in the previous section are likely to be the most effective ways for governments to control farm prices. However, in the intervening years, it was also prevalent for governments to come up with sectoral policies with the implicit objective of changing the price level of agricultural products. The following can be a list of these techniques:

- Administered prices;
- Minimum guaranteed prices;
- Price stabilization schemes;
- Commodity taxes.

The rationalizations given for such strategies include:

- Keep the price for food low to the benefit of consumers;
- Increase farmers' income;
- Stabilize farmers' income to offset the high variability of agricultural production;
- Provide fiscal revenue.

The inferences that can be drawn after years of practice with price control systems in different parts of the world is that they are always a less effective way to achieve the primary objective. That is why they are increasingly being discarded worldwide.

7.4.1 Administered Prices

With this term, we indicate all the policy interventions aimed at maintaining the market price of a commodity at a predetermined level, somewhat independent of the real supply and demand balance. It was used particularly for food prices, because they should be reduced significantly to support poor consumers, who are those for whom the higher share of their budget is food spending. The government needs to put a complex regulatory structure in place to directly control rates, which means that no transaction is done at a cost other than that set by the government. For instance, in Syria, in the context of cotton, sugar beet, and tobacco, farmers have to offer their products at a controlled price to the government processing facilities.

Governed prices pose a lot of issues. First, maintaining successful project management is operationally challenging. Sometimes, either oversupply or excess product demand may arise at the regulated rate, as it is hard for the government to properly assess the supply and demand equilibrium. Excess supply will be observed by growing private and public inventory, while the common side effect of deficits will reveal the excess demand with waiting in a queue. Secondly, trade barriers must also be in place with increased administrative costs in order to guarantee a fixed price. Third, and most relevantly, fixed prices will almost certainly result in resource misappropriation, as they will radically change the comparative terms of trade between products and sectors.

7.4.2 Minimum Guaranteed Prices

With this tool created to protect farmers' earnings from dropping, the government is trying to ensure that the price received by producers does not drop below a preconceived minimum level, while at any level it is left free to rise. Implementation is another very complicated scheme, as it demands that the government be prepared to purchase any excess supply at the guaranteed price point (Figure 7.3).

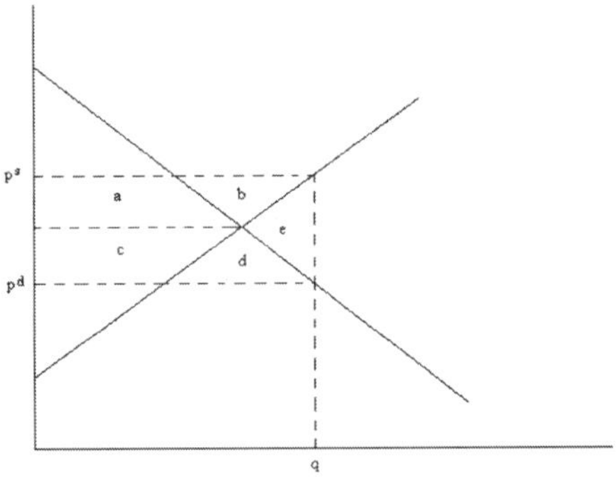

Figure 7.3. Minimum guaranteed price.

Source: Frank Ellis (2014).

In relation to Figure 7.3, presume that the minimum guaranteed price is p^s, above the market equilibrium price. In order to enforce it, the government must undertake to purchase any excess supply produced at that price.

Production will be q, and the government will buy all of it paying p^s. Then, the government might sell the amount to the consumers, which will be willing to pay p^c. As a result, producer surplus will increase by (a + b), consumer surplus will increase by (c + d); while the government's net expenditure will be (-a-b-c-d-e). The overall, net efficiency loss will be (-e). This type of intervention is sometimes referred to as a deficiency payment, given that it is equivalent for the producers to sell their production on the market, at price p^d, and then the government would pay the difference between whatever this market price and a fixed level of support price, p^s. Guaranteed prices are usually utilized to ensure an adequate remuneration to farmers' resources. The major issue then is to determine which level of minimum guaranteed price is appropriate. Normally, one operating procedure is to try to set the support price at a level that encompasses the estimated average cost of production of the crop concerned and to increase the price from year to year as an average cost increase, which is equivalent to rewarding inefficiency. In addition, normal compensation for land and family labor should be included in the determination of the cost of production. Land prices, however, depend on the price of production and, by linking the price to the average cost, could lead to a circular upward spiral in cost and price levels.

The most important concern with the guaranteed price is that it frequently sets the wrong incentives for production, which tend to specialize in supported production, making the intervention more expensive for the government. For this purpose, it is important for many countries to manage and also regulate the quantities generated, with additional administrative costs. The implementation of a guaranteed price system in the European Union has resulted in a change from a place of net importers of cereals to one of the world's major exporters. The European Union has introduced a variable import levy scheme, with the goal of sustaining border costs at domestic support rates. Imports were tariffed according to the difference between the domestic target price and global price (so price support, as well as stabilization, was achieved). With the passing of time, production increases gradually contributed to an excessive surplus in the European Union. The increased cereal supply has prompted the implementation of export subsidies (referred to as export refunds) to be able to sell it on the world market. The scheme of guaranteed prices in Europe has lately been abolished, mostly due to the high budget costs and the pressure from the WTO. As a general conclusion on price support schemes, we can conclude that direct price support schemes should be removed where possible because they change competitive advantage relative trends. Indirect means of maintaining agricultural production, such as combined tariffs on imports and export subsidies, or a policy of restricted exchange rate devaluation, should be preferred to direct control schemes in conditional circumstances.

7.4.3 Price Stabilization

The stabilization of the price is another justification for government involvement on domestic prices. The contention here is that uncertain prices can cause farmers to have unstable incomes, which is considered a risk. It should be noted, however, that volatile prices do not automatically mean variable incomes: in addition, one of the fundamental reasons for variable prices is the fluctuation of demand due to weather variability: prices tend to be high when output is low and vice versa. It means income is much more stable than costs, offering what is known as a natural hedge. Only when prices are not associated with domestic production will a market stability scheme help to stabilize incomes. This is the case, for example, for tradable goods, the price of which is determined on the world market (Figure 7.4).

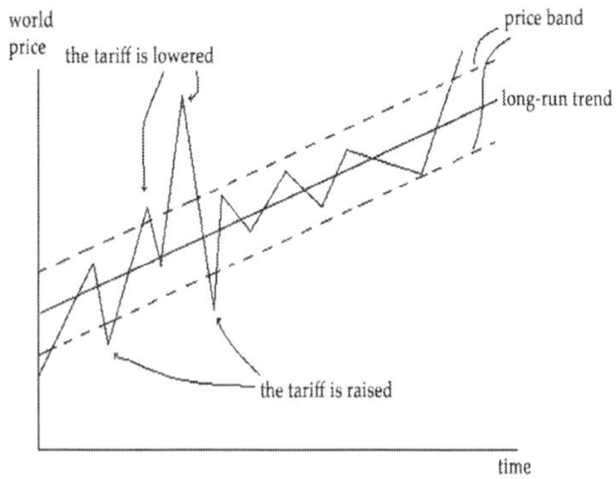

Figure 7.4. A price band scheme.

Source: Frank Ellis (2014).

In several countries, the easiest price stabilization scheme used is the use of buffer stocks. The principle though is that the government would set a lower and upper price limit and be willing to buy commodities at the lower price whenever the market price falls below the minimum price, thus accumulating stocks to be released on the market when the price is higher. To operate a buffer inventory scheme efficiently, the cost boundary rates should be set appropriately. For example, if the lowest price is set too high, the concern is that the public stock will rise too much. The state should typically be prepared to retain huge reserves, with proportionately high overheads. Price stability could be done more efficiently using price band systems rather than with buffer stocks. Price bands are a system of variable tariffs on imports. When the foreign price increases by more than a previously defined percentage or sum above its traditional trend line, the resulting tariff are reduced. On the opposite, the tariff increases once the world price falls under the long-term trend (See Figure 7.4). In this manner, relative to the international price, domestic prices are stabilized without triggering distortions in the relative comparative advantage. Price bands should not be mistaken for the European Union's adjustable levy scheme. The variable levy is intended to ensure that domestic support rates are equal to border prices. There must be no support rate under a price band, as the tariff fluctuations are not related to any domestic level, but only to the consistent pattern of international prices.

7.4.4 Commodity Taxes

To attempt to provide the state with tax revenue as an alternative to income tax, agricultural commodities can be subject to sales and output taxes. For example, taxing export crops to countries where income tax systems are not well established has been a common practice. One of the reasons of product taxes is that they wouldn't significantly change production. Nevertheless, product tax (similar to discriminatory tariffs) will undermine opportunities by breaking the relationship between domestic demand ratios and comparative external prices. Alternatively, if a state needs to directly tax the agricultural sector for distributive reasons or tax revenue, a tax on primary factors (land, labor, capital) or revenue would be a better option. The comparative productivity of plants would not be modified, and the distribution of capital would not be skewed.

7.4.5 Input Policy

So far, we have been debating policies aimed primarily at changing the price of produce. There are other opportunities for government input pricing and availability to impact the rewards for producers. We will address the array of input policies briefly. Providing subsidies on input prices is one of the most obvious ways to support producers. Variable input payments such as fertilizers, pesticides, other additives, but also water and electricity are the cost of a farm. The expense of the farm will be lowered by subsidizing the price of inputs. The output would therefore increase, and the surplus of suppliers would increase if the product price is kept constant. Nevertheless, if input subsidies are applied to the whole industry, it is not clear whether or not producers are going to benefit. It depends on the relative supply and demand elasticity. However, if the demand feature is very inelastic, the advantages of production subsidies could be fully passed to customers. Between inputs, there is a special focus on agrochemicals (such as fertilizers and pesticides) and plants.

There are generally large economies of scale in the chemical industry. For this reason, the chemical industry has historically been privately regulated as a natural monopoly, as a single large corporation can reach lower marginal costs than many smaller companies. When the nation wants to promote and increase agricultural production, it is better to provide such inputs to peasants at a reduced price. Nonetheless, it is important that the agrochemical supply is successful if the subsidy has to communicate its maximum benefits in terms of increased production. In the evolution of agricultural development, one of the productive factors that allowed productivity growth was the introduction of new and improved varieties. Switching to the new variety, however, typically needs a total technological change, such as abandoning the practice of using self-produced seed and buying licensed, certified grain. Smallholders may have issues with the introduction of the new technology, and it may be important to provide discounted inputs to provide opportunities for uptake. For instance, farmers may be risk-averse, and the benefits of the new technology would be ignored. Furthermore, the adoption of new technology may need to be followed by an increased awareness of input use and cropping technologies.

For all these purposes, policy input incentives and input delivery are best designed within a more specific input kit exchange that involves crops, fertilizers, chemicals, and technical knowledge about best farming practices. The dimension of the subsidized inputs is the inherent imbalance which they cause in the allocation of resources. For example, by providing cheap pesticides, an opportunity is being created to replace chemicals for labor. This may run counter to the comparative advantages of the nation in an agricultural system of ample labor.

7.5 POLICIES THAT PROMOTE ACCESS TO RESOURCES

7.5.1 Land Tenure Policies

The land is one of the factors of production with which agricultural production depends more heavily. Of a country's resources, the land is also the one that cannot be modified in quantity. Whereas population increase and the concentration of capital ensure that over time the proportion of labor and capital tends to increase, land cannot grow in a country. The only option to contribute to a nation's economic overall growth is by increasing productivity with defined availability of land. As can be seen, soil productivity has a direct connection to the land ownership system, which is why we can research tenure forms and policies that can improve it. By tenure, we mean a bundle of rights for a person, a household, or a community in relation to land, water or other resources. This encompasses rights of ownership, as well as rights that are permanent or seasonal. We limit the importance of land tenure to land rights, their sources, and operations (Forni, 2000).

Land reforms are major political and social processes designed to change land tenure. They have political, social, economic, and, more recently, environmental objectives. The political aims are the attempt to influence the power structure in the country and they can be both the forum of radical and liberal political parties. The primary societal objective is generally 'social justice' as the uneven allocation of a country's most important resource is perceived from all viewpoints as unfair. Here, the main focus will be on the economic goals of land tenure reforms, and briefly discuss the growing crucial environmental goals. The two most important economic goals are:

- Reduction of absolute poverty; and
- Increase of agricultural productivity.

Agricultural reform could alleviate poverty. Most types of old land tenancy are characterized by heavy landlord labor exploitation, rendering them similar to slavery. For these reasons, large proportions of the population remain below the level of poverty under feudal estates and endowing them with land may be the first step to escape it. The higher proportion of poverty among the landless rural population is seen in many developing countries, and the main reason for land reform is to reduce the number of poor people. If poverty is less of a concern, land reform's main economic aim is to have a positive impact on land productivity. Land productivity is only up to a certain point a natural phenomenon. Some soils are better than others for natural reasons, such as chemical composition, depth, slope, etc. However, even better soil will lose productivity if it is not well managed over time. For this reason, what is relevant for productivity is the security of the right on land use. Only when a farmer is guaranteed on the continued right to the product of the land, there will be enough incentives to keep and increase land productivity.

Also, the productivity of land depends on use. Land can be utilized for many various activities, and land should be easily shifted from less to purposes that are more useful in order to boost overall productivity. And lastly, the third factor contributing to land productivity is to enhance the quality of the land by means of fixed investment. The irreversibility of land loss is an essential aspect relevant to land quality. Several of the potential harm that may end up causing productivity loss is irreversible. In other words, the land is not a resource that is completely renewable. The truth is a mildly degraded soil can replenish is left fallow if it is subordinate to organic fertilization and if it is safeguarded from erosion, however, regeneration may take too much time to be regarded as an option when the damage is intense. Soil erosion, which is the degradation of the top part of the soil, which is the one that really is responsible for agricultural output, can result in serious productivity loss, as is seen, for instance, by the land that is stripped bare from the vegetation as in the hillsides of Haiti or even in some parts of the Amazon Basin, where deforestation has disrupted the natural cycle of accumulation of nutrients. This disruption has a worldwide impact on the environment, such as reduction of water supply, biodiversity risk, and local or global climate change. The comprehensive policy goals of equity and land use productivity are therefore reflected in the operational goals of:

- Provide equitable access to land.
- Secure the rights over land use.
- Enable land markets and other assignment structures to operate smoothly.
- Giving farmers access to capital for investment.
- Stop over-use.

Land access is achieved by one of three instruments:

1. Land settlement, which means the occupation of land over which no one has yet claimed rights.
2. Land redistribution, which means the expropriation of

fundamental land rights from those currently in possession of the property, compensation for such rights and the allocation of expropriate rights to others.

3. Tenancy reform, this includes changing the rules on legal and illegal types of contracts between farmers and landowners.

As can be seen, access to land does not necessarily require the property right over land, provided efficient land markets are operational. Nonetheless, the rights must be clearly defined and safeguarded by institutions such as laws and regulations in order for a market to function. There are various forms of land rights that can be classified into six basic types (Norton, 2002):

- **Open Access Land:** If no one can claim land ownership, no one can be excluded from access to it as well. It is more typical for marine resources, although it may be characteristic of some forest or countryside.
- **Communal Land:** It's just like open access land, but access is restricted to individuals of a particular community, and community rules and regulations may govern the use of land. Their use is usually defined in traditional land regimes, based on historical traditions.
- **Collective Land:** The property is typically owned by the government and it is used by a community of farm families for joint production activities. As in the collective farms of the former Soviet Union, decisions on what to grow and how to handle the land are left to the centralized authority.
- **Individual Land Rights Under Associative Tenure:** In both customary and collective tenure regimes, this right embraces individual plots. For example, individual households may be given the right to decide what to cultivate in a communal or collective land area on limited plots of land.
- **Private Land Rights:** It is the most popular form of land rights in capitalist economies, including private ownership as well as user-friendly rights such as rent, leasing, and sharecropping. Private owners may willingly choose to pool their land into cooperatives or other forms of the joint operation.
- **State Land:** This is when the state (any regional or central authority) preserves the right to own the land.

What is meaningful for agricultural activities is the protection of the right to land-based income, rather than direct ownership. A complete ownership is more closely related to the position of land as a capital asset. For instance, land ownership enables access to loans to be used as collateral, while leased land cannot be used for that purpose. Therefore, land tenure policies are intended to establish and preserve the protection of land use rights. The critical question of policy, therefore, is: 'what should the nature of land rights be?,' 'Should the traditional land tenure regimes be maintained, or should tenure reform be introduced?,' 'How can the rights agreed upon be protected?,' And, most significantly, how can it be ensured that land rights can be exchanged in such a way that land can be used often in a more productive manner? Once again, the question is not how to substitute the state with the market, but how the government can allow land markets to work smoothly. The following points can be summarized as broad conclusions that can be taken from the study of experiences with land tenure structures in different parts of the world (Norton, 2002). Social conservation in developing countries often tends to be weak, and communal land tends to degrade more quickly than private land. Although the scientific proof on the type of collectively owned farms is significantly negative in many countries around the world. Observation from a wide variety of countries (Honduras, Nicaragua, El-Salvador, China, Hungary, Ethiopia, Vietnam, Peru, Cuba, etc.) has shown that collective farms are unable to provide high land returns:

1. Lack of property ownership and therefore the farm members' inability to pursue usual selling, lease, and mortgage options.
2. The history of government interference in unit management stopped land from being intended for the best use.
3. The absence of a sufficient internal incentive structure to motivate farmers to work on communal plots as rigorously as they do themselves.

Additionally, the state land history offers a limited success story. For several purposes, the government may wish to retain ownership of the land:

- Historical reasons;
- Ideological principles;
- Concern that privatization may lead to concentration of landholdings in relatively few hands;
- Concern that private ownership might encourage the speculative holding of land that is left idle;
- Concern on possible overexploitation of land because of failure

to recognize negative externalities.

However, the government has not traditionally demonstrated to be a competent manager of agricultural land. Generally, state officials who determine what to produce and what to do lack the appropriate knowledge about the actual value of the land. There are also limited options for managers who are unable to lease, buy or sell land and make the necessary investment decisions. Lower productivity thus typically overcomes the possible beneficial effects of state ownership. Private land rights appear to be the type of land rights that offer higher productivity levels to be achieved. The public authority can perform multiple essential functions in safeguarding private rights, which are therefore the main components of modern land tenure policy. First, land titling can be done to acknowledge ownership. Building a land cadastre, a land title record, is a very crucial step in any land tenure policy. Furthermore, regulations can be implemented to allow and control contracts for rent, lease, and sharecropping. These types of contracts are common, as they provide four main benefits:

1. Even families with low incomes who do not have sufficient money to purchase land can also have access to extra land;
2. Rental agreements move the use of the land plot from the hands of someone who is less motivated or willing to use it to another individual who is more involved or competent, so it is very possible that short-term profitability will improve (although long-term productivity may be affected if the rental agreement does not last long enough to internalize long-term returns.);
3. The possibility of temporarily renting land lowers the landowner's income risks so they can secure at least a minimum income flow in the event that health, family finances, or other factors prevent the landowner from being able to grow the land. If rent were not possible, the only alternative would be to sell the land, thus also losing the preservation of capital represented by the land; and
4. Location or shareholding agreements are inclined to avoid the pitfalls of asymmetric labor effort information for large-scale landowners by avoiding the supervisory costs of hired labor.

Third, the state can reduce land purchase transaction costs by, for example, eliminating size restrictions on land sales or enforcing inheritance laws. Indeed, rigorous land privatization, when land sales markets do not function smoothly due to transaction costs, may give rise to the problem of fragmentation, resulting from the average farm size being too small to exploit economies of scale due to mechanization.

7.6 CREDIT POLICIES FOR AGRICULTURE AND RURAL AREAS

7.6.1 Importance of Credit for Agriculture

Three rationales why farmers require funds:

- **Working Capital:** Because production is only attained by the end of the season and costs are maintained throughout the season, farmers must anticipate money.
- **Consumption Smoothing:** Agricultural production varies greatly year by year, while consumption must be maintained constantly. Farmers may have to take out a loan for tough years and save money for good years.
- **Investments:** Whenever money is invested, its cost is paid at the earliest stages, whereas the benefits are obtained only after many years.

Farmers could use personal savings for all of these purposes. Personal savings are just not enough, however, particularly for investment, and they require a long time before an investment can be made. Saved capital is also immobilized and can therefore not be put into productive use until enough investment has been made. Lastly, who can save is usually who doesn't need the resources to make investments. High productivity within the market could be accomplished by enabling the credit market to move the capital from those who have saved it to those who need it.

7.6.2 Sources for Credit

There is always a financial market in any country, whether formally or informally. Those who have access to excess capital, in exchange for a remuneration, may look for ways to lend it to those in need. The formal credit is usually only feasible when the private lender and the borrower have personal knowledge and reciprocal trust. Nevertheless, the informal types of credit may never be enough, because the prospective lender and the possible borrower may fail to meet, or they may lack the personal relationship necessary to allow the exchange.

Because of this purpose, we generally observe the emergence of financial middlemen, whose role is to allow credit supply and demand to be met. The banking system plays the role of financial intermediation in modern economies. The market interest rate should be the amount that clears the market when supply and demand meet, which is at which there is no excess supply or excess demand. Moreover, there is always a rate of return between the interest rate paid when taking out loans and that received when lending money when there is a financial intermediary sector. The rate of return should encompass all the intermediary's costs, such as the wages of the people working in the bank, the security guards needed to protect the money. Most costs can be identified as costs for transactions (see below). The financial intermediary sector is usually highly monopolized (both formal and informal). In addition to the operating costs, therefore, the margin will likely include a more or less relevant monopoly rent. In order to avoid these profits, governments have typically decided to intervene either by directly controlling the banking sector or by strictly restricting the activity of the banking system.

7.6.3 Transaction Costs in Financial Markets and Credit Problems for Small Farms

Operational costs are not the only costs that financial intermediaries must pay. The most relevant part of the costs is linked to the transaction costs generated by the administrative and legal system needed to permit the operation of credit. The banking intermediary will justify charging a risk premium above the interest rate to negate the risk of default, so that the interest paid by the debtor can be much higher than the interest received by the creditor. In addition, real guarantees can be requested in the form of collateral in order to reduce the risk of default, which also causes a cost to the borrower. Finally, it would be appropriate to provide extremely complex legal agreements and administrative procedures. All transaction costs tend to be more expensive for small credits when calculated as a percentage of the amount of the credit transaction. There are two implications for the existence of transaction costs: they decrease the effective interest rate that savers can end up receiving for their money and increase the interest rate that borrowers must pay when borrowing money. As a result, the credit market can be severely restricted to total disappearance for two possible explanations: first, because there will be an inadequate supply of capital from those with savings, and second, because there will be limited demand from those who need capital.

7.6.4 The State's Historical Action in the Sector of Rural Finance: The 'Old Credit Policy'

Nearly all governments globally have deemed it necessary to provide farmers with credit for rural development. Experience has shown that nearly everywhere there was insufficient availability of credit to farmers. Generally, governments have acted through state agricultural banks (for instance, the Agricultural Cooperatives) effectively assuming the role of financial intermediary in agriculture. Therefore, by granting credit at low marginal interest rates, they will seek to increase the amount of credit. The explanation for this form of incentive is the assumption that farmers have a highly elastic demand for credit, that is, it is highly responsive to the interest rate. This method of offering credit can be objected to in many ways: First, even if the nominal interest rate may be low, the transaction cost occurrence may be such that the cost-effectiveness of the borrowed money, especially for small farmers, can continue to be extremely high. Second, a low-interest money lending program does not provide savers with ample opportunities to provide sufficient capital supplies so that it can only be sustainable by continuing external subsidies. Another common goal of conventional agricultural credit policy has been to aim for both users of credit. (for instance, small farmers instead of large farmers) and to use (Through, for instance, offering a kind of loan, the State Bank could directly provide input instead of money required to buy input if this loan is intended to fund input purchase.). Such focusing can be accomplished by easily avoidable mechanisms: for instance, the government can impose restrictions on the maximum amount that may be borrowed with a single contract to support small farmers. This, however, is not sufficient to prevent the money being spent on large farms from really doing so: large credit could indeed only be made by entering into several agreements which would only have the effect of increasing transaction costs. Therefore, if the farmer wants money instead of a commodity for sale, he could still re-sell government supplies to earn cash. Again, the only consequence will be by pushing the farmer to make another payment to increase transaction costs. Ultimately, credit distribution can be related to plant marketing in order to reduce the risk of default. In the context of Syria, debt settlement typically takes the form of a deduction from the farmer's price for produce, which is sold through the same credit-providing organization (the Agricultural Cooperatives).

7.6.5 New Credit Policy Objectives and Tools

In several nations, the experience gained from subsidized agriculture loans was negative. Farmers never find the lending process enough, and the government budget always has been so burdened with unsustainability. What can then be done to make rural households more creditable in a self-sustainable way? Community saving mobilization must be the first goal. It is easily wrong to believe that farmers cannot save by noting that farmers are able to smoothly consume, even with great production variance. If in one way or another they could not save, how could they endure times of low harvest or eat something while waiting for the next harvest to come? Clearly, something must be saved by the farmer. Sometimes, the high cost of doing so is what keeps farmers from relying on structured savings (such as bank saving accounts). Their saving capacity also includes very limited amounts, so they can't afford to pay the transaction costs connected with formal credit (including time and distance costs to reach a bank branch, lack of confidence based on limited process performance data, etc.). For lack of suitable tools, the peasants do not formally save, rather than because of low saving potential. Households prefer to keep their wealth in bovine animals, in grain stocks, or in gold rather than in the bank, particularly when the bank seems untrustworthy.

The second goal should be to reduce the financial intermediary's margin, in particular by decreasing transaction costs. What really matters is the appropriate interest rate for the farmers' incentive. Instead of reducing the overall nominal interest rate on borrowing, lowering transaction costs would stimulate much more demand. When high overheads, over-employment, low morale of bank officials, and similar inefficiencies inflate the administrative costs of the banking system, the effective interest rate to be paid by farmers is necessarily high. Nonetheless, what is most difficult is to reduce transaction costs due to the risk associated with any credit agreement. Second, to both structured saving and lending, the amount of administrative costs and paperwork should be reduced. For instance, door-to-door collection of regularly scheduled small savings amounts might be a realistic option for rural villages where there is no bank's local branch. Administrative costs can also be reduced by decreasing bureaucracy and red tape. By creating incentives and marketing mechanisms in line with official success (designed to attract savers, making loans, retrieving delinquent payments, etc.), by decentralizing branch decision-making, and so on (Ellis, 1991). Probably the primary rationalization for the large overhead provided by banks around the world is that they are a prerequisite to compensate for the costs due to the low rates of loan recovery. Therefore, a valuable goal for public involvement in the credit market is to focus on increasing the rate of loan recovery so that banking institutions cannot use it as an excuse to justify high margins, which could merely hide monopoly rents.

7.6.6 Successful Rural Lending Experience

A variety of successful strategies for building viable rural finance programs are now being observed. Saving mobilization has proven to be a powerful mechanism to induce viable credit networks to grow. Savings could be mobilized easily simply through the implementation of a safe and convenient liquidity store network. It was also possible to reduce default rates. One fruitful way of doing this is by community loan schemes in which a group of farmers instead of individual farmers are responsible for the loan repayment.

7.6.7 Reform of the Traditional System of Credit

Nevertheless, given their success, micro-finance programs cannot be the solution to the credit requirements of the entire agricultural sector. Medium-sized farms tend to be too large to have access to microfinance and too small to have access to formal loans. In terms of reforming the conventional, structured banking system, much needs to be done to make it more effective in providing loans to agriculture in many developing countries. Rural bank authorization, which is commercial banks specifically dedicated to the demands of the agricultural sector, is a sustainable initiative, stipulated that the main issues of agricultural credit are evaluated:

- Covariant yield threat, which makes it very probable that all farmers in one region will also need credit around the same time, or that they may find it difficult to pay back loans, is a widespread drought or other widespread reduction in production.
- Limited local savings, which must be supported with enough opportunities to be mobilized.
- Lack of flexibility in addressing farmers' interests with the correct interest rate and repayment terms.
- In the absence of initial investment funds to create a rural bank.

This and many other problems affecting rural banks may be solved by (Norton, 2002):

- Extending the user base to a broad geographic area to minimize the covariant threat.
- Adopt strategies for targeting clients and establishing reimbursement opportunities similar to those implemented by micro-finance organizations, such as community loans or ties between access to credit and past repayment records.
- Decentralize the choice-making of loans to local branches as often as possible, including having loan committees made up of local citizens.
- Create modern information systems to allow loan officers to track clients when loan payments are delayed by even one day.
- Take into account creative forms of collateral, such as antichresis or mobile possessions; an antichresis is an acceptable form of land use as collateral. It allows the lender to immediately transfer control over land in the case of a loan default. The move would last only until the loan is repaid from the land's harvests.
- Keep providing opportunities for the choice of good customers and the recovery of loans.
- Provide the rural population with a variety of financial services.
- To set up a financial company, using donor funds or other existing funds. In addition, the bank's ownership should be transferred to farmers over time.

As one can see, there are many choices for designing and maintaining a sustainable rural finance system. Needless to say, the examples of such programs in developing countries are still too small. The financial sector is often either still heavily regulated by the government or in the hands of powerful individuals that have an interest in the manufacturing sector or the oil sector.

7.7 WATER UTILIZATION AND IRRIGATION POLICY

Irrigation is a perfect example of market failure from an economic point of view, and thus government intervention of one kind or another has always been present in most cases of irrigation development plans. The loss of the industry results from:

- The failure to identify property rights under private ownership.
- The effect of externalities arising from the effects of individual

user activity on collective user water access as a community.

As a consequence, a market will not emerge and therefore there will be no market price, and there will also be a difference between the marginal private costs and the marginal social costs of water supply for agriculture. Irrigation, on the other hand, is crucial to agriculture because it allows for a huge potential increase in agricultural production. Water also becomes more important due to the ties between irrigation and other policies. First of all, irrigation water is often a supplement to other inputs like fertilizers or improved crops. As a consequence, input subsidies' overall effectiveness is linked to irrigation quality. Irrigation policy is therefore specifically related to the process of inputs. In addition, the most productive use of irrigation water typically requires the adoption of new machinery procurement techniques and other fixed investments that may require credit. Irrigation policy is therefore directly related to credit policy. In addition, the availability of irrigation water can increase the variety of plant patterns available to farmers. When they can use irrigation, farmers would have the opportunity to grow many different crops. This versatility would improve the supply elasticity of all crops, as farmers can move from one crop to another more effectively. As an outcome, the reaction time of farmers to price policy is enhanced by irrigation availability, which provides a connection between irrigation policy and price policy. Lastly, the utilization of irrigation is purely linked to land use: if people have challenging access to land, irrigation water will not be available to them. Three issues can be identified as the most relevant when it comes to irrigation water throughout the world and throughout the history of public policy in agriculture:

1. The option of irrigation technology, in comparison to conventional irrigation technologies, which are typically labor-intensive but do not require large-scale investment, and modern irrigation technologies, such as drip and sprinkler irrigation, which save water, require much less effort, but also some investment.

2. Institutional system for controlling access to and management of broad irrigation facilities for water use. Irrigation installations are often distinguished by economies of scale that make them ideal candidates for state monopolies, and their operation requires constant maintenance (such as keeping channels dry, preventing damage in the pipes, etc.) for which private incentives may not be adequate.

3. The rate of the commitment of farmers to the expense of supplying food. Farmers are often given essentially free use of water. This has detrimental effects on the level of use, which appears to be excessive, and on water availability and performance for other uses, (externalities can be produced by agricultural use of water). Hence, the concern is how much to start charging farmers for use to send them the right signals about the effective value of water and save sufficient water for other use (particularly for consuming and other personal uses).

Let us discuss separately each of these topics.

7.7.1 Irrigation Types and Choice of Technology

The use of human technology to enhance and regulate the supply of water for crop production can be described as irrigation. In most situations, because of runoff, irrigation is equivalent to the naturally occurring water supply to crops. Nevertheless, there are significant examples where there would be no irrigation-free agricultural production (such as in desert or arid regions where rain is concentrated within a limited period of the year). Human imagination has been developing irrigation technology since time immemorial: irrigation projects have flourished in Asia, the Middle East, and North Africa for thousands of years. Kudos to irrigation, the very first human settlements of the Euphrates and Tigris valleys are possible. Egypt's influence was driven in prehistoric times by the prospect of irrigating the Nile River. We have to differentiate between:

- Technology for water collection;
- Technology for water distribution.

It is possible to capture water from surface water (ocean, rivers, glaciers, or even just the lakes) or from groundwater (by digging wells that draw water from aquifers). The expense of water collection varies greatly, depends a lot on the relative abundance of the water source, the depth at which the aquifer is situated deep into the earth, the quality of the water (for instance, water can be used for irrigation in theory, but only after desalination, which can be very expensive). When the water has been accumulated, it must be dispersed on the cultivated land to be used for irrigation. Some methods of simple water distribution innovations, such as redirecting a river's flow to flood land, have lasted for thousands of years and are still being used in the same way today. The main feature of traditional water supply mechanisms is that the monitoring and control of water flow require significant amounts of human labor. Also, traditional technologies' water efficiency is very low.

Huge amounts of water are necessary because the land will hold only a small portion of it and will be beneficial to the plants. Due to run-off or deep percolation, lots of water will be lost. The primary reason why traditional technologies are still being used in developing countries, specifically by small farms, is that they do not require multiple investments. In other words, the farmer's upfront cost of irrigation is very minimal with traditional technologies. To summarize, the limits of traditional technologies are that:

- Of course, it is only possible where there are abundant surface water sources (rivers, lakes, etc.). To make it available in other areas, it is necessary to construct large water distribution systems (such as dams, reservoirs, and long canals).
- Modern irrigation technology's running costs are low only when labor is relatively cheap for resources.
- Relatively large quantities of water are required.

Because of these considerations, when both water and labor became sparse and therefore more precious, modern alternate solutions of water distribution technologies were developed, which essentially substituted labor for capital and technology. Such inventions respond to two key aspirations: saving labor and saving water. Sprinkler irrigation systems replace work with power pumps and pipes to spread water on the surface, while drip irrigation is intended to reduce water loss due to run-off and deep percolation as much as possible. All types of irrigation systems also have the advantage of being able to operate them by automated systems, thus further minimizing labor requirements.

The method of irrigation to be used in the absence of government regulation depends on private incentives. If labor is relatively affordable (just like in small farms with bountiful family labor, for instance), whereas the availability of investment capital is limited, traditional irrigation systems will be common. Sadly, this will indicate that water usage capacity will also be reduced, and therefore irrigation will only be genuinely practicable where there is plenty of water. Unless the water is scarce, it will be impossible to spread irrigation between small farms. When labor is proportional to capital relatively scarce, there will be a powerful incentive to implement modern technology for irrigation. Savings in labor costs would account for the initial value of the necessary investments. Modern communication technology (especially drip irrigation) will allow irrigation to spread even in areas where water is a limited resource due to higher water use efficiency. Intervention by the administration can have a major impact on private opportunities to change from traditional to modern irrigation. For instance, by offering better access to credit, the government can also allow small-scale farmers to implement modern technology, and in effect, this could help to save water and encourage irrigation to expand to larger areas. In addition, presenting rural people with appropriate employment opportunities, the motivation to modern irrigation will improve due to the increased cost of family labor opportunities.

7.7.2 Public Spending and Agencies to Manage the Distribution of Water

Whenever it becomes available, farmers will utilize the water. The competitive price of labor and capital will decide whether to use conventional or modern structures. Because of economies of scale and the common property aspect of irrigation facilities, however, providing, and increasing the availability of irrigation water is usually a public responsibility. Water availability for irrigation can be improved by building dams, excavating wells, and, most significantly, by constructing a distribution channel network that will carry water from the point of collection to the points of use. Such installations are distinguished by large economies of scale: the building of a big dam would usually be economical than many small ones. Often, once a network of channels is in place to add more channels, the main reason is that typically. Therefore, it is very challenging to restrict access to water once it has been made available in canals. Generally, it will cost even more to put in place systems that can accurately measure the amount of water used, or to stop farmers from using it at the outskirts of the irrigation scheme. This element is what renders irrigation systems have common property resources attributes.

A private water source is very unlikely to develop for the combination of these two factors. In reality, a private company would find it very hard to pay a price that represents water quality. The common property feature may not be a major issue if water was not a limited resource, or if there were no market failures related to water use. Regrettably, there is generally a problem of over-exploitation when water availability is low and consumers are not charged a price. Over-exploitation signifies that each individual user tends to use as much water, thereby minimizing everyone else's availability. Therefore, when water usage creates externalities, the loss of productivity will be compounded. To demonstrate the market failure associated with such a challenge, economists use the prisoner's dilemma, which is supposed to highlight why selfish behavior on the part of all individuals will not lead to maximization of welfare, thus contradicting the fundamental theorems of welfare economics. The dilemma of the prisoner is generally discussed as follows. Imagine there are two inmates, A, and B, charged with a burglary that the judge believes they have done together. There really is no evidence, however, that they have done and, so if neither of the two prisoners testify, they will only be punished with a small fine. If either of the inmates accuses the other, he might be released while the other could be convicted with a severe sentence. Nonetheless, both of them will be punished if they seek to blame the other. Suppose the two prisoners are unable to interact with each other, but they must determine what to do on the basis of what the other prisoner feels will do. Neither of the two confessions would correlate to the highest possible social welfare. But each prisoner's best interest is to continue to blame the other. So, the social outcome will be the worst possible if both follow their individual incentives. In regard to water use, there will be an opportunity for each individual user to use more water. When all the consumers do this, it will negatively impact all farmers (because of water rationing, increased salinity, etc.). Nonetheless, if only one farmer wants to use less water, he must bear the full expense of this decision, while everybody benefits. Economic experts then anticipate that the result is always that all farmers will attempt to get as much water as possible, thereby overexploiting the resource. These would necessarily imply, however, that individuals involved do not care about what happens to others, and that they are unable to communicate and commit to cooperation with each other, which could improve social welfare.

Therefore, one of the primary objectives of irrigation policy is how to prevent over-exploitation by supplying farmers with the right motivation for water use. The important aspect of the irrigation scheme is how it pays for its value. Farmers have historically been granted the right to use water practically free of charge, or after payment of charges that do not represent the actual cost of water supply. On the other hand, water supply involves large-scale investments that cause the government to incur large costs. This kind of expenditure is composed of two elements: the initial investment expense to build the dam, or the other water-collecting facility, and the canals, tubes, weirs, and all other facilities, and the consequent operation and maintenance and maintenance costs. Prolonged water availability relies in particular on the plant's efficient operation and maintenance. The carrying capacity of the channel may be impaired if canals are not kept clean from weeds and soil. Additionally, if routine servicing is not performed, there may be severe water losses along the system due to perforations in the pipes, canal breaks, and so on (in Italy, for instance, in some southern regions, it is predicted that more than 30% of the water is lost due to the poor state of the tubes). Generally, the government pays for these expenses, with only small farmers' contributions. For instance, farmers incur just a minimal fee to connect to the network, mainly in the form of a land tax on irrigated land, which is sufficient to cover only part of the initial cost. The construction and operation of the irrigation system are usually carried out by a parastatal under the supervision of the Ministry of Agriculture and the Ministry of Public Works. Therefore, farmers only accrue a relative cost of distributing water on their land parcels, which usually does not depend on the actual amount of water being used. On the opposite, if conventional systems are used and labor is inexpensive, the quantity of water needed is greater and the distribution cost is lower. This lack of participation by farmers in the costs of running and sustaining water facilities has several negative consequences. To begin with, the government can incur budgetary issues that prevent the program from being efficiently maintained. Second, there is no economic motivation for farmers to conserve water, resulting in overuse.

Number three, bribery, and rent-seeking behavior on the part of irrigation authorities, which have been usually poorly compensated, may characterize the parastatal administration. This in effect could cause distributing equity problems for the water, particularly when the water is rationed in draughts. Fourth, if that same authority is supposed to be in charge of capital construction as well as operation and maintenance, there may be an inclination for a higher preference towards new capital constructions over recurring operation and maintenance. As a consequence, maintenance in many irrigation projects is usually poorly funded, with the consequence of large water supply inefficiency. For all the above reasons, reforming irrigation policy has become important in several countries to give farmers greater involvement in both cost and irrigation plant management. Privatization of irrigation infrastructure is not a realistic solution: as mentioned previously, that would be very challenging, if not impossible, for any private operator to regulate water use in order to charge the correct user fee. Due to varying river levels, spillage, and other canal losses (such as evaporation), varying rainfall, etc., water supply in the canal system cannot be fully controlled. Demand will also be difficult to control: most farmers obtain their water mostly through the fields of other farmers, or through field channels that are diverted according to local water needs from one filled to another. Therefore, it is necessary to develop strategies other than privatization. These could involve:

1. **Participation of Farmers:** The risk of inadequate management and unequal distribution can be reduced if farmers are directly involved in the management and maintenance of the facilities that provide irrigation water. One proposal might be to give farmers the responsibility of choosing a representative among themselves to patrol and regulate water flows as needed.
2. **Function Separation:** Most writers indicated that the responsibility for investment and development should be divided from operation and maintenance. The benefits of such a split would include that the time-and resource allocation differences between ongoing operation and maintenance of new projects and devoting more resources to the maintenance of existing facilities, which is currently underfunded.
3. **Charges for Water:** Farmers should be charged for their participation in the irrigation scheme in a realistic manner. Recovery of capital costs and recurring maintenance costs should be passed on through fees to farmers.

The strategies by which fees are collected must be structured in such a way that the entire payment is connected to the use of water. A yearly fee, for instance, depends on the amount of land and crop type.

In conclusion, the effective use of a country's water resource depends heavily on the capacity of governments to formulate an appropriate set of policies that provide the right opportunity for farmers. Irrigation policy is closely linked to other agricultural policies, such as input policies, credit policies, and pricing policies. A very interesting point to note is that while water is considered a domestic commodity that cannot be traded, water can be exported indirectly by agricultural commodities exports. For instance, if a country supports exports of irrigated crop commodities, it indirectly distracts water use from other domestic uses. If, when making a decision which crops to promote, both farmers and governments fail to appreciate the opportunity cost of water, the actual comparative advantages can be downplayed. Indeed, reducing water availability for domestic crops is one of the most negative effects of excessive support for export crops. The price of water in farming should be considered the lower of the two costs:

1. The price of providing water or; and
2. The cost opportunity to remove water from other uses.

One or the other of the two costs may be higher depending on the relative scarcity of water and the competition with urban water needs. Failure to internalize agricultural water costs will always lead to over-exploitation problems.

8

CASE STUDIES

CONTENTS

8.1 Patterns In Agricultural Policy In Various Regions 162
8.2 Initiatives For Helping Producers 163
8.3 Policy Support Measures For Consumers 189
8.4 Policy Coherence, Integration, And Harmonization at National And Regional Levels 227

8.1 PATTERNS IN AGRICULTURAL POLICY IN VARIOUS REGIONS

The section below is based on reports by FAO food and agriculture policy decisions analysis (FAPDA) initiative, led by the Agricultural Development Economics Division (ESA).

8.1.1 Policy Monitoring

Policy monitoring involves collecting data on a policy while it is being instituted, making it possible to use the recommendations when determining the future course of action. Policies can be perceived as a process; thus, tracking them is important to provide proof and create an environment for public discourse, shining a light on arising issues. The following section will be based on empirical research, document reviews, and country-level surveys on government policy decisions over three biennia (2007/08; 2009/10; 2011/12). This provides a wide range of policy decisions on food and agriculture adopted in 71 developing countries. Selected policy choices have been examined (Table 8.1).

Table 8.1. The Countries Reviewed

Region	Countries Included
AFRICA (27)	Ghana, Algeria, Zambia, Mozambique, Burkina Faso, Kenya, Cameroon, Democratic Republic of Congo, Egypt, Ethiopia, Lesotho, Liberia, Malawi, Mali, Mauritania, Nigeria, Morocco, Rwanda, Senegal, Sierra Leone, South Africa, Tanzania, Togo, Tunisia, Uganda, Chad, Zimbabwe
ASIA (24)	Vietnam, Azerbaijan, Bangladesh, Bhutan, Cambodia, China, India, Indonesia, Iran, Iraq, Kazakhstan, Lao PDR, Lebanon, Nepal, Oman, Pakistan, the Philippines, Saudi Arabia, Afghanistan, Sri Lanka, Syria, Tajikistan, Thailand, Yemen
LAC (20) Latin America and the Caribbean	Uruguay, Argentina, Brazil, El Salvador, Chile, Colombia, Costa Rica, Cuba, Dominican Republic, Ecuador, Guatemala, Bolivia, Haiti, Honduras, Mexico, Nicaragua, Panama, Paraguay, Peru, Venezuela

The emphasis is on national, regional / sub-regional and global policy patterns, common strategies, and evolving issues. Since food, security risks have prompted policymakers to rethink food and agricultural development liberalization policies and to extend or introduce programs for social protection. Below are the patterns focused on agricultural policy categorization by FAO.

8.2 INITIATIVES FOR HELPING PRODUCERS

Initiatives to help farmers depend on a variety of policies to raise domestic food production to improve farm income and strengthen food security. This chapter deals only with those that are most commonly the subject of policy decisions to decrease production costs, stabilize prices, minimize the risks, and guarantee producers' tenure security, especially smallholders, i.e., input subsidies, agricultural credit, price support, agricultural insurance, and land policies.

8.2.1 Input Subsidies

An input subsidy is a government resource reimbursement to reduce the price of inputs purchased by the farmer to be used on the farm. The goal of using input subsidies differs, but the most likely explanations are: increasing production and achieving food security, making inputs accessible to farmers who are unable to actually buy them (as a significant part of an optimized package of inputs and services) and social equity (transfer of income to farmers). The trend in using input subsidies and strategies for enhancing input subsidy programs performance is discussed below.

8.2.1.1 The Scale and Trend of Input Subsidies

Input subsidies are some of the most widespread support initiatives to improve the production of staple food crops by smallholder farmers. regardless of the criticism that input subsidies disrupt markets and represent inadequate resource utilization, the percentage of countries with subsidy programs in the sampled countries for which information was available over the reference period has increased. Virtually all governments managed to maintain input support programs that were implemented or re-launched after the food crisis of 2007/08 (Figure 8.1).

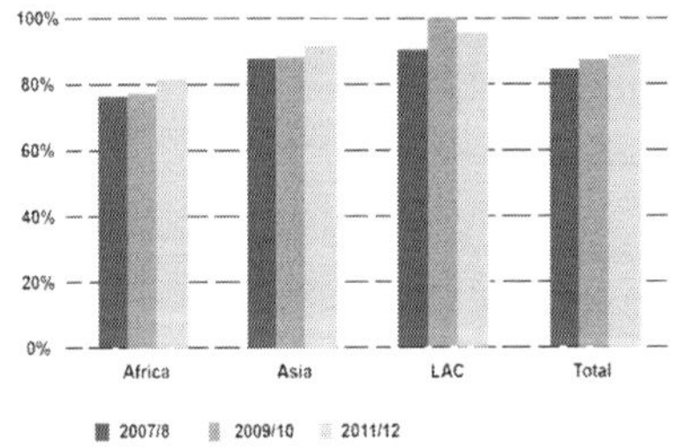

Figure 8.1. Percentage of countries with subsidies for inputs (2007–2012).

Source: FAO, FAPDA 2013.

Input subsidy initiatives are relatively more common in Asia and the LAC than in Africa: the percentage of input-subsidizing countries in Asia and the LAC approached or surpassed 90%, likened to 76 to 81% in Africa. The percentage of nations with input subsidy programs rose in all three regions relative to 2007/08 in 2009/10 and 2011/12. In Africa, after the first African Fertilizer Summit in Abuja, Nigeria in 2006, the reinstatement of large-scale input subsidy programs has gained popularity. The forum urged on Member countries to enhance the access of farmers to fertilizer through targeted subsidies, with particular reference to poor farmers (Druilhe and Barreiro-Hurlé, 2012). Some nations have developed national initiatives and extended government support for programs for input subsidies, while others have limited or ad-hoc programs (Table 8.2).

Table 8.2. Input Subsidy Schemes for Selected Countries (2007–2012)

Region	**Ad-Hoc/Small-Scale Subsidy Programs**	**Large-Scale Programs**
Africa	Sierra Leone, Chad, Mauritania, Lesotho, Mozambique, Algeria, Tunisia, Zimbabwe	Kenya*, Malawi*, Mali*, Egypt*, Ghana*, Senegal, Burkina Faso, Morocco*, Togo, Nigeria, Rwanda*, Tanzania, Zambia*
Asia	Thailand, Lao PDR, Cambodia, Nepal, Tajikistan, Bhutan, Vietnam,	China*, Lanka*, Syria, Yemen*, India*, Indonesia, Iran, Iraq, Lebanon*, Azerbaijan, Bangla-desh*, Oman, the Philippines, Saudi Arabia, Sri Kazakhstan
LAC	Colombia, Costa Rica, Argentina, Cuba, Haiti, Panama, Peru, Uruguay, Bolivia, Nicaragua, Brazil, Chile	Ecuador*, El Salvador, Guatemala, Honduras, Mexico*, Paraguay, Venezuela*
* Enlarging programs		

Source: FAO, FAPDA 2013.

Throughout Asia, input subsidies were a big part of the green transition programs and between 2007 and 2012; most governments maintained and extended their input subsidy programs. India, China, Philippines, and Indonesia are known for their broad subsidy programs for inputs. In contrast, input subsidy schemes in other Asian countries are either limited or ad-hoc (like Bhutan and Cambodia) or actually non-existent as in Pakistan and Afghanistan. In LAC, input subsidy initiatives in many countries, along with Brazil and Argentina, are comparatively small or ad hoc, which are all substantial exporters of the area's agricultural commodities. Brazil's 2011 Plano Brazil Sem Miséria (Brazil Without Misery Plan) disseminated free seed to small and rural owners. In 2008, Chile began implementing a similar strategy via the Program for Rural Development (PRODESAL) that puts an emphasis on initiatives in rural development that include input subsidies. From its Program de Desarrollo Territorial Indígena (PDTI), Chile also uses a unique input subsidy arrangement to help indigenous communities or associations with farming, forestry, and related activities. Additionally, all through the study period, some countries extended their large-scale domestic input subsidy systems, including Mexico (mostly diesel and irrigation electricity), Venezuela, and Ecuador (Table 8.2). Certain countries (e.g., El Salvador, Honduras, and Guatemala) still maintained their national programs for input subsidies. In 2009/10, all LAC states had either large or small national subsidy programs.

8.2.1.2 Improving the Efficiency of Input Subsidy Programs

The development of input subsidy programs around the globe has changed in the last decade from a universal coverage with localized benefits and huge costs to a more effective system utilizing identified households and/or staple grains utilizing voucher systems and decoupled payments. Small-scale rice farmers are by far the most widely known beneficiaries in Asia (like Nepal, Bangladesh, and Sri Lanka), while subsidies are often directed into smallholder farmers growing staples such as maize (e.g., Kenya, Tanzania, Zambia, Mozambique, and Malawi) in Africa. In LAC, small and medium-sized farmers growing food crops are the customary targets group, but in some countries (e.g., Peru, Colombia, and Costa Rica), cash crops such as coffee and cotton are also included in input subsidy programs. In some African countries, however, un-targeted subsidy programs still exist, such as Egypt, Burkina Faso, Togo, Senegal, Mali, Nigeria, and Ghana. Nearly all farmers are offered input subsidy programs among Asian countries, China, India, Iran, Iraq, Lao People's Democratic Republic (Lao PDR), and the Philippines. In LAC, universal input subsidy systems were only introduced in Mexico in 2007/08 and 2009/10, and the universal method was discontinued in 2011/12. In order to mitigate the deleterious effect of subsidized or free dissemination of inputs on market development, steps have been taken to implement input voucher systems, making it possible for targeted farmers to purchase inputs from neighboring private vendors. Voucher schemes, however, are not commonly used. It is confirmed that only Tanzania, Malawi, Mozambique, Kenya, Nigeria (pilot phase in several states) and Rwanda from Africa and Asia-based Bangladesh have used voucher systems. Ghana trialed then scrapped a voucher program in 2010. In countries such as Mexico and India, options to the traditional system of input delivery have been implemented. For example, Mexico has maintained its regional-based agricultural support payments (The Procampo Program) to reduce inequalities and increase the income of farmers. Starting in 2012, India started to replace the current input subsidy scheme with a direct deposit into the bank accounts of farmers.

8.2.1.3 Provisions on Agricultural Finances

The difficulty of access to finance in developing countries is a significant limitation on investment by smallholders and, correspondingly, on both agricultural production and income generation (Figure 8.2).

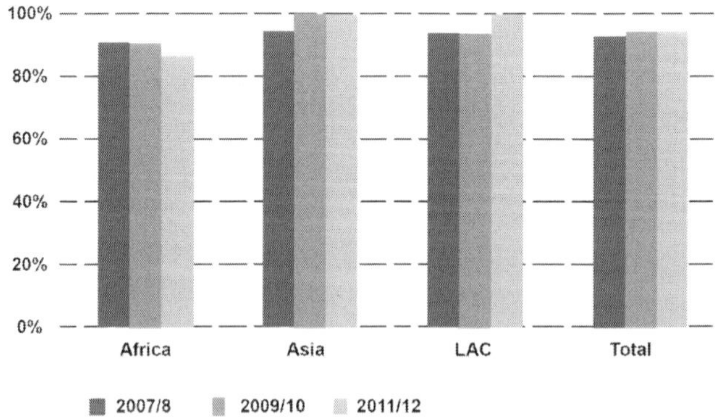

Figure 8.2. Percentage of nations adopting steps to increase smallholders' credit access (2007–2012).

Source: FAO-FAPDA 2013.

A correlation between the three nations examined indicates that Africa is lagging behind in promoting agricultural credit provisions: 100% of Asian and LAC countries had agricultural credit schemes in 2011/12, compared to 88% in Africa (Figure 8.2). There was no explicit rural credit program in Africa, Liberia, and Sierra Leone, and there was an info asymmetry on credit initiatives in countries like Mauritania, Burkina Faso, Democratic Republic of Congo (DRC), and Chad. Other concerns, such as peace and stability and lack of resources, seem to have limited credit use in many African countries to improve food production. Included are the major credit techniques to support producers:

1. Unique projects to enhance the flow of loans to farming;
2. Agricultural credit risk management initiatives (credit support schemes; credit guarantee schemes (CGSs));
3. Safeguards to develop or maintain financial institutions for agriculture.

Customized financial institutions have also been used by many nations to make rural credit accessible and affordable. The tendency and pattern in the application of these techniques, as shown below, differs from area to country.

8.2.1.4 Unique Projects to Enhance the Flow of Loans to Farming

In most Africa, with the support of special schemes, some nations have expanded the credit fluidity to agriculture, while other countries have supplied interest rate subsidies, or combined both. The Agricultural Credit Support Scheme, which has been in place since 2006, and the Commercial Agriculture Credit Scheme, which was developed in 2009, provides funding for the agricultural value chains of the state. The Ministry of Agriculture in South Africa has rearranged the Agricultural Credit Program into South Africa's Micro-Agricultural Finance Schemes (MAFISA), which was piloted in 2005 and eventually expanded to include micro and retail financial services to local farmers and budding entrepreneurs. In 2011/12, Egypt put in place credit programs that included debt reduction and interest exemptions. Through the Social Fund for Growth, which provides cash financing and advice to small farmers, it also funded small and micro-businesses. Morocco launched long-term loans for farmers without a bank account with interest rate subsidies. Identically, in 2011, the Kenyan government lowered interest rates for small farmers and agro-dealers (from 24% to 10%). Nonetheless, agriculture still receives only a small share of total credit in Africa, leaving smallholder farmers to dependent on low savings and informal credit sources (MFW4A, 2012).

Many Asian nations took action during the period 2009/10 and 2011/12 to extend credit and lower interest rates to support small farmers (Table 8.3). In India, agricultural loans grew from 2005/06 to 2009/10 at a compound annual growth rate of 18.5% (FAO, 2013a). In China, a sharp increase in the number of industrial, cooperative, and other banks in recent years (e.g., 2011) has greatly increased the volume of agricultural loans. In many countries (especially India, Nepal, Bhutan, the Philippines, and Cambodia), the growth of microfinance institutions (MFIs) has also played a key role in the expansion of agricultural credit (and other financial services). Cambodia, India, and the Philippines have acknowledged microfinance's special features and provided effective regulations and supervisory practices for banks engaged in the provision of microfinance products. It is stated that the Philippines is the first country in Asia to develop performance standards in microfinance for banks, cooperatives, and MFIs (Table 8.3).

Table 8.3. Major Credit Instruments Adopted in Selected Countries (2007–2012)

Region/ Measure	Credit Expansion	Interest Rate Subsidy	Both
Africa	Rwanda, Malawi, Lesotho, Mauritania, Zambia	Tunisia, Kenya, Uganda, Zimbabwe	Mozambique, South Africa, Nigeria, Algeria, Egypt, Ghana Morocco, Tanzania
Asia	Cambodia, China, Bangladesh, Thailand	Saudi Arabia, Indonesia, Iraq, Nepal, Syria, Iran, Vietnam	Pakistan, India, Lao PDR, the Philippines, Sri Lanka
LAC	Cuba	Mexico, Chile, Costa Rica, Argentina, Dominican Republic, Guatemala, Nicaragua, Paraguay, Panama	Peru, Colombia, Ecuador, El Salvador, Bolivia, Brazil, Venezuela

Source: FAO, FAPDA 2013..

Some countries in the LAC adopted measures to enlarge agricultural loans and lower interest rates for more countries (Table 8.3). Specific credit programs for small and medium-sized farms have been designed to improve access to credit. As part of MERCOSUR's family farming program, several countries adopted credit controls. As an integral approach to boosting agriculture (including credits, input subsidies, and technical assistance) for small and medium-sized farms, Ecuador launched the Socio Siembra Program in 2008. Since 2007, Peru has instituted various schemes with major credit elements (among others, the Agro-Peru Program, and the Agroequip Plan), while more attention has been paid to rural producers and family farmers, with credit disbursements almost doubling between 2007 and 2010 (CEBRI, 2012). Microfinance development and sustainability also triggered microfinance activity in rural areas in Latin American urban areas. An adequate climate has enabled this itself: a sustainable macroeconomy, appropriate organizational strategies, reasonable property rights, and an adequate regulatory framework (Jaramillo, 2013).

8.2.1.5 Credit Guarantee Schemes (CGSs)

Over the reference period (FAO, 2013a), the use of CGSs as a risk management mechanism to tackle market failure in credit services and to facilitate loans to the agricultural sector has gained significant attention. Well-managed CGSs have the ability to expand access to credit for smallholders. CGSs are not widely available in Africa, but new pilot projects have arisen during the reference era through collaborations between governments, the private sector, donors, and NGOs. For example, in 2009, a collaboration between an international commercial bank and various organizations culminated in a pilot loan guarantee scheme in four African countries (Ghana, Mozambique, Tanzania, and Uganda). Small-scale CGSs are found in a few countries, mostly operated as partially governmental or non-governmental. On the other hand, during the period under scrutiny, only Ethiopia, Egypt, Morocco, and Nigeria were reported to have fully owned CGSs by the government. The government has financially backed banks in Ethiopia to shield farmers from payment default. In 1977, the government set up the agricultural credit guarantee scheme fund (ACGSF) in Nigeria to provide some measure of risk protection and to enable commercial banks to increase their lending to farming. A new program, the Nigeria opportunity-based risk-sharing system for agricultural loans (NIRSAL), was also launched in 2011 with the aim of de-risking farmers' agricultural loans and reducing bank lending costs.

Throughout Asia, many countries have public CGSs (Table 8.4), but they are mainly intended to serve small and medium-sized enterprises (SMEs). In India, the micro and small enterprises' credit guarantee fund trust (CGTMSE) meets the lender's loss up to a maximum of 85% of the default amount. While the coverage of the scheme has steadily increased since its introduction in 2000 (both in the number of people reached and the volume of credit distributed), the CGTMSE does not cover agricultural loans (FAO, 2013a). Depending on the CGTMSE observation, the Indian Reserve Bank suggested an Agriculture Credit Risk Guarantee Program for Small and Marginal Farmers to be established in 2012. Cambodia's government has consistently reported that it is investigating the possibility of setting up a CGS and risk-sharing facility to encourage the production and export of paddy rice (GAFSP, 2011).

CGSs are more widely accessible in LAC than in Asia or Africa: during the reference period, nearly all surveyed LAC countries had one or more government CGSs. A number of individual and partial credit guarantee operations are provided by many LAC countries. In Brazil, for example, under the umbrella of the Brazilian Development Bank, three different CGSs for agriculture and agro-processing are managed. The most significant of these funds is the Fundo Garantidor para Investimentos, which operates with 12 intermediary banks funding investments, primarily in large-scale agricultural production (FAO, 2013b). Several countries have increased their CGS size. Mexico, for example, with one of the world's oldest and largest guarantee funds, the FideicomisosInstituidosenRelación con la Agricultura (FIRA) Trust Funds for Rural Development-provided nearly $6 billion in guarantees in 2010, helping 1.08 million players in agriculture and the agricultural value chain (FAO, 2013a) (Table 8.4).

Table 8.4. Examples of Countries With Public, Partially Public and Non-Governmental CGSS

Region	Credit Guarantee Schemes (CGSs)
Africa	South Africa**, Egypt*, Ethiopia*, Ghana***, Kenya ***, Morocco*, Mozambique***, Nigeria*, Tunisia**, Burkina Faso **, Tanzania**, Uganda**, Senegal***
Asia	Thailand*, Saudi Arabia**, Indonesia*, Iraq***, Lebanon**, the Philippines*, Cambodia*, India*, Syria*
LAC	All countries have public CGSs except Cuba, Dominican Republic, and Haiti ***
*public CGSs, ** partially governmental, ***non-governmental	

Source: FAO, FAPDA 2013.

8.2.1.6 Financial Institutions for Agriculture

Sophisticated financial institutions for agriculture are widespread in all regions and are increasingly operating alongside private commercial banks and cooperative banks. Specialized institutions such as government-owned agricultural development banks (ADBs), community banks, or rural banks have been required to improve access to affordable credit by small farmers. The argument that private commercial banks offer intermittent and restricted services and appear to target wealthy farmers is often used to justify setting up specialized public financial institutions. Multiple public agricultural financial institutions in Africa have endured economic reform programs and during the period under consideration played an important role in the rural credit market (Table 8.5). In Rwanda, the Rwanda Development Bank has been reformed and expanded to provide loans to MFIs and cooperatives. During the course of the study, a government fund for microfinance refinancing and growth increased (the Republic of Rwanda, 2011). Recently reinvigorated and enlarged the Principal Bank for Development and Agricultural Credit in Egypt and Morocco's Crédit Agricole du Maroc. MAFISA funds are handled by the government-owned Land Bank in South Africa, which conducts fund and treasury management roles on behalf of the agriculture department (WTO, 2009). The decision to close specialist banks has been reversed by other nations. For example, after almost two decades of liquidation of Cameroon's Crédit Agricole, Cameroon announced in January 2011 the creation of the Cameroon Agriculture Financial Rural Corporation with the objective of funding agricultural projects (Pibasso, 2011).

In Mali, the Banque Nationale de Développement Agricole (BNDA) National Agricultural Development Bank-keeps playing a role in agriculture, although its credit licenses for rural areas have declined substantially in recent years, primarily due to the cotton sector crisis and the high indebtedness of actors in the two main sub-sectors, rice, and cotton (Michigan State University, 2011). Nearly all monitored countries in Asia have specialized banks serving farming. Every country (except Afghanistan) has retained one or more main long-standing financial institutions to serve the rural sector, and the position of cooperatives (often supervised and funded by governments) has increased significantly in recent years. The Vietnam Bank for Agriculture and Rural Development (Agribank) is the country's largest commercial bank, with a dominant role in Vietnam's economic development, particularly in agricultural and rural investment. The payment of Agribank credit has expanded rapidly in recent years. As of March 2011, the Bank for Agriculture and Agricultural Cooperatives of

Thailand expanded its outreach to 6.25 million farm families, accounting for almost 98% of the total number of farm households in the country. Government banks (e.g., China's ADB) and different kinds of advanced banks, including rural commercial banks, rural credit cooperatives, and township banks, provide financial services to agriculture, rural areas and farmers in China (People's Bank of China's Financial Stability Analysis Group, 2012). In Bangladesh, a partnership agreement with NGO-based MFIs enables state-owned specialist banks, state-owned commercial banks, private commercial banks, and international commercial banks to expand lending facilities to agriculture (Rahman et al., 2011). In India, the agricultural sector receives credit from several government schemes and the production has greatly surpassed targets in recent years. The regulations of the Reserve Bank of India make it compulsory for domestic commercial banks to channel 18% of their modified net bank credit to agriculture and related sectors. Several countries have specialist banks participating in the LAC (Table 8.5). Financial development institutions (FDIs) are the primary funding sources for the agricultural sector. Over the years, the DFIs supporting the agricultural sector have been redefining themselves. In many situations, they have strengthened their management as state or public-private financial institutions and shifted their focus, switching from a concentration in agriculture to a multi-sector approach and from direct loans to farmers (first tier) via intermediaries to a second-tier credit line. Under the Ministry of Agriculture, Chile's Instituto Nacional de Desarrollo Agropecuario(INDAP)National Agricultural Research Institute of Chile is a specialist agency. It is a major credit provider for preferential tariffs for small-scale agriculture, and its position has become more important over the years, mainly due to the various credit initiatives implemented since 2009 (e.g., special credit for medium-sized farmers and a program for financial support for farmers). INDAP loans rose by 31% in 2011 compared to 2010. The Banco Nacional do Des envolvimentoEconômico e Social (BNDES) National Bank for Economic and Social Development-is the largest state-owned development bank in Brazil, supplying the bulk of the country's long-term credit (more than 70%) and funding operations in the farming, manufacturing, and service sectors. BNDES, South America's largest lender, offers subsidized finance in a world where credit is globally costly and still yields huge profits. Among the effective public-private agricultural banks is the Banrural SA from Guatemala, which serves both rural poor and non-agricultural clients. Banrural SA remained a competitive public-private bank in which the public sector owned initially 30% of the shares and the remaining private shareholders (Trivelli and Venero, 2007). The share of the agricultural portfolio of Banrural SA has been steadily increasing over the reference period (Jaramillo, 2013) (Table 8.5).

Table 8.5. Countrics of Financial Institutions for Agricultural Purposes

Region	Public Agricultural/Development Financial Institution	Cooperative Banks and Other Forms of Financial Institutions Serving Agriculture
	Kenya, Nigeria, Burkina Faso, South Africa, Mali, Mauritania, Morocco, Mozambique, Algeria, Cameroon, Egypt, Ethiopia, Ghana, Rwanda, Senegal, Tanzania, Tunisia, Uganda, Zimbabwe	Kenya*, Algeria**, Rwanda*, Tanzania***, Uganda*
	Arabia, Syria, Thailand, Bhutan, Bangladesh, China, India, Indonesia, Iran, Cambodia, Iraq, Lao PDR, Nepal, Oman, Pakistan, Sri Lanka, Saudi Vietnam, Yemen	Cambodia****, Bangladesh****, China***, India****, Pakistan***, the Philippines***, Vietnam***
	Paraguay, Peru, Brazil, Colombia, Costa Rica, Dominican Republic, Chile, Ecuador, ElSalvador, Guatemala, Honduras, Mexico, Nicaragua, Panama, Venezuela	Argentina**, Cuba ***, Guatemala*, Uruguay**
*Public- private partnership, ** Public commercial banks, *** Cooperative banks, **** Private commercial banks		

Source: FAO, FAPDA 2013.

8.2.1.7 Price Stabilization and Government Aid

Price stabilization and support policies often refer to a minimum price supported by the government to protect farmers against low and fluctuating commodity prices. Price support is a government-based price risk management tool employed to achieve self-sufficiency in key grain commodities, support farmers' income, and builds grain stock for public distribution to vulnerable groups (Figure 8.3).

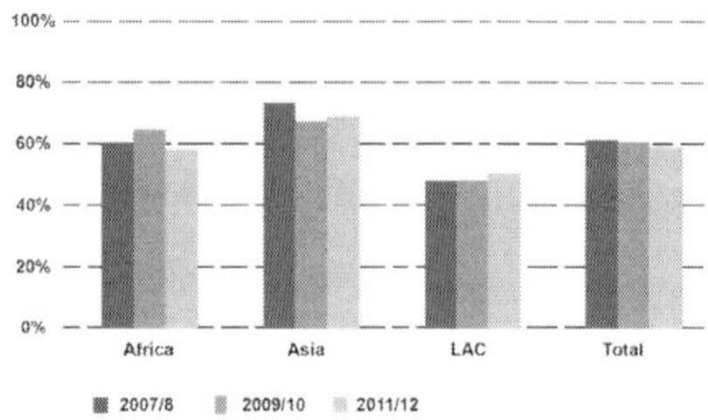

Figure 8.3. Proportion of countries implementing Price stabilization and support schemes (2007–2012).

Source: FAO, FAPDA 2013.

Price stabilization and support programs are more widespread and comprehensive in Asia than in Africa or LAC. In 2011/12, about 68% of the Asian countries implemented price support schemes, compared to 58% in Africa and 50% in LAC. Price support and stabilization programs, which were universally applied throughout Asia during the drive to adopt 'green revolution' technologies in the 1960s and 1970s (Demeke et al., 2012), appear to have been sustained during the period under review. However, the pattern and scope of price interventions varied from one country to another within each region. In Africa, price support programs have attracted greater attention in recent years (Table 8.6) but comprehensive and consistent national price support programs are not very common. Many countries in East and Southern Africa retained state-controlled marketing parastatals that led to an uneasy coexistence with the private sector (Oyejide et al., 2012). In Mala with the main objective of the minimum support pricing (MSP) scheme is to protect the farmers but the quantity of maize purchased by the parastatal, Agricultural Development, and Marketing Corporation, has been minimal relative to production and has declined in recent years (Ricker-Gilbert et al., 2013). In Zambia, the government purchased maize at above-market prices through the Food Reserve Agency during the bumper harvest period of 2009/10 to 2011/12. In Kenya, the government intervenes intermittently in the maize market through the National Cereals and Produce Board (NCPB). For the 2011 harvest, the NCPB raised its buying price and protected farmers from falling prices but maize prices decreased markedly after NCPB stopped buying the commodity in January 2012 (Kamau et al., 2012). Nigeria introduced a guaranteed minimum price (GMP) scheme in 2009 but the level of procurement by the National Food Reserve Agency (NFRA) fluctuated sharply. In 2010/11, market prices were far higher than the GMP and farmers preferred to sell at the prevailing market price (Olomola, 2013). In North Africa, Algeria, Egypt, Morocco, and Tunisia used price support programs during the period 2007/08 to 2011/12 but not on a regular basis.

In Asia, most of the major agricultural economies have price support schemes and the level of support is increasing over time. To better support grain production and provide farmers with incentives to grow grain, the Chinese government has been raising minimum purchase prices for wheat and rice. The Food Corporation of India has bought wheat, rough rice and milled rice for MSPs that have been announced well before the planting seasons. In response to rising international prices and declining wheat stocks that began in 2005, the Indian government raised the MSP for each staple grain. The procured food grains are used for distribution to poor consumers or for export at times of surplus. Similarly, in Bangladesh, domestic procurement serves the dual purpose of building rice stocks for the Public Food grain Distribution System and providing income support to farmers. The fixed MSP for rice in Bangladesh is well above the market price and is the highest among Asian countries (Table 8.6).

Table 8.6. Examples of Countries with Price Support Measures for Staple Commodities

Region	Price Support Measures
Africa	Malawi, Mozambique, Tanzania, Zambia, Rwanda, Zimbabwe, Algeria, Burkina Faso, Nigeria, Ghana, Togo, Morocco, Kenya, Egypt, Mauritania, Tunisia
Asia	Bangladesh, China, India, Indonesia, the Philippines, Pakistan, Ukraine, Iraq, Syria, Lebanon, Iran, Nepal, Thailand, Sri Lanka, Vietnam, Yemen, Kazakhstan
LAC	Brazil, Ecuador, Venezuela, Costa Rica, Cuba, Argentina, Mexico, Honduras, Dominican Republic, Colombia

Source: FAO, FAPDA 2013.

Price support programs are applied intermittently in some Middle East economies. The Government of Lebanon, for instance, guaranteed prices for farmers, purchased wheat at a higher price from local producers in 2007 and 2009 and then sold it at lower prices. In 2008 and 2010, market prices were higher; farmers sold directly to the market, and the government bought only a small quantity of locally produced wheat. Iran, Lebanon, Iraq, and conflict-affected countries such as Syria and Yemen, implemented price support programs sporadically. In LAC, price support programs are less popular than credit, input subsidies, or insurance programs. Only a few LAC countries, such as Brazil, Mexico, Ecuador, the Dominican Republic, and Venezuela operate large-scale price support programs. Brazil uses its national food reserve system to stabilize local prices of staple crops such as maize, and to foster and support smallholder agriculture and family farms. The Companhia Nacional de Abastecimento (National Supply Company, CONAB), which manages food supply, stocks, and distribution, along with the Program de Aquisição de Alimentos (Program for the Acquisition of Food, PAA), guarantee a minimum price to small food producers and buy grains from smallholders at subsidized rates. The food purchased is then donated and re-circulated through local food security-related organizations or lodged in the national or local food reserves (IATP, 2012). Price support levels have tended to increase in recent years (IATP, 2012). Mexico provides market price support to some commodities, and payments based on output (through the IngresoObjetivo program). Mexico has significantly reduced market price support in favor of direct historical payments and more recently increased expenditure on payments based on inputs. The country has large direct payment programs and subsidy schemes to inputs and crop insurance (OECD, 2011). In general, countries that responded to the 2007/08 food crisis with price stabilization and support measures did not change their market intervention policies in 2009/10 and 2011/12. However, the measure is applied more consistently and systematically in Asia for the purpose of increasing farm income, ensuring food security, or boosting production for export.

8.2.1.8 Agricultural Insurance Provisions and Risk Management

Agricultural activities are particularly prone to risk, especially in relation to extreme natural events (e.g., droughts, floods, pests, and diseases) that have a significant impact on yields and in turn on price volatility. High levels of risk in agriculture prompted many governments to get involved in agricultural insurance programs and disaster risk management (DRM) schemes during the study period. About 74% of the surveyed countries with available data had provisions for improving access to insurance and DRM in 2011/12. The proportion consistently increased: from 68% in 2007/08 to 71% in 2009/10 and 74% in 2011/12. The incidence of agricultural insurance and DRM schemes is higher in LAC and Asia than in Africa; of the surveyed countries with data available about 80% of the LAC and around 90% of the Asian countries had national agricultural insurance and risk management schemes in 2011/12, compared to around 56% in Africa. Governments with national programs have relied on two major approaches in support of insurance programs: public insurance and related schemes, and premium subsidies (Figure 8.4).

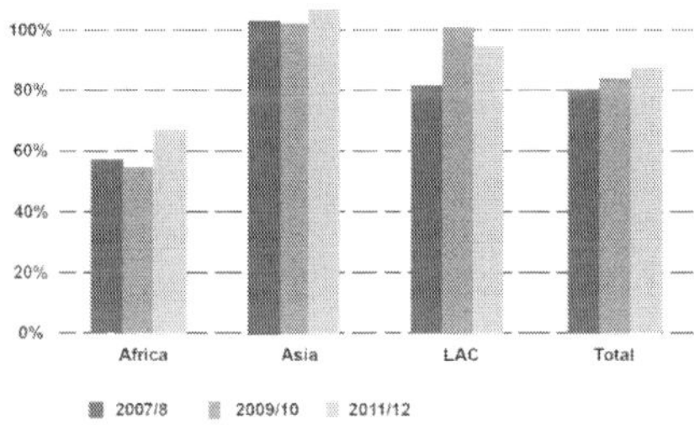

Figure 8.4. Fraction of nations with government insurance and catastrophe risk management programs (2007–2012).

Source: FAO, FAPDA 2013.

8.2.1.8.1 Agricultural Insurance and Associated Programs

Progressively, government intervention in agricultural insurance and reinsurance and calamity management has favored public-private partnerships. Government insurance and related services apply to state-owned insurance companies, government-based (last resort) re-insurance plans, and state-run disaster management systems. Many public sector schemes' poor performance and minimal penetration among farmers have led several governments to reassess and redefine the position of the public sector in agricultural insurance. In LAC, state-owned insurance companies have become prominent, but operate with private insurance companies, providing special services such as reinsurance and insurance. The Ministry of Rural Development and Land in Bolivia has implemented the Pachamama Agricultural Insurance Act, which was enacted in 2011 and came into force in February 2012. Ecuador's national agricultural insurance scheme (NAIS), AGROSEGURO, was founded in 2009 to safeguard the investments of farmers from natural catastrophes and the impact of climate change. Agroasemex, which is owned by Mexico, offers insurance and reinsurance products across the region. Parastatal insurance companies operate in conjunction with private insurance companies except for AGRODOSA (AseguradoraAgropecuariaDominicana) in the Dominican Republic. In other words, in the region, state-owned insurance and reinsurance firms are subject to the same legal framework as private insurance and reinsurance firms. A common trend in the area is also a public-private partnership. For instance, in 2008, the Brazilian government enacted a law creating the Fundo de Catástrofe Rural, a public-private partnership which involves the Brazilian government, the private insurance industry, agro-industries, and cooperatives, to develop frameworks to assess potential losses incurred by insurers and to enable them to help agricultural business in risky geographical areas and risky crop. Sheer market-based private insurers, typically supported by private reinsurers, bid to underwrite agricultural insurance in all LAC countries. In circumstances where agricultural production is subjected to the risk of devastating windstorms, excessive rains or famines, the insurance industry may not have the enthusiasm to underwrite agricultural risks, and governments usually take action after the disaster (in ex-post fashion). Many Caribbean nations, as well as Bolivia, Mexico, and Brazil, rely on government post-disaster aid. In addition, agricultural insurance complements more complex financial markets (such as Brazil and Mexico) with post-disaster assistance from governments in LAC countries. In many LAC countries (e.g., Colombia in 2010, Mexico in 2001, Peru in 2010 and Argentina in 2009), the public sector (at the national and sub-national level) has recently started to purchase private agricultural insurance cover to transfer catastrophic agricultural risks to international markets and to protect small traditional and semi-commercial farmers.

In Asia, a combined effect of public, private, and public-private agricultural insurance designs and government-based natural catastrophe risk management programs have emerged. In terms of the number of farmers covered, India administers the world's largest crop insurance system. About 18 million farmers, or 15% of all producers, are covered annually by the NAIS. The Indian government agreed in 2010/11 to amend NAIS and switch to a market-based insurance scheme from a public social insurance program. Throughout China, where China's People's Insurance Company maintained a near-monopoly on agricultural insurance, the government encouraged a significant expansion of private sector-led agricultural insurance and by 2008, all agricultural insurance was provided by private and/or mutual insurance companies (no public-sector agricultural insurance companies). In Iran, the Government Insurance Fund for Agricultural goods (a monopoly) higher insurance coverage, jumping in the reporting period about 30% of the total hectares of farmland under cultivation. Operating in India, Pakistan, the Philippines, Thailand, and Vietnam, market-based agricultural insurance companies operate. Many private businesses, however, are small and have recently started running as pilot schemes. In Sri Lanka, Thailand, China, Vietnam, and India, the government is involved in agricultural reinsurance. It is understood that the Sri Lankan government is the only supplier of agricultural reinsurance. In the meantime, governments in China, Vietnam, Thailand, and India are serving as a reinsurer for disaster, but their markets are also open to competition from national reinsurers and/or foreign reinsurers. Agriculture in Asia is highly vulnerable to significant climatic risks, including typhoons, floods, droughts, and tsunamis, and a large proportion of rural households are therefore dependent on public post-disaster. Many nations have government-based risk management systems for natural disasters that integrate preventive measures with post-disaster response programs in the form of relief, rehabilitation, and restoration operations. Farmers generally receive reimbursement for lost livestock and free seeds and fertilizers for replanting their crops after the disaster. Vietnam has an exceptionally well-developed system for managing natural disasters as well as post-disaster emergency relief and recovery scheme, partly funded by central and local government (provincial and district governments). Asian countries are also known for other forms of state-sponsored agricultural risk management tools such as public irrigation schemes and state-sponsored lending to farmers that are often linked to compulsory crop insurance, as in India and the Philippines (FAO, 2011a) (Table 8.7).

Table 8.7. Different Insurance and Risk Management Project

Region/ Measure	**Insurance**					**Disaster Risk Management**
	Public Insurance	**Public Private Insurance**	**Reinsurance**	**Premium subsidy**	**Technical Support**	
Africa	Morocco*, Nigeria*	Senegal*+, Algeria, Tunisia, Morocco, Ghana, Malawi+, Mozambique, South Africa, Kenya*+, Ethiopia +	Morocco			Algeria, Mozambique*, Malawi, Mauritania, Ethiopia, Ghana

Asia	Nepal*, the Philippines*, Iran, India*, Syria, Saudi Arabia, Oman, Sri Lanka	China*, India, Indonesia, Nepal, Pakistan*+, Vietnam, Thailand, Sri Lanka, the Philippines	Sri Lanka, Vietnam, India, Iran, Thailand, China, Kazakhstan	India, China	Indonesia, Sri Lanka, India, Vietnam, Bangladesh, China, Thailand	India, Oman, Thailand, Vietnam, Lebanon, Iran, Saudi Arabia**, Syria**, Iraq**, China
LAC	Bolivia*, Brazil*, Ecuador*, Nicaragua, Costa Rica*, Panama, Uruguay*, Dominican Republic*, Mexico*, Peru*	Dominican Republic, Mexico, Brazil, Costa Rica, Argentina, Uruguay, Paraguay, Venezuela, Peru, Chile, Colombia*	Brazil, Dominican Republic, Mexico, Costa Rica, Peru	Argentina, Brazil, Chile Uruguay	Uruguay, Argentina*, Chile, Brazil, Paraguay, Peru, Ecuador, Panama, Nicaragua, Honduras, Mexico, Dominican Republic	Honduras, Costa Rica, Cuba, El Salvador+, Dominican Republic, Guatemala+, Panama, Bolivia, Nicaragua, Brazil, Mexico
* Includes premium subsidies, ** Sporadic funds, + pilot						

Source: FAPDA, Mahul, and Stutley, 2010; World Bank, 2012a; and FAO, 2011a.

There is almost no tradition of national agricultural insurance stipulation in Africa, with the exception of South Africa, Nigeria, Algeria, Morocco, and Tunisia. The government-owned Nigeria Agricultural Insurance Corporation maintains a de-facto agricultural insurance monopoly in Nigeria, but its coverage remains very limited (Eleri et al., 2012). In addition, there is a long history and better agricultural insurance products in South Africa. Seven private commercial or cooperative firms and underwriting companies currently offer coverage for crops and livestock or both to commercial farmers (DHNA Foundation) (Mahul and Stutley, 2010). However, South

Africa has no insurance program for small farmers. In North Africa, Morocco expanded the coverage of its national insurance program (the Mutuelle Agricole Marocained'Assurances) in 2012. Public-private and private models of agricultural insurance have emerged in several African countries. In Ghana, the Agricultural Insurance Program was launched in 2011 and developed the first agricultural insurance products to protect farmers from the negative impacts of climate change. It is an example of government-private partnership in the agricultural insurance system, as the program coordinating steering committee is made up of representatives from the public sector, the private sector, and development agencies. Insurance products are available in Algeria and Tunisia in North Africa based on public-private partnerships. In 2010, Algeria's agricultural insurance coverage increased by 98%. Nevertheless, only 1% of the domestic insurance market accounts for agricultural insurance (Mena Insurance CEO Club, 2013). Many African countries have pilot insurance programs that only cover a small number of farmers and herders. There is also under development in the provision of public agricultural reinsurance in Africa.

Calamity risk management relies on the goodwill of donors, but in many African nations is being restructured and institutionalized (African Union (AU) Commission, ISDR, and World Bank, 2008). A number of countries have taken steps to improve their national management of disaster risk (DRM) and devise national policies, strategies, and courses of action. For example, in Malawi, Mozambique, and Ghana, projects were planned between 2007 and 2010 (in collaboration with the World Bank (WB)) to incorporate DRM into strategic plans and business development policies. Some countries have started to look for mechanisms to finance the projects for contingency funding. For the 2008/09 to 2011/12 agricultural seasons, the Government of Malawi bought drought support in the form of weather derivative contracts that covered the risk of severe drought during the critical rainfall season with donor co-financing support (World Bank, 2012a). In Ethiopia, the government first implemented conditional funding mechanisms.

8.2.1.8.2 Premium Subsidies

Subscription subsidies are some of the most prevalent forms of public involvement in support of agricultural insurance, referring to the percentage of the total premium subsidized by the government. Agricultural premium incentive policies are often designed to increase farmers' interest in buying insurance coverage and draw private insurers to agricultural insurance programs. In LAC, premium vouchers are commonly used and in recent years have received increased allocations from the public budget. In 2009, government spending on premium subsidies in Brazil and Mexico increased significantly (World Bank, 2010a). Most LAC countries have developed policies channeling premium subsidies to improve the objectives of food security. Costa Rica provides to small and marginal farmers higher premium subsidies than to larger farmers. Argentina and Uruguay are channeling premium funds to unique crop insurance schemes. At present, premium subsidies account for 60% of the premium value in Colombia. Many countries, like Chile and Brazil, have a limit (cap) on the maximum number of premium subsidies each farmer may earn, preventing large farmers from receiving a disproportionate share. Numerous LAC governments also provide technical support units to encourage and assist agricultural insurance markets in their growth.

Premium support is less popular in Asia than in the LAC and has taken on various forms and sizes (FAO, 2011a). India's government policy is to enable agricultural insurance as readily accessible and affordable as possible for small farmers using a premium subsidy of up to 75% and technical support (e.g., crop-cutting experiments (CCE) in the fields used to assess the average yields for each crop used to compensate for area-yield losses). It must be observed that India deployed the first weather index insurance (WII) program for micro-level or individual farmers in 2003. Since then, with support from a government premium subsidy, it has been scaled up by both public and private insurance companies. China provides adjustable premium subsidies and has dramatically increased the level of premium agricultural insurance subsidies in recent years (FAO, 2011a). In order to support rice farmers, Vietnam performs comprehensive research and development on climate index coverage. A few pilot cases that occurred during the reference era in Africa often used premium incentives as a method for insurance promotion. The farm-specific insurance agency, Compagnie Nationaled'Assurance Agricole du Sénégal, was founded as a pool company in Senegal in 2009. It is public-owned, regional insurers and banks and earns a federal premium subsidy of 50%. Almost all of the pilot farm insurance programs function with the assistance of agribusiness companies and donors. Half of the premium for the Killimo Salama agricultural insurance scheme in Kenya, for example, is paid by agribusiness partners such as Syngenta East Africa Limited. For the most part, there is a shortage of capacity-building activities and technical support in insurance products in Africa. There are no regulations for insurance or risk management tools on the continent for agricultural development techniques and investment plans. Lately, this void has prompted the New Partnership for African Development (NEPAD) Comprehensive Africa Agricultural Development Program (CAADP) to initiate an initiative to incorporate risk management tools, including agricultural insurance, into national and regional agricultural investment plans (RAIPs) (NEPAD, 2012).

8.2.2 Measures Relating to Land Policies

Ultimately, from 71% in 2007/08 to 82% in 2011/12, the percentage of countries adopting land-related initiatives increased. With increasing population density and increased interest by lenders in land acquisitions, land markets have grown, and governments have been required to implement policies to ensure sufficient access and tenure protection for local communities over the land they develop. Regional variations, however, exist: the percentage of countries adopting land policies during the comparison period was higher in LAC (88% on average) and Asia (85%) than in Africa (61%). Many countries in Africa have yet to take further action, but also several governments are reforming their land policies, and in recent years the proportion of counties introducing new legislation has risen sharply from 43% in 2007/08 to 70% in 2011/12 (Figure 8.5). Land policies aimed at improving access to land for smallholder farmers and minority groups have used different tools, from extending credit for land acquisitions to land distribution. Several recent land policies are being used to address foreign land investment governance.

8.2.2.1 Land Policies for Improving the Access of Farmers to Land

Policymakers have a number of strategies at their disposal to boost small farmers' access to land: land allocation for the incredibly poor and downtrodden, land titling for traditional holders, and credit facilities for low- and mid-income households earning their living from farming (Figure 8.5). Numerous countries in Africa have reviewed land policies and legislation with the aim of making sure equitable access to land, facilitating security of land tenure, particularly for smallholder farmers, and offering some form of legal recognition of customary property rights. For example, in 2009, Burkina Faso introduced a rural land law and in 2012 revised the existing land tenure law. A strong pattern is reflected in the new land policy. Concerning local land management and promoting formalized land rights, including those based on customary claims.

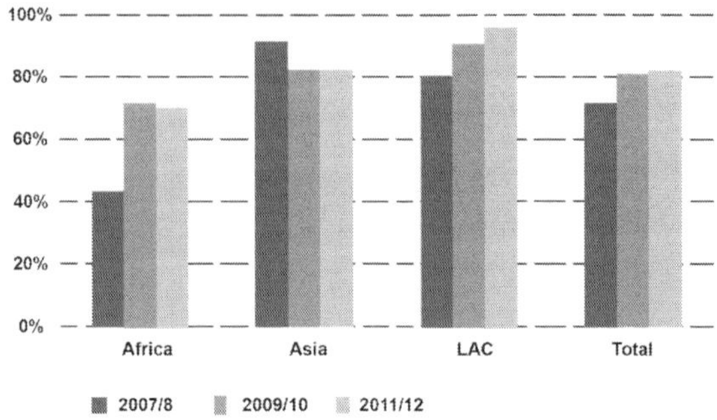

Figure 8.5. Percentage of nations applying land policies (2007–2012).

Source: FAO, FAPDA 2013.

Other countries have taken various steps to improve land access: extending land procurement micro-credits in Uganda, subsidizing land purchases in Malawi, or developing better conditions for the land market in Zimbabwe and Morocco. Nearly all governments are tackling land ownership problems in the LAC by introducing land distribution and titling or wider land reform programs (Table 8.8). Traditionally, uneven land holdings and a large consolidation of land (latifundios) in the hands of a few people were a major problem in the region, so in the 1960s and 1970s, some countries started reforming their land tenure. The 2007/08 crisis exacerbated this pattern, i.e., most countries acknowledged that the LAC undernourishment issue was not due to the availability of food, but a question of food access. As an outcome, marginalized groups have been targeted for land titling, specifically indigenous peoples. In almost all LAC countries, land distribution and titling programs are registered. Several other countries have adopted ambitious land reform initiatives: in 2010 Colombia unveiled its land reform (primarily to resolve the problem of its displaced communities following its internal armed conflict); in 2009, while seeking agrarian reform since the 1970s, Brazil expanded its efforts with major land transfers undertaken through Instituto Nacional de Colonização e ReformaAgrária (INCRA); In 2009, Ecuador implemented major reforms, adopting a new constitution specifying that land has a social value and therefore unproductive land can be expropriated; Bolivia undertook land reform since 2006, creating the likelihood of expropriating land 'not serving its social value' in 2009 and launching the Plan Nacional de TitulaciónMasiva de Tierras in 2011; Argentina has placed a cap on non-citizens' ownership of land; and Venezuela has implemented a radical land reform; since 2006, the Instituto Nacional de Tierras, founded in 2001, has been introducing large-scale land expropriations and redistributions to small farmers.

Many countries in Asia have tried to address land problems mainly through the use of legislative and bureaucratic structures. Most countries have introduced new policies or changed existing policies on land (Table 8.8). In India, in February 2009, an amended Land Acquisition Act was passed with the intention of minimizing forced displacement and ensuring greater compensation and an enhanced legal system for, among others, those whose land is being removed. Sri Lanka's National Land Title Registration Program (2007–2022) is underway for surveying and demarcating land, issuing titles, and increasing land ownership within 15 years. By 2010, the Vietnamese government concern approximately 31.3 million land use right certificates (LURCs), covering approximately half of Vietnam's land area, to improve the security of tenure. In order to improve access to land (Iraq, Oman, Thailand, and Yemen), new land legislation was approved. Throughout 2007, Iraq also welcomed foreign land investments. Yemen passed a law that allowed foreigners to own land but then limited foreign ownership to 49% (Table 8.8).

Table 8.8. Examples of Countries with Policies Related to Land (2007–2012)

Region	Policies for the Allocation of Land and/or Protection of Tenure for Small Farmers
Africa	Ethiopia, Zimbabwe, Kenya, Rwanda, Morocco, Rwanda, Senegal, South Africa, Tanzania, Burkina Faso, Liberia, Malawi, Ethiopia, Mauritania, Tunisia, Cameroon, Kenya, Uganda, Zambia, Algeria
Asia	Indonesia, Iraq, Kazakhstan, Afghanistan, Azerbaijan, Bangladesh, Bhutan, India, the Philippines Thailand, Cambodia, Iraq, Vietnam, Yemen, Oman, Sri Lanka, Tajikistan, Thailand, Ukraine
LAC	Nicaragua, Venezuela, Costa Rica, Colombia, Ecuador, Paraguay, Uruguay, Cuba, Dominican Republic, El Salvador, Argentina, Bolivia, Brazil, Chile, Guatemala, Haiti, Honduras, Mexico, Panama

Source: FAO, FAPDA 2013.

8.2.2.2 Policies for the Management of Direct Foreign Investment in the Country

Demand in foreign direct investment (FDI) in the land is driven primarily by long-term goals such as increased food and biofuel consumption in the context of insufficient arable land, water, and energy availability. Investors are seeking safe access to food and other agricultural commodities as well as desirable financial returns, while host countries hope to benefit from job creation, higher foreign exchange earnings, and an increase in local market food supplies. There may be risks associated with large-scale acquisitions of land, however. Fund managers may be assigned land and water corresponding to local communities that receive little or no payment, leading in social and political conflict, particularly in countries with weak governance and poorly defined land tenure systems. Land allocated for exporting food and biofuels may not only reduce food supplies to local markets but may also contribute to land degradation and deforestation. These issues have resulted in three different levels of policy responses: participating countries, host countries, and international communities.

1. **For Investing Countries:** FDI in agriculture comes primarily from emerging economies (example Brazil, Malaysia, South Africa, India, and Korea), the region of the Middle East and North Africa (MENA) and developed economies (which are the United States and European). Stakeholders from North and South America and Europe are almost predominantly private firms, although state-owned industries are the main players from the Middle East, and to a lesser degree from China and South Korea. For example, some MENA countries, which are among the most contingent on imported food, have established special institutions in foreign countries to support the purchase of farmland. Regarding the transition away from the costly agricultural self-sufficiency strategy (due to insufficient water resources), Saudi Arabia introduced a package of private investor support measures in 2008 and developed the Saudi Agricultural Investment Abroad Initiative for King Abdullah in 2009. The first initiative provides credit facilities in targeted countries through public financial institutions and finances infrastructure projects. The initiative of King Abdullah, a public body, selects appropriate host countries, signs bilateral agreements, and creates the Saudi Agricultural Investment and Animal Production Company (Cotula et al., 2009; Green, 2012; Hallam, 2010). In addition, the Chinese government started issuing several regulations as well as financial incentives and concessions to encourage the acquisition of land in foreign countries for development purposes in an effort to overcome domestic resource shortages (land and water) and

prevent over-reliance on international markets to guarantee food imports (Hongzhou and Zhang, 2013).

2. **For Host Countries:** Over 80 nations are forecasted to be targeted by foreign investors, but 11 of them, as per the Land Matrix, account for 70% of targeted surface areas. Approximately two-thirds of the identified farmland area is located in Africa, primarily DRC, Sudan, South Sudan, Tanzania, Ethiopia, Madagascar, Mozambique, Liberia, and Zambia. LAC and Indonesia's Argentina and Brazil and Asia's Lao PDR are also among the target countries for land investment. The beneficiary countries' policy response has ranged from offering generous incentives to enforcing conditions on foreigners' ownership of land with few restrictions. Some countries have special policies to attract FDI in agriculture. In Ethiopia, the government expects FDIs to grow export crops, thus increasing foreign earnings, encouraging technology transfer, creating job opportunities, developing social infrastructure (such as highways, hospitals, and schools), and fostering energy security through biofuel production. Therefore, a number of policies to generate investors have been put in place. In Ethiopia, a large area of land in the southern and western parts of the country is clearly marked as free and readily available to interested investors; land rent is set at a very low rate by the government and the process of acquiring land for foreigners is highly simplified without contractual obligations. Investors are eligible for different tax exceptions and financial amenities, including exclusions from customs duties and taxes on capital goods imported goods; and exceptions from land-use fees for up to five years and the right to full repatriation in convertible currency, profits, and dividends. Tanzania has also authorized a program that offers a five-year tax-free status for investors, encourages residency and work permits for immigrant workers, and grants the right to extradite funds. In Iraq, the 2009/10 reforms to the investment law mentioned the need to evaluate all state-owned land with the intention of moving state land to the National Investment Commission for investor allocation. In collaboration with Iraqis, the amendments chosen to allow investment firms/individuals to rent Iraqi lands. In Yemen, in September 2007, the cabinet passed a law allowing foreigners to buy and own property. In 2008, the government passed a law on massive land

registration as it was a major impediment to investment. As a result of domestic political pressure and global efforts to protect local communities' land rights, some countries have taken steps to protect local communities' interests and recipient countries' interests. The proposed changes were continued to allow investment firms/individuals to rent Iraqi lands in collaboration with Iraqis. The cabinet changed the law in Yemen in September 2007 enabling foreigners to purchase and own property. The state passed a law on massive land registration in 2008 as it was a major obstacle to investment. Some countries have taken steps to protect the interests of local communities and recipient countries as a result of domestic political pressure and global efforts to protect the land rights of local communities. Also, Bolivia and Ecuador put a ceiling for the maximum size of a farm's land. Demands for land deals to be scrutinized have prompted some African governments to issue new laws that acknowledge local communities' interests and/or restrict foreigners' ownership rights. For example, Kenya's new constitution forbids the right to own land for non-citizens—they can only rent land for 99 years. There was no political agreement between October 2007 and October 2011 on new concessions, over 10,000 hectares in Mozambique, and in 2008, the government approved a set of guidelines on the type of investment it wanted to attract. Tanzania has introduced new land deals with ceilings: up to 5,000 hectares for rice and up to 10,000 hectares for sugar cane.

3. **For Global Responses to Land Deal Concerns:** Concepts and recommendations were established at the international level to resolve the dangers associated with FDI in the property. The Concepts for Accountable Agricultural Investment Respecting Rights, Livelihoods, and Resources (PRAI) were established by FAO, United Nations Conference on Trade and Development (UNCTAD), International Fund for Agricultural Development (IFAD), and the WB in 2010. The concepts include, but are not limited to, respect for established land and property rights, openness, and good governance and enabling climate for investment in agriculture, and consultation and involvement of all those significantly affected by the project. In May 2012, over 100 UN Committee on World Food Security (CFS) member countries adopted the National Food Security Voluntary Guidelines on

Responsible Governance of Land, Fisheries, and Forests. The Voluntary Guidelines are a reaction to tenure concerns and poor governance in many countries. These were established in an inclusive and collaborative phase that lasted over three years, offering standards and procedures that are internationally recognized to strengthen tenure governance. At the moment, several countries are calling on the UN to help them incorporate these concepts into their national legislation, as every aspect must be well handled.

8.3 POLICY SUPPORT MEASURES FOR CONSUMERS

The dual-track approach to rural development seeks to improve production and efficiency while at the same time taking advantage of the vital role of social welfare and social policy in shielding vulnerable groups from hunger and food insecurity. Market support measures are part of broader social security policies aimed at ensuring equal access to food with a focus on protecting poor and vulnerable people from high and unpredictable food prices. Market initiatives addressed are incentives related to customers, nutrition support programs and cash transfer (CT) programs. During the triple wave of food, finance, and fuel crises from 2007 to 2009, the way in which these policies were incorporated, and subsequent emerging issues are also discussed.

8.3.1 Consumer-Related Subsidies

Universal demand subsidies and untargeted subsidized commodity purchases are initiatives aimed at regulating food prices and other essential goods, such as petroleum products (Grosh et al., 2008).

The main objective of consumer-related subsidies is to ensure that access to these goods is open to all or all classes of households at rates they can afford. The reason for using subsidies rather than CT may be to create incentives for particular product practices as well as operational considerations (Alderman, 2002). It is possible to generalize (i.e., universal) and seek consumer-related subsidies. The most typical model is an untargeted subsidy that lowers all consumers in a country's food or fuel prices (Alderman, 2002). Governments, however, also use structured subsidies to reduced prices for some families, targeting groups by level of income, or other factors such as children's number or geographic location (High-level panel of experts (HLPE), 2012).

8.3.1.1 Food Subsidies

Specific food subsidies are government-subsidized purchases of staple food products in unrestricted or rationed amounts. Such instruments are popular in all locations, particularly in Africa and Asia where, during the reference period, nearly 80% of the countries surveyed used direct food subsidies.

Additionally, in 2007/08 the proportion of LAC countries applying direct food subsidies was lower than other regions and in 2009/10 and 2011/12 decreased further. Indirect food subsidies apply to tax exemptions or cuts (value-added tax (VAT) or sales tax) are often perceived to be untargeted cost subsidies (Alderman, 2002).

To alleviate the burden of rising food prices on poor households, most countries in Africa, Asia, and LAC implement some form of exclusion or zero-rating on staple or unprocessed food. Overall, over the reference period (2007–2012), about 73% of the countries surveyed had a VAT or sales tax exemption regime on basic food items (Figure 8.6).

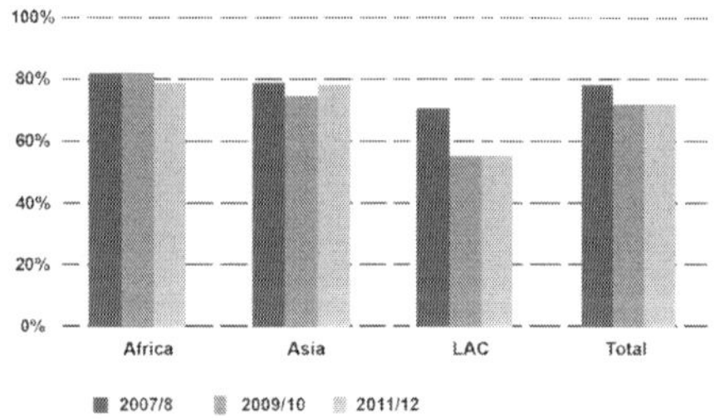

Figure 8.6. Fraction of states providing direct food subsidies (including price control measures) (2007–2012).

Source: FAO, FAPDA 2013.

1. **Direct Food Subsidies:** These are one of the most prevalent responses in Africa to soften the impact of high food prices over the reference period. Many sub-Saharan African (SSA) countries have introduced selective food subsidies and ad-hoc or provisional food commodity price controls. In reaction to the 2007/08 food crisis, emergency subsidies were implemented by several SSA countries. Several of them did so via subsidized sales to millers, including Kenya, Ethiopia, Senegal, and Zambia. Some, including Burkina Faso, Cameroon, Chad, and Malawi, responded to price controls, while Ethiopia and Senegal combined

food subsidies with price controls. Many nations, however, have opted to set the price of the main staple food products on a regular basis (e.g., Senegal for wheat, Zambia for maize, Liberia for rice), while others have adopted price control as an ad-hoc measure to address specific circumstances. For example, in Burkina Faso, in response to the socio-political crisis of early 2011, the government established and approved a list of 19 items subject to price regulation (November 2011). Eventually, through regulation and profit margin limits enforced on the selling of imported consumer goods, retail prices of basic food commodities were set. Likewise, price ceilings for rice were set in Mali during the lean period of 2008, 2009, and 2012 (usually from March to May), and suppliers decided to sell rice at or below this ceiling price in order to have exemptions on import duties and taxes.

As compared SSA nations, there have been mandatory food subsidies for several decades in North Africa. In certain nations, in reaction to the increasing prices of 2007/08 and the political unrest of 2010/2011, commonly known as the 'Arab Spring,' there was a noticeable trend of greater public spending on food subsidies. New food items have been included in the list of subsidized products for 2007 and 2008 in Algeria, Morocco, and Tunisia. Egypt increased the amount of food provided under the national ration card scheme (unchanged since 1988) and included new groups as qualifying recipients (e.g., veterans, and people with chronic diseases). The scheme hit around 64 million individuals (as of July 2011), comprising almost 79% of the total population of Egypt in 2008 (Ghoneim, 2012). Following some governments' recent attempts to improve targeting (for example in Tunisia), food subsidies in North Africa remained universal.

Direct food subsidies in Asia are normal practices and have remained popular over the reference period (similar to Africa). Several countries in South and East Asia have had broad targeted food subsidy programs in place for decades that have been extended recently (in India, Indonesia, and the Philippines) or scaled down in favor of other food safety networks (in Bangladesh). India, which has one of the largest food subsidy systems in the world, significantly increased the overall program budget over the past six to seven years, representing approximately 5% of the 2010/2011 agricultural GDP (Sharma, 2012).

There is already an aggressive National Food Security Bill anticipating parliamentary approval. It seeks at extending the scope of subsidized food grains from 27% to approximately 67% of the population. Indonesia's in-kind 'RASKIN' benefit initiative distributes rice on a monthly basis to the poorest families at a subsidized price. Following a first-time increase in subsidized rice prices in 2008, the program's budgetary costs tripled between 2007 and 2010. The Philippines has also extended its rice subsidy program (which has been running for over 50 years) to increase poor people's coverage (from 26% in 2006 to 48% in 2009). These changes can be traced to policy measures to increase the distribution of beneficiaries (Fernandez and Velarde, 2012). The Public Food Distribution System operates in Bangladesh across two channels: in-kind (see paragraph 3.2.1) and subsidized sales of food (open market). The latter has lately been cut back as the private sector has played an increasingly prominent role in stabilizing supplies and prices on the market, particularly in times of natural disasters. Countries in the Middle East have taken a different path within Asia. Including North African nations, they depended heavily on unconditional food subsidies and, in reaction to both the food crisis of 2007/08 and the 2010/11 protests, most of them increased these subsidies. Food subsidies and price controls were in place for the main staple food commodities (mainly wheat, wheat flour, and sugar) in all the seven countries examined over the reference period (2007–2012). The governments, however, are justifying (Iraq) or phase out (Iran) subsidies in two of them.

Direct food subsidies are much less prevalent in LAC than in Africa or Asia and have lost support overtime over the reference period: the proportion of LAC countries with direct subsidy programs fell from 70% in 2007/08 to 55% in 2011/12. During the 2007/08 recession, food subsidies and, in general, price control measures were used predominantly. After the crisis, many countries continued to use them, often as a temporary or longer-term strategy.

Countries such as Colombia and Mexico (2008), Honduras (2007 and 2010) and Ecuador (2008, 2009, and 2010) also briefly set the prices of several food products included in the basket (canasta básica de alimentos). Some dictate the price of the primary food products daily, such as Costa Rica and the Dominican Republic for rice and Ecuador for popular pan (popular bread). In order to maintain domestic supply and control retail prices of staple food commodities, Argentina has also developed a system of compensation for producers (initially targeting only wheat and maize mills) since 2007. A number of food products currently receive subsidies, although the largest share of payments goes to wheat mills and meat producers. Other countries, such as Venezuela, Honduras, Nicaragua, and Bolivia, are interfering in food markets through articulated public acquisition, storage, and distribution systems.

Bolivia founded the government organization de Apoyo a la Producción de Alimentos (Food Production Support Company) in 2007 with the objective of promoting food production and supplying internal markets on the basis of fair prices. During the same year, Nicaragua reinstated the company Nicaragüense de Alimentos Básicos, which also works through the entire supply chain, purchasing produce from local farmers, building food stocks and distributing products to consumers across the world at affordable prices. Since 2003, Venezuela has introduced price controls on staple foods utilizing Mercados de Alimentos, C.A., a government-run company that sells subsidized consumer goods via a countrywide chain of stores. Productora y DistribuidoraVenezolana de Alimentos (Venezuelan Food Producer and Distributor) was also created in 2008 to cover the entire value chain and cope with the final sale at set prices of essential food products.

2. **Indirect Food Subsidies:** Throughout the observation period, however, the number of nations utilizing indirect food subsidies increased overall. Lowering domestic food taxes in Africa is a more popular policy tool than in Asia or the LAC. In order to respond to the 2007/08 crisis, numerous governments retained exemptions or reductions that were already in effect (before 2007), while VAT or sales tax exemptions or reductions served only a temporary purpose in many cases, some other countries adopted the step.

   The measure was either administered temporarily (e.g., Ethiopia in 2008 and DRC 2012) or with a longer-term viewpoint (e.g., Cameroon, Mauritania, and Sierra Leone) (Table 8.9). Throughout Asia, the need for VAT or sales tax adjustment to minimize the effects of rising food prices is constrained; during the study period, only a few governments have reported using VAT/sales tax adjustment. Indonesia and China have both implemented and maintained a VAT reduction/exemption policy on basic foodstuffs, while Cambodia has only temporarily adopted a VAT exemption policy (on agricultural products) in 2008. Within LAC, during the time under review, a few countries adopted VAT modifications while several countries already had VAT exemptions in place before 2007. A VAT exemption on essential food products was authorized by Ecuador and Venezuela in 2007, and the measure was in place until 2012. Brazil lowered national taxes on staples like wheat, wheat flour, and bread in 2008 and preserved the policy until 2012. From 2008 to 2009, and again in 2011, Uruguay temporarily stopped VAT on certain consumer goods (Table 8.9).

Table 8.9. VAT Exemptions/Reductions on Basic Food Items (2007–2012)

Region	Exemptions/Reductions Introduced	Exemptions/Reductions Already in Place (Before 2007) and Retained
Africa	Sierra Leone**(exemptions from 2010), Ethiopia (temporary suspension in 2008), Mauritania (exemptions from 2008 and 2009), Cameroon (exemptions from 2007), DRC**(temporary suspensions in 2012)	Zimbabwe, Lesotho, Mali, Morocco, Nigeria, Rwanda, Ghana, Kenya*, Uganda, Malawi, Senegal, Algeria, Chad, South Africa, Tanzania, Zambia
Asia	Cambodia (temporary suspensions in 2008), Indonesia (exemptions from 2007), China (temporary suspensions in 2008)	Sri Lanka, Nepal, Thailand

LAC	Uruguay (temporary suspensions in 2008, 2009, and 2011), Ecuador (exemptions from 2007), Venezuela (exemptions from 2007), Brazil (reductions from 2008)	Honduras, Mexico, Argentina, Dominican Republic, Nicaragua, Panama, Paraguay, Colombia, Costa Rica,
* The new VAT Bill 2012 predicts a 16% VAT for some products which were formerly exempted, such as wheat, wheat flour, bread, and processed milk. **The VATs, or goods and services tax (GST), in Sierra Leone and DRC, were introduced in 2010 and 2012 respectively.		

Source: FAO, FAPDA 2013.

8.3.1.2 Fuel Subsidies

Almost all tracked countries have been impacted in recent decades by dramatically increasing world market oil prices. For this purpose, fuel subsidies are widely used, often as universal subsidies that favor all consumers in a country to lower the price of energy used for cooking, heating, lighting, and personal transportation as well as the energy used as input for goods and services output. Fuel subsidies include direct price subsidies where the cost paid by companies and households is less than the supply price, and tax subsidies where taxes are lower than their efficient level International Monetary Fund (IMF), 2013). Frameworks for price regulation, like price caps, set or freeze rates, and price adjustment steps, such as stabilization fund methods, are mechanisms for indirect consumer support (Kojima, 2013). Global prices of oil and oil products increased sharply in 2007, challenging countries and triggering their energy costs to rise. The worldwide spike in consumer subsidies followed closely the sharp rise in international prices of fossil fuel (IMF, 2013). Between 2007 and 2012, over 80% of countries regulated direct fuel subsidies). The percentage of fuel subsidy countries continued to rise and constant between 2007 and 2012, regardless of the fact that many countries across all three regions tried to decrease or reform their subsidy systems to ease the burden on government spending, strengthen energy efficiency and security, boost investment in clean energy sources and address climate change (Figure 8.7).

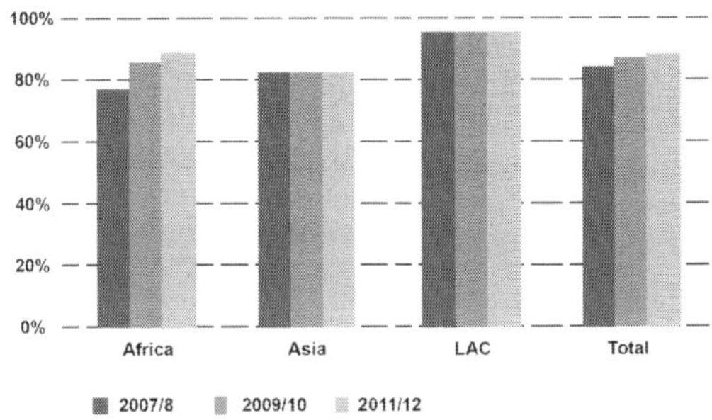

Figure 8.7. Percentage of fuel-subsidizing nations (2007–2012).

Source: FAO, FAPDA 2013.

Within LAC, throughout the review period, many governments retained direct subsidies or price control measures to reduce consumers' fuel prices. In the 1990s, reforms were implemented to minimize subsidies in the region (e.g., Brazil, Argentina, Chile, and Mexico), but price control and adjustment strategies are still a widespread practice. The energy sector in Argentina was liberalized in 1989, but in recent years, through indirect price control steps on petroleum products and heavy oil export taxes, the government has kept fuel prices high (Kojima, 2013). In January 2002, prices in Brazil were privatized by law, but in practical terms, the national oil company, Petrobras (that currently holds 98% of the country's refining capacity), has frozen ex-refinery prices for years. In recent years, price stabilization measures have also been utilized in Bolivia and Venezuela, while resources have been implemented in Colombia and Peru to reduce and regulate fuel prices. In countries such as El Salvador, Chile, Mexico, and Peru, efforts to reduce or change fuel subsidies have been recorded. In Asia, between 2007 and 2012, direct fuel subsidies and price control initiatives were in place in most of the countries surveyed, although some of them tried to reduce or rationalize their fuel subsidy systems. Southeast Asian countries have a high average subsidization rate (as a share of GDP): In terms of dollars, Indonesia, and Thailand are the top 20 oil subsidizers in the world. Fuel markets are more deregulated in South Asian countries than in Southeast Asia, but subsidies are commonly used in Bangladesh, Nepal, and Sri Lanka. In the Middle East, incentives are high for oil-exporters as well as importers: oil-exporting countries such as Iraq (14.30% of GDP) and Saudi Arabia (13.27% of GDP) display the highest subsidy levels. Multiple Asian countries, which include Bangladesh, India, Indonesia, Iran, Iraq, Kazakhstan, Nepal, Sri Lanka,

Syria, and Yemen, reported price control measures to lower fuel prices. In times of high world prices, Thailand, and Vietnam control oil funds to lower prices. Bangladesh, China, India, Indonesia, Iran, Lebanon, and Syria have taken steps to reduce fuel subsidies among the countries surveyed. In Indonesia, the government is making multiple efforts to reform its fossil-fuel subsidies since the 1997 economic crisis. In 2008, together with the fuel price adjustment, a range of payment steps was implemented in the form of unconditional cash transfers, distribution of rice to the needy, financial support for children in the lowest ranks of civil servants, and interest subsidy loans for SMEs (APEC, 2012).

Many of the countries surveyed in Africa depend on direct subsidies or price control measures to reduce fuel prices. Countries like Cameroon, Egypt, Ethiopia, Ghana, Malawi, Morocco, Mozambique, Nigeria, and Rwanda have for several months or longer frozen petrol, diesel or both costs. Others, such as Kenya, Rwanda, and Senegal, have lowered taxes and charges on diesel and kerosene. Some SSA countries, however, have been trying to reform their fuel subsidy policies in recent years. Reforms have been followed in Ghana, Nigeria, and Mozambique by the extension of targeted social spending initiatives to shield lower-income households from increasing fuel prices. The significant decrease of gasoline subsidies was declared in Nigeria in mid-2011 and consequently, the Subsidy Reinvestment and Empowerment (SURE) program was introduced to offer a variety of social security network measures to minimize the impact of eliminating subsidies on the poor (IMF, 2013). The Nigerian government ended the gasoline fuel subsidy in January 2012, resulting in prices more than doubling. This price surge, however, particularly affected Nigeria's low wage and led to protests, forcing the government back down (Hickey, 2013).

8.3.2 Food-Based Safety Net Programs

Food-based safety net services are applied in various ways, promoting adequate utilization to reduce hunger and malnutrition. In this chapter, three forms of the food safety net are considered:

- Free dissemination of food and nutrition to vulnerable individuals, school feeding programs.
- Free dissemination of food and nutrition to vulnerable individuals, food for work programs.
- Free distribution of food usually involves the direct distribution

of food and extra feeding for vulnerable populations (usually targeted).

Clear and specific nutrition initiatives may be included in order to maximize the nutritional impact of this type of support. School feeding is a form of supplementary feeding that incorporates providing free food for children at school (excluding a few cases where governments may solicit small donations). Food for work is the direct supply of food rations for a fixed volume of work (basically self-targeting). Such programs vary in terms of length, size, and targets. Whereas delivery of food assistance to vulnerable people is mostly introduced with a short-term goal in crisis situations, school feeding and food for work programs are usually more complex strategies with a medium to a long-term goal. Only government-led initiatives and projects that have a significant role in government are analyzed below, including donor-funded food distribution research. During the reference period, over 80% of countries investigated used food-based safety net programs. Such methods are standard procedure in all regions that are more prevalent in LAC (which over the reference period all observed countries adopted some possible combination of this type of program) than in Africa or Asia. Evidence indicates that between 2007/08 and 2011/12 countries have not amended their food-based support policy (Figure 8.8).

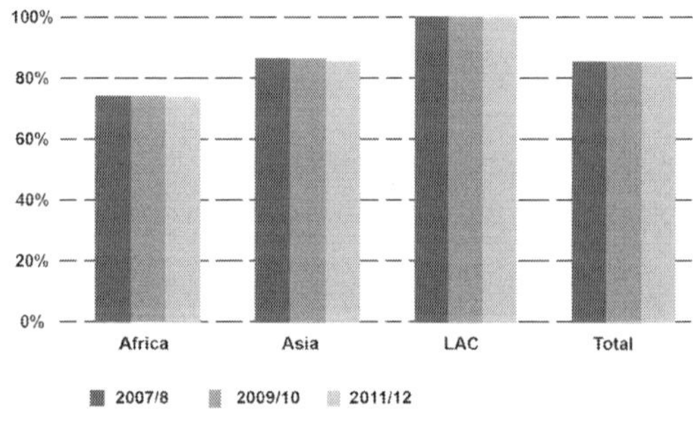

Figure 8.8. The proportion of countries that distribute food (2007–2012).

Source: FAO, FAPDA 2013.

Generally, food aid is more commonly done for vulnerable individuals and school feeding than food for work programs. In addition, food-based support services strategies and activities vary from region to region and country to country (Table 8.10).

Table 8.10. Food Safety Net Implementation of Services in Specific Countries (2007–2012)

Region	Free Food Distribution to Vulnerable People	School Feeding Programs	Food for Work Programs
Africa	Lesotho, Burkina Faso, Malawi, Tanzania, Egypt, Mauritania, Cameroon, Chad, Tunisia, Senegal, Togo, Ghana, Mali, Nigeria, Zimbabwe, Ethiopia, Kenya	Morocco, Cameroon, Mali, Kenya, Senegal, Togo, Burkina Faso, Ghana, Mauritania, Rwanda, South Africa	Kenya, Ethiopia, Mauritania
Asia	Bangladesh, Cambodia, China, India, Oman, Iraq, Syria, Indonesia, Nepal, the Philippines, Yemen, Sri Lanka, Thailand, Vietnam	Indonesia, Lao PDR, Saudi Arabia, Yemen, Syria, Bangladesh, Bhutan, China, India, Nepal, Sri Lanka, Thailand, Vietnam	India, Bangladesh, Bhutan, Cambodia, Nepal
LAC	Mexico, Bolivia, Colombia, Ecuador, Paraguay, El Salvador, Guatemala, Peru, Uruguay, Brazil, Chile, Venezuela, Dominican Republic, Haiti, Honduras, Nicaragua, Panama	All countries	Nicaragua, Haiti, Bolivia, Guatemala

Source: FAO, FAPDA 2013.

8.3.2.1 Free Nutritional and Food Distribution Schemes for Vulnerable People

Over the reference period, almost all of the countries surveyed offered free distribution of food to vulnerable people. Distributions have been targeted and put into effect ad-hoc in most cases. Amongst other items, the African nations of Mauritania (2009 and 2010), Cameroon (after 2008), Chad (throughout the reference period) and Togo provided food transfers in kind to help people and regions impacted by natural disasters or chronic malnutrition. The National Food Distribution project for relief and restoration in Kenya consumed about 53% of all protection net spending between 2005 and 2010; although the program was largely funded by international partners (71%). Some LAC nations, including Chile (2010), Paraguay (2012), and Mexico (2012), provided free food in response to disasters. Particular groups such as native people and people affected by natural disasters have also received large-scale food aid in Brazil. Free food distribution was also prevalent in Asian countries, which include Syria (2008, 2009), Cambodia (2008, 2011), Sri Lanka (2007–2012), Pakistan (2010), China (2012), Thailand (2011) and Vietnam (2011), in emergency contexts or in response to high food prices over the period of analysis. Under the Vulnerable Group, Bangladesh has been apparently running the distribution of food to vulnerable groups.

Some countries are integrating food and nutrition interventions into their social safety net programs as part of medium and long-term poverty alleviation strategies. Among LAC countries, Brazil's excellently-known Popular Restaurants, or Community Kitchens (established in 2003 and strengthened during the reference period), provide free or subsidized food to low-income people. Over time, the budget for these community kitchens has steadily increased. The Brazilian administration has agreed to enforce the De Alimentación del Trabajador Program-Worker Feeding Program (established since 1975)—to provide employees with free meals under the minimum wage. National programs have been developed in Ecuador (since 2009) and Guatemala (since 2008) to institutionalize ad-hoc free distribution of food. Many LAC countries have institutionalized specific long-term dietary initiatives to tackle hunger, targeting children and mothers in their national programs. These services are often introduced as health care for mothers and children, food, and micronutrient distribution, dietary extension and training. Several Asian countries have set up and broadened national programs to fight hunger and malnutrition. Vietnam has a robust system of public health and nutrition that involves community health workers and a particular structure called 'food partners.' These health and nutrition workers test children for malnutrition and educate mothers on breastfeeding, balanced diet, hygiene, and sanitation. As a consequence, Vietnam is almost certain of meeting the 2015 MDGs 4 and 5 goals for infant and maternal mortality (Save the Children, 2012). Mali's government in Africa has kept going to use community health workers with coaching on several nutrition-related strategies to improve child survival by providing vitamin A to women and children under the age of five. Malawi has put tremendous energy and resources into strengthening nutrition and health services for its people, particularly those living in rural areas (Save the Children, 2012).

8.3.2.2 School Feeding Programs

Throughout Africa, throughout the reaction to the food crisis of 2007/08, school feeding systems have been put in place or improved in several countries. The Cameroon state, for example, increased school feeding expenditures by 51% compared to 2008 in 2009. The school feeding system in Ghana began before the crisis in September 2005 on a pilot basis, but was extended nationally during the 2007 crisis, with the government paying for around 75% of the total cost. In 2011, Kenya extended the school feeding system and Rwanda's school feeding program was also scaled up from 14% in 2011 to include 50% of children in primary and secondary schools (Anand et al., 2012). Recently extended school feeding initiatives in South Africa, which have been in effect since 1994, concentrating steadily on nutritious characteristics of meals, and providing up to 30% of daily nutritional requirements (Anand et al., 2012). South African school feeding programs have led to spill-over consequences for local economies, generating work employment opportunities, and encouraging them to create small businesses that provide food for the school feeding system in a given area (Bundy et al., 2009).

Most school feeding systems in LAC, which have been in place for decades, have during the comparison times been improved. Brazil expanded its national school feeding program, Merienda Escolar, since 1955, in 2009. Coverage has been expanded to children and adult students studying in public schools (of all basic education), benefiting 45 million students in 2012. In addition, in 2009, a national law declared that 30% of the overall school feeding budget had to be invested in directly purchasing products from family farms (see Box 1), thus benefiting small-scale production and local economies as well as providing high-quality food. In Chile, the Escolar Food Program (established in 1964) targets children from poor and vulnerable families, while in Ecuador, in 2011, the School of Food Program (started in 1999) was expanded. In 2007, Colombia also strengthened its program. In 2008, Colombia started to distribute milk to schools and to families in poor areas, the Leche para TodosProgramme. A school feeding scheme launched in Paraguay in 2007 was halted in 2008 (because of budget limitations) but re-introduced in 2009 to administer a glass of milk to school kids. El Salvador (2010) and Honduras (2011) introduced a new program to offer milk to students called Vaso de Leche ('Milk Glass'). Milk is bought from small domestic producers for the programs, like the Brazilian experience. One component that brings these initiatives in the LAC region robust sustainability is that they are run by highly trained institutions or units (often under the Ministry of Education) dedicated to the management of the programs. Other than Argentina and Bolivia, whereby school feeding is performed by provinces or municipalities, school feeding in LAC is provided by huge government initiatives through which governments try to fulfill their responsibility to guarantee the right to education, the right to food and at the same time confirm the right to health of school children. Over the reference span, many Asian countries had a public-school feeding program in place, and in some of them (e.g., China, Thailand, India, and Bangladesh), penetration has been especially wide, with significant expansion in recent years. In 2007, China introduced its Rural Compulsory Education Nutrition Improvement Plan. Its exposure is the world's third-biggest, second only to India and Brazil's school feeding services. Bangladesh's program allocates micronutrient-fortified food snacks to primary school kids, while Thailand's school lunch program includes free lunch for all kids in remote rural areas and for low and underweight kids in suburban schools, middle-income neighborhoods, or semi-rural areas. India has the world's largest program for school feeding. In 2011, the mid-day meal which has been in effect since 1995 hit 113.6 million school kids. The priority is making sure that all children receive adequate nutrition and primary education.

8.3.2.3 Food-for-Work Programs

Food for work programs focused on the government has become less common compared to food and school feeding programs. Only about 17% of the countries covered introduced these initiatives, often for a limited period of time or part of the year, in unstable, persistent poverty or post-conflict settings. The current debate on the use of cash instead of food frequently raises concerns about the impact of food distribution on local food markets, the transaction costs involved and beneficiary preferences (Alderman, 2002). Food-for-work systems have the ability to draw labor away from their own farms of consumers, disrupt food markets or alter habits of consumption (Barrett, 2006). Food-for-work initiatives are put into place in Africa in reaction to circumstances of emergency or chronic food insecurity. In Ethiopia, the Successful Safety Net Program, that saw a 33% increase in spending in 2008, offers food, and money transfers in drought-prone parts of the country via public works (at a cost of 15 kg of cereal in cash or grain for five working days a month). The food for work program in Kenya, which has been in place since 2000, was discontinued in 2009, and substituted by a Food-For-Asset program that began successfully in 2011, providing food to rural households and helping rural communities create resources. The policy was introduced mainly in arid and semi-arid lands (ASALs) to mitigate the impacts of probable hazards (floods, droughts); while in Mauritania, there was national food for work programs.

Through LAC, many countries depend on food for work to tackle major emergency situations of hunger. In 2011, Bolivia launched the Food Security and Urban Road Development Program (Programa de SeguridadAlimentaria y Desarrollo Vial Urbano) in El Alto Region. Guatemala's Alimentos por Trabajo initiative and similar schemes in Haiti and Nicaragua are among other food for work programs in the country. In the referred period, some of these initiatives, which have been in place since the last one or two decades, played a significant role. Bangladesh has two initiatives among the Asian countries, including the Food-for-Work and Test Relief, which provide food grains (rice and wheat) as wage payments to male and female workers in labor-intensive public work programs. There is also food in Cambodia and Bhutan for job programs. Throughout slack agricultural seasons, Nepal introduced seasonal food for work schemes while rural people are waiting for the next harvest and wage workers are beginning to face food shortages. Since 2005, India has put into place a nationwide work food program in the lowest income rural districts (rebuilt in 2009 as the Mahatma Gandhi National Rural Employment Guarantee Act). The scheme, which is 100% federally funded, offers services for technical and unskilled labor in the form of cash and food grains to the rural poor.

8.3.3 Cash-Based Consumer Support Programs

Cash-based transfer programs "require offering support in the form of cash and other essentially money-like measures that can be used to move funds to the vulnerable or to those who, in the absence of transfer, are likely to be at risk of poverty" (Grosh et al., 2008). FAO describes CTs as "payment of money or vouchers to vulnerable individuals, households, or companies in the private sector" (FAO, 2012b). Such transfers also apply to regular non-contributory cash payments made to individuals or households by the government (sometimes in collaboration with donors). The study does not discuss contributory benefits, which allow the recipient to make matching contributions. Only government-led projects are discussed below, and systems in which the government plays an active role. In over 90% of the Asian or LAC countries, surveyed, cash-based transfer programs were put into effect to support the poor and in about 80% of the African countries monitored. Through the use of CTs is noticeable from the larger percentage of countries implementing the measure compared to 2007/08 in 2011/12. One of the major benefits of a CT that is frequently described is the choice it gives recipients to use additional revenue compared to other transfers and reduce governmental specifications or lower operating costs (Grosh et al., 2008).

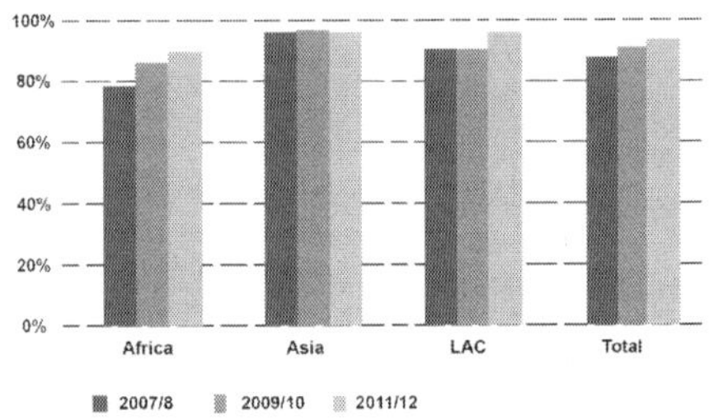

Figure 8.9. Percentage of countries pursuing cash transfers (2007–2012).

Source: FAO, FAPDA 2013.

Cash-based transfer programs first emerged in the 1990s as a mechanism for consumer support in middle-income countries and expanded rapidly around the world. In recent years, low-income countries are gradually introducing CT schemes in the context of a contingent or unconditional cash transfers, cash vouchers (for food) and cash-for-work programs, in some cases with donor assistance. CTs are more common (conditional or unconditional) than cash vouchers or cash-for-work programs (Figure 8.9).

8.3.3.1 Conditional and Unconditional Social Cash Transfers (SCT)

There may be contingent or unconditional non-contributory cash transfers (NCT). Conditional cash transfer (CCT) policies are designed to provide money to poor people in exchange for the fulfillment of particular behavioral conditions, including children attending school and regular visits by pregnant women to a health care facility, etc. These initiatives are focused on supporting human development, human capacity building, and economic productivity and growth enhancement. Unconditional cash transfers provide money; either based on their earnings (e.g., social support) or targeted recipients, such as care for infants, for poor families or individuals. CTs are widely deployed in LAC and are often used as CCTs. In 2011/2012, 19 of the 20 surveyed countries had one or more types of CTs. New CT systems have been implemented or extended in recent years (e.g., grants to parents, children, and older people), since LAC governments view CT schemes as the primary policy tool against poorness and food insecurity. In the course of school support and the conformance with medical checks for pregnant women and children, many conditional CCTs are designed. In Argentina, for instance, a social program dubbed Assignation for Maternity Security Social was launched in 2011 and offers conditional maternity benefits to women aged 12 weeks after regular medical tests have been completed. In 2004, the administration introduced a Familias Por Inclusión Social program, but CCT was substituted in 2010 by the universal child benefit of the Asignación Universal por Hijo for disadvantaged families with children (under 19). In 2010, a universal child benefit was provided. Bolivia has also incorporated multiple CT programs: the RentaDignidad, a non-contributory state pension for poor citizens over 60 years old, was instituted in 2008; the Bono Madre Niño-Niña 'Juana Azurduy de Padilla' was launched in 2009, a CCT for children aged 0–2 years, and the RentaSolidaria was introduced in 2012. In 2012, Peru replaced the monthly appreciation bonus program with Pensión 65 for people over 75 years of age living in extremely poor circumstances, where the limit was lowered to 65 years.

In 2012, Colombia revamped Familias in Acción (2001) and changed its name to Más Familias in Acción to raise the amount of transfers for new school students, encouraging eligibility for higher education. Many LAC countries reported an improvement in GDP during the reference period (gain from high raw and agricultural commodity prices) and were able to boost their budget for social protection, addressing the lengthy-standing issues of distribution of income and food insecurity in the region (FAO, 2012a). The Bolsa Família in Brazil is the best overall and undoubtedly, the largest of all CCT schemes in the developing world. The Bolsa Família provides financial aid for poor families who are expected to make sure their children go to school and are vaccinated. The goal is really just to minimize short-term poverty through direct CTs but also to tackle long-term poverty through increasing human capital among the poor through linking education and health services to CTs. Correspondingly, over the years, the Brazilian government has steadily increased the budget and signed new applicants to the scheme; reaching 13.7 million poor households in 2012, (the transfer volume also rose by 45%). In 2011, Bolsa Família developed a new sub-program of CCTs, Bolsa Verde ("Environmental Conservation Support"), to support families engaged in conservation projects in national forests as well as indigenous peoples, afro-descendants, and other local groups. Aid for CT services in Africa is growing. These are often introduced as unconditional cash transfers and draw attention in supporting families who care for orphans and other children afflicted by AIDS owing to their 'protective' aspect (UNDP, 2008). Throughout the study period, 14 of the countries studied implemented CT systems, while established CT programs were enhanced in other countries (Table 8.11). For instance, Ghana's government launched the program livelihood empowerment against poverty (LEAP) in 2008. LEAP is a visionary in West Africa's NCT. This provides very poor households with money and free health insurance. The NCT program of Kenya, the Orphan and Vulnerable Children program, increased its transfer value by 33% in 2011 and reached 150,000 households across the country by 2012.

In 2007/08, in relation to the food crisis, national unconditional and contingent CT schemes were either launched or extended in Asia. In 2007, China's Minimum Livelihood Guarantee Scheme (the urban Di Bao program) increased the maximum level of income (below which people are eligible for payment) by 23%. The system, initially designed to serve urban residents, has been extended to rural areas, reaching a total of 53 million in 2011 (Qian, 2013). In Vietnam, a monthly CT scheme was extended in 2007, launched in 2004 to assist elderly people aged 90 and above with no contributory pension: the minimum qualifying age was lowered to 85 years and the minimum monthly payout was increased. The mandatory qualifying age was again lowered to 80 in 2010, with a further increase in the minimum monthly income. In 2007, the Philippines launched a CCT program: the PantawidPamilyang Pilipino program offers cash awards to recipient households pursuant to education and health conditionality compliance. (e.g., Kids attending school on a regular schedule, pregnant women, and children visiting health facilities to monitor their wellbeing). Over the years, this initiative has developed to become the largest social assistance scheme in the Philippines: it began with 360,000 household beneficiaries in 2007 and reached 2.3 million in 2012, accounting for about 44% of poor households (Table 8.11).

Table 8.11. Recently Introduced and Extended or Maintained Cash Transfer Services in Selected Countries (2007–2012)

Regions	Recently Introduced Cash Transfer Programs	Cash Transfer Programs Expanded (Resources and New Vulnerable Groups) or Retained
Africa	Senegal, Tanzania, Burkina Faso, Morocco, Ghana, Lesotho, Zambia, Malawi, Zimbabwe, Nigeria, Mozambique, Uganda, Rwanda, Sierra Leone	Cameroon, Mozambique, Ethiopia, Tanzania, Nigeria, Zimbabwe, Uganda, Kenya, Malawi, South Africa, Morocco, Tunisia, Egypt, Algeria, Mauritania, Liberia, Zambia

Asia	Indonesia, the Philippines, Pakistan	Oman, Yemen, Pakistan, Indonesia, Bhutan, Sri Lanka, China, Iran, Iraq, Saudi Arabia, India, Cambodia, Afghanistan, Bangladesh, the Philippines, Lao PDR, Nepal, Tajikistan, Vietnam, Kazakhstan, Syria
LAC	Haiti	Peru, Honduras, Uruguay, Argentina, Bolivia, Brazil, Colombia, Ecuador, Dominica Republic, Nicaragua, Paraguay, Venezuela, Guatemala, El Salvador, Mexico, Chile, Costa Rica, Panama

Source: FAO, FAPDA 2013and World Bank 2011a.

8.3.3.2 Cash Vouchers (for Food)

Cash vouchers are intended to improve the purchasing power of vulnerable groups who spend a large share of their income on food. Vouchers are more likely to increase food consumption than CTs (because of the food link). Nonetheless, they require a functioning system for exchanging vouchers for cash from banks and/or post offices or local stores. The absence of an effective voucher redemption scheme can undermine these programs' effectiveness (Fiszbein and Schady, 2009). This is perhaps one of the reasons that few countries use voucher systems in the three regions. In LAC, Uruguay, Panama, and the Dominican Republic adopted cash voucher programs providing debit cards to be used in designated shops with the goal of ensuring that the payment is only used for food purchases. In 2006, Uruguay launched Tarjeta Uruguay Social, a government-charged magnetic card for buying basic food in activated shops by poor people across the country. During the timespan under evaluation, the African nations of Mozambique, Zimbabwe, and Senegal used vouchers. ProgramaSubsídio de Alimentos, monthly CT program in Mozambique, helps recipient households pay for food. An online voucher program designed to eliminate malnutrition among people on antiretroviral therapy has helped vulnerable people living with HIV in Zimbabwe (IRIN, 2011). A Few Asian countries have a voucher program, and this can be credited in part to controlling the food marketing system and consumer prices, which are a more common way to provide affordable food. China uses coupons as a way of handing out food supplies to poor households, but a network of 'simple' food stamps where stamps/vouchers are used to buy food from private retailers at market prices (Josling, 2011).

8.3.3.3 Cash-for-Work Programs

Cash-for-work schemes generate part-time work for the most vulnerable sections of the population in public projects (such as road repairs, debris removal, and re-building infrastructure). Such activities allow poor households to obtain paid employment, thereby enhancing their access to food. A mixture of money (cash-for-work) and in-kind (food-for-work) payment methods are used in some public work programs, whereas in recent years cash payment is perhaps the most common form of payment (Subbarao et al., 2013). In Africa, cash is comparatively more common for work programs than in LAC or Asia. Cash for work schemes was adopted over the review period by an increasing number of African countries (e.g., Ethiopia, Rwanda, Malawi, Tanzania, and Mozambique). The productive safety net program (PSNP) in Ethiopia creates transfers of food and cash through its public works. The state pays close attention to cash payments as the majority of the PSNP's budget is allocated to cash for work. The Vision 2020 Umurenge Program (VUP) was introduced as a cash-for-work program in Rwanda in 2008. It was upgraded in 2009 and expanded through two main strategies to CTs for the most vulnerable: public works and direct support. Designated beneficiaries earn a regular wage under the portion of public works in return for their work on labor-intensive community building or reconstruction projects. Labor-scarce households (especially the elderly and people with disabilities) receive direct aid through a monthly CT. India, Yemen, and Afghanistan have cash for work programs between Asian countries. India has a strong history of using cash for work programs to combat extreme poverty, provide humanitarian assistance, and address problems of unemployment/underemployment during sluggish agricultural seasons. In addition, the Mahatma Gandhi National Rural Jobs Guarantee Scheme has introduced the public work system.

Table 8.12. Cash Transfer Typology in Selected Countries

Re-gion	Non- Contributory Unconditional Cash Transfers	Non-Contributory Conditional Cash Transfers	Cash for Work	Cash Vouch-ers

Africa	Zambia, Sierra Leone, Zimbabwe, Ghana, Lesotho, Tanzania, Ethiopia, Rwanda, Uganda, Mozambique, Algeria, Mauritania, Egypt, South Africa, Tunisia	Senegal, Malawi, Tanzania, Kenya, Ethiopia, Morocco, Tunisia, Nigeria	Cameroon, Burkina Faso, Ethiopia, Rwanda, Liberia, Malawi, Mozambique, Lesotho	Mozambique, Zimbabwe, Senegal
Asia	Bangladesh, Bhutan, Cambodia, China, India, Nepal, Pakistan, Sri-Lanka, Thailand, Vietnam, Kazakhstan, Tajikistan, Oman, Saudi Arabia, Iraq, Iran, Syria	Afghanistan, Bangladesh, Cambodia, India, Indonesia, Nepal, Pakistan, the Philippines, Sri Lanka, Thailand, Yemen	India, Yemen Afghanistan, Indonesia, Cambodia, Sri Lanka, Lao PDR, Bangladesh	India, Bangladesh, Pakistan, Sri Lanka, China
LAC	Bolivia, Colombia, Ecuador, Paraguay, Peru, Uruguay, Venezuela, Guatemala, Honduras, Mexico, Nicaragua	Cost Arica, Argentina, Chile, Colombia, Paraguay, Peru, Uruguay, Venezuela, Dominican Republic, El-Salvador, Guatemala, Haiti, Bolivia, Brazil, Honduras, Mexico, Nicaragua, Panama	Argentina, Paraguay	Uruguay, Panama, Dominican Republic

Source: FAO, FAPDA 2013and World Bank 2011a.

Throughout the reference period, Argentina, and Paraguay introduced cash-for-work systems at the LAC. Argentina initiated the Jefes y Jefas de HogarDesocupados (Unemployed Heads of Household Program) in 2002, which had been in place until 2009, after the country was hit by an economic crisis. While, in 2010, Paraguay initiated the regional Ñamba'apo program. The beneficiaries are vulnerable unemployed, low-education, and at least three-member families. The plan hires recipients employed in construction and community work for a total duration of six months. The program also provides the recipients with job training to mainly (but not only) promote their employment in large public infrastructure works (Table 8.12).

8.3.3.4 Government Steps for Trade and Business Growth

Government agencies in developing countries have used trade and market growth interventions to minimize the impact of rising and unpredictable food prices in reaction to the global food, financial, and fuel crises from 2007 to 2009. Nevertheless, as international food trade (along with agricultural commodities and natural resources) is at the center of several new threats to multilateral and regional trade structures, in recent years, trade policies have experienced many changes and even reversals. Although introducing stringent trade policies as a short-term solution (i.e., 2007/08), most countries opted to loosen trade restrictions and increase local market efficiency; their overall goal was to enhance medium-term national food safety (i.e., over 2009/10 and 2011/12).

8.3.4 Trade Policies

Once governments interfere in the commercial sector, they aim to control markets for the benefit of either producers or customers. In 2007/08, policy choices to benefit consumers were more common than steps to benefit producers by placing restrictions on imports and export bans through increased imports and increasing exports. Nevertheless, a rising number of countries continued to reduce import tariffs over the period 2009/10 to 2011/12 with the goal of securing domestic food supply and/or relaxing restrictions on exports to benefit producers. We contemplate trade policies related to the primary staple food crops in this section, namely wheat, maize, and rice.

8.3.4.1 Import Policies

In contexts of their policies towards staple grain imports, two groups of countries have been identified: those that maintain their policies prior to 2007/08 and those that change their import policies during the period under consideration. The evidence gathered from all three regions and some major food grain exporting countries (e.g., Argentina) in several food import-dependent countries shows that there was no particular political or economic reason to change import policies in response to the 2007/08 crisis. Countries that have changed their policies have adopted variable import tariffs, imposed import bans, or pursued import quotas in order to influence grain prices for consumers or producers.

8.3.4.1.1 Import Bans

Regarding the rising food prices of 2007/08, only slightly among those countries in which information was available was enforced import bans on basic food products. A significant number of countries did not remove imports: on any of the three staples, just seven out of the 71 surveyed countries implemented import bans. The bans were often applied as ad-hoc, short-term interventions aimed at protecting domestic producers from unfair trade, international competition, or overseas cheap food dumping. Within Africa, there were only three countries within place during the reference time, namely Algeria, Nigeria, and Zambia. For example, in April 2009, Algeria enforced a ban on wheat imports quoting good domestic harvest as the primary reason for the lifting of the import ban in 2011 as the country returned to international markets to meet its demands for durum wheat. Before September 2008, Nigeria had an import ban on maize and wheat flour. In March 2012, it suspended imports of cassava flour to promote the replacement of wheat flour with domestic, high-quality bread-making cassava flour. Throughout Asia, during the study period, only Thailand, Indonesia, and Iran introduced import bans. Thailand terminated maize imports from the Ayeyawady-Chao Praya-Mekong Strategy for Economic Cooperation Countries (Thailand, Lao PDR, Vietnam, Cambodia, and Myanmar) for a few months in November 2008 to protect farmers from falling domestic prices. Indonesia implemented periodic bans on imports of rice, generally one month before and two months after the harvest season (March to June), in order to guarantee better prices for producers in a bountiful supply period. During the study period, Colombia was the only LAC country to impose a temporary import ban on one of the selected staples. In August of 2010, the Colombian government implemented a temporary import ban on rice with the objective of ensuring higher prices for producers.

8.3.4.1.2 Import Tariffs

The most popular response to the world's food crisis of 2007/08 was the decrease and/or disqualification of import tariffs on staples: nearly 60% of countries surveyed with information available suspended import tariffs with the aim of lowering consumer prices. Some of these countries safeguarded the post-crisis suspension/reduction, while others brought back domestic production import tariffs. A third-country group maintained a variable approach, introducing, and suspending tariffs on an intermittent basis. The direction in tariff policies in Africa has varied: some countries have retained the suspension/reduction implemented during the 2007/08 crisis; others have reinstated tariff protection to help domestic producers, while some countries have maintained a flexible tariff policy. Tanzania, for example first lowered import tariffs on wheat in 2008 (from 35% to 10%) and then finally lifted them three years later in 2011. In January 2009, South Africa had zero-rated the 2% import duty on wheat and wheat flour. Whereas the duty was abolished by South Africa's International Trade Administration Commission, it restored the 1999 variable tariff with the provision that the tariff only comes into effect if the wheat price falls below US$ 157 a ton. Senegal and Burkina Faso, on the other hand, temporarily suspended rice import tariffs in 2008. A couple of months later, both countries restored import tariffs. Both Mali and Nigeria have taken a variable approach. In 2008, 2009 and 2012, Mali frequently terminated import tariffs and rice taxes during the lean season (usually from March to May). Likewise, in 2008, Nigeria temporarily halted and dramatically reduced its rice import tariff for three months (from 109% to 30%). Import tariffs on rice, wheat, and wheat flour, were consequently increased in 2012. Many countries' tariff policies (e.g., Nigeria) imagine a high degree of unpredictable nature and point to a unilateral policy that may limit the potential for private trade participation.

Across Asia, as a reaction to the food crisis of 2007/08, most countries have not changed their import policies. Nevertheless, among those who did, the most changed their strategy to the conditions, while a limited number of countries either retained their tariff reduction/suspension policies for 2007/08 or reintroduced tariffs on imports. Afghanistan and Bangladesh retained their policy on wheat and rice in 2007/08, respectively, removing import tariffs. In 2011, Pakistan brought back rice import tariffs that had previously been discontinued. Indonesia's tariff legislation on staples appeared to differ from year to year: the country re-imposed tariffs on wheat (2009/10), after their elimination in 2008, while rice tariffs were first decreased, increased, and then again reduced during the reference period. Many countries in LAC have terminated or decreased import tariffs, while others have not changed their import policies due to the food crisis of 2007/08. Of those that made changes, Brazil cut import duties on yellow maize for the first time (2008) and then indefinitely suspended (2009). Bolivia abolished import tariffs (2008) on many staple foods (such as wheat, wheat flour, maize, and rice), and then lifted tariffs on wheat flour permanently (2010). In addition, Ecuador first reduced import tariffs on wheat (May 2008), then removed (2009) and eventually reintroduced (2012).

8.3.4.1.2 Import Quotas and Tariff Rate Quota (TRQ) Regimes

Import quotas have often been connected to tariff structures to create tariff rate quota (TRQ) environments with lowered (sometimes zero) tariffs imposed on imports below a quota threshold, and higher tariffs applied once a defined quota threshold has been reached.

The key purpose is to protect domestic producers from cheap imports while ensuring an abundant supply of staple grains is available to consumers at a reasonable price. Export quotas were used more commonly in LAC and Asia than in Africa, often used as tariff-rate quota systems. Several LAC states, including Brazil, Colombia, Costa Rica, Guatemala, Honduras, Mexico, Nicaragua, and Panama, have commonly used TRQ regimes (Table 8.13). Only quota systems are introduced by other LAC countries (e.g., Ecuador). China (wheat, maize, and rice), the Philippines (rice), and Thailand (maize) introduced TRQs in Asia, while other countries, such as Pakistan, India, and Sri Lanka, used only a quota system. No government in Africa has introduced a TRQ for basic food products, but during the study period, Zambia, and Kenya adopted some import quotas.

Table 8.13. Variations in Import Tariff Policies (2007–2012)

Region	**No Change in Import Policies Pre-2007/08 Policies Sustained**	**Changed Import Policies in Response to the 2007/08 Food Crisis**				
		Import tariffs			**Imposed Import Ban (ad-hoc)**	**Pursued Quota Systems**
		Tariffs Reduction/ Suspension Maintained After 2007/08	**Variable Trends After 2007/08**	**Import Tariffs Reintroduced After 2007/08**		

Africa	Togo** Ethiopia* Egypt Lesotho* Mozambique**	Uganda (wheat), Tunisia****, Algeria (durum wheat), South Africa (wheat and wheat flour), DRC (basic food items such as wheat), Sierra Leone (rice), Liberia (rice), Rwanda (wheat, maize), Tanzania (wheat, cereals)	Mali (rice), Nigeria, Morocco,	Kenya (wheat, maize), Zimbabwe (maize), Chad, Malawi (wheat flour), Burkina Faso (rice), Senegal (rice, wheat), Mauritania***(rice), Ghana (rice, maize, wheat), Cameroon (wheat, wheat flour, rice)	Nigeria, Algeria, Zambia	Zambia, Kenya
Asia	Nepal** Lebanon Oman** Yemen** Iraq** Tajikistan Bhutan* Cambodia** Lao**	Arabia (wheat), Kazakhstan (wheat), Afghanistan (wheat), Bangladesh (rice, wheat), Saudi	Indonesia, Sri Lanka, India, the Philippines, Thailand, Syria (wheat maize)	Pakistan (rice), China (staples) Vietnam, Azerbaijan (wheat)****	Thailand, Indonesia, Iran	Sri Lanka Thailand***** Bangladesh, China*****India, The Philippines****
LAC	Costa Rica, Dominican Paraguay, Argentina, Republic, Chile, Uruguay	Brazil (maize, basic food items), Peru (maize, rice), Bolivia (wheat flour), El Salvador (wheat flour, maize), Mexico (wheat, rice, maize), Nicaragua (beans), Panama (basic food items, such as rice), Honduras (wheat flour)	Ecuador (wheat)	Guatemala (wheat flour) *** Colombia (rice)	Colombia	Brazil***** Costa Rica***** Panama***** Nicaragua***** Guatemala***** Ecuador Mexico***** Honduras***** Colombia*****
*No tariff system for basic food items; **Tariff system in place and maintained throughout the reference period; ***Tariffs maintained at a lower level; **** Import VAT suspension; ***** TRQ in place.						

Source: FAO, FAPDA 2013.

8.3.4.2 Export Policies

Export-related steps relating to basic foodstuffs:

- Export bans;
- Export restrictions (export taxes, minimum export prices (MEPs), and quotas).

8.3.4.2.1 Export Bans

During the world's food crisis of 2007/08, export prohibitions on wheat, maize, and rice have been widely used. Nevertheless, the use of export restrictions has declined over the years to keep prices low for consumers. In both 2009/10 (around 30%) and 2011/12 (around 20%), the percentage of governments restricting exports dropped. This pattern shows that public support for export prohibitions has receded over time least in part because of the revelation that any motivation to expand production is negatively affected by such measures (Figure 8.10).

Figure 8.10. Percentage of countries that accept export bans (2007–2012).

Source: FAO, FAPDA 2013.

More than half of the countries tracked in Africa (around 56%) prohibited exports of staple grains in 2007/08, but this percentage dropped to around 36% in 2011/12. Most countries only used short-term export bans. For example, in 2008 only ad-hoc, short-term export bans were implemented on Burkina Faso (on cereals), Mali (on wheat, maize, and other cereals) Sierra Leone (on grain) and Togo (on maize and others). Several countries instituted export bans on an irregular basis, including Tanzania, Malawi, Chad, and Sierra Leone. The ban on rice exports in Egypt continued for four years, with only brief disruptions during the time of research. Since 2009, Nigeria has had an export ban on maize. In Asia, more than 40% of export bans imposed by countries during the global food crisis in 2007/08, but by 2011/12 the figure dropped to around 13%. Numerous Asian countries are sizeable exporters of food (India, Kazakhstan, Pakistan, Cambodia, Thailand, and Vietnam) and all of them, with the exception of Thailand, have used export bans for a short period of time and only as a reaction to a major threat. For example, due to an abnormally low stock level, Kazakhstan implemented export bans from April to September 2008. In other nations, export bans have been used intermittently. For example, India sometimes used export bans in combined effect with quotas and MEPs. Non-basmati rice exports were first prohibited (2007/08 and 2009/10) and then removed (2011). A prohibition was applied in 2007 with respect to wheat, temporarily lifted in 2009, fully re-imposed, and finally lifted in 2011. In 2008, maize was also susceptible to a three-month temporary ban. Bangladesh has intermittently enforced export bans on rice throughout the reference period, allowing small quantities to be exported from time to time. In LAC, export bans have typically been less common than in Africa or Asia. In LAC, in 2007/08, just six out of the twenty countries tracked implemented export bans, and by 2011/12 their number dropped to one (Brazil on rice in April 2011). Only in 2007/08 did Argentina (maize and wheat) and Ecuador (rice) introduce temporary export bans. On the other hand, during the period 2007–2012, Bolivia (maize) and Brazil (rice) intermittently introduced export bans.

8.3.4.2.2 Export Restrictions: Export Taxes, Minimum Export Prices (MEPs) and Quotas

Some governments have shifted from a policy of prohibiting exports to limiting them by using initiatives such as export taxes, MEPs, and quotas to maintain adequate domestic supply and keep domestic prices down. Export taxes on staples were figured to be less prevalent in Africa (only one country, Egypt, administered the measure) than in Asia or the LAC, among those nations for which information was available, while export quotas were relatively more prominent in Asia than in Africa or the LAC. Export taxes have often been enforced in Asia on a short-term, ad-hoc basis, sometimes in confluence with MEPs and/or quotas. Vietnam, coupled with raising taxes and quota systems during the reference period, switched from a policy of a rice export ban to a MEP system. Lebanon, India, Pakistan, and Syria have lifted their food crisis maximum export bans and began to implement quotas and MEPs to regulate export flows. In 2010, in Pakistan, when the export ban was withdrawn, export taxes were introduced in conjunction with a quota system and MEPs. China's grain export tax policy has changed several times: export VAT rebates were abolished in 2007/08; export taxes increased in early 2008 (from 5% to 25%) but were largely abolished in December 2008; some grain export taxes were abolished in June 2009; export tax rebates on maize flour were abolished in 2010 and export quotas were introduced; and grain export quotas/tax poles were abolished in June 2009.

There was no common thought in the use of export taxes or export quotas amongst nations in the LAC. During the reference time, Argentina increased export taxes on some food items, including wheat and maize, while in July 2008, Uruguay abolished a 5% export tax on rice (in place since 2004). Argentina (on maize and wheat) and Ecuador (on cotton) retained export quotas throughout the time, whereas in 2009/10 and 2011/12 Bolivia implemented its export quota system. Many countries in Africa have not used export control measures. In Malawi, Ethiopia, Egypt, Tanzania, Zimbabwe, and Zambia alone, export quotas were administered. Egypt used export taxes on a number of occasions to influence the price and supply of selected staple grains: grain export taxes were imposed in 2007; export taxes increased in February 2009; and an export ban was lifted as an export tax was introduced in July 2009. However, in October 2009, Egypt also brought together export prohibitions and rice taxes with constrained monthly export quotas.

8.3.4.3 Market Development Policies

Policymakers have tried to use various policy instrumentation to influence local grain markets since the food, fuel, and financial crises of 2007–2009. The administration of public grain stocks and the growth of market institutions at the national and international level have been given greater importance. Common stock policies are aimed at fixing inventory-management market failures and securing food supplies to avoid price volatility, whereas 'new' market creation structures are typically aimed at reducing knowledge asymmetries which lead to reducing transaction costs for manufacturers, customers, and other economic agents.

8.3.4.3.1 Food Grain Stock Management

Until the world food shortage of 2007/08, there has been a great deal of interest in public food reserves in developing countries by both governments and development partners. During the period under evaluation, more than

65% of the survey countries managed to maintain public grain stock. In some cases, the procedure was also extended after 2007/08. Food grain reserves have predominantly been used for two main objectives: price control in domestic markets and emergency response in severe weather or other catastrophe situations. In addressing price inflationary pressures and food security, the function of food stocks has become the central topic of ongoing political discussion and has been addressed in high-level forums such as the G8 and G20 summits and the High Level Panel of Food Security and Nutrition Experts of the United Nation (HLPE, 2011), as well as analyzed in a wide range of publications. Furthermore, in the ongoing conversation on including food stocks on the agenda of the WTO Ministerial Conference in Bali in December 2013, the G-33 group of developing countries proposed to remove the trade distortion status of supplying producers with price support, as these types of measures enable the government to stock grains for food safety or distribution purposes as food aid (Figure 8.11).

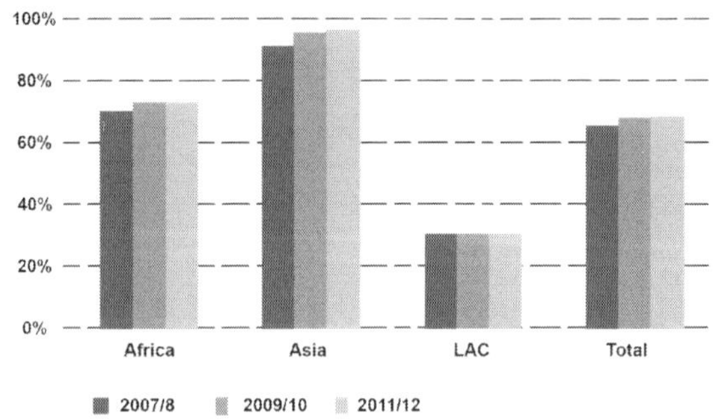

Figure 8.11. Percentage of nations with a national reserve of food in operation (2007–2012).

Source: FAO, FAPDA 2013.

Most countries in Africa (about 70% of investigated countries) managed to maintain public food reserve systems over the reference period. Many countries have been unwilling to give up their food reserves' price stability target entirely and attempt to interfere with varying levels of success in grain markets. Zambia's Food Reserve Agency, for example, has maintained an active participant in purchasing maize abundance in the country over the reference period (holding a reserve of over 350,000 tons). The nation had an excess of 1 million tons in 2010, which could not be effectively stored or exported, leading to a plunge of the cost. Recently, new public organizations have been set up to manage food reserves and take action in some countries' grain markets. In 2007, Nigeria set up the NFRA and adopted a policy to keep 15% of the total yearly grain harvest in the reservation. The department is to keep 5% as a key strategic grain reserve and a further 10% is to be held by individual states, known as 'state buffer stocks,' to guarantee supply in case of a food crisis. Ghana also set up a parastatal under the Ministry of Agriculture in 2010 to reduce post-harvest losses, ensure price stability, and strengthen reserves for emergency grain. Certain African countries have agreed to increase their grain reserves: in 2011, Kenya expected to double its reserve capacity from 4 to 8 million 90 kg sacks; Malawi voted to increase its food reserve from 60,000 tons to over 100,000 tons in 2009; and in 2010, Rwanda, which had disbanded its parastatals during the Structural Adjustment Program period, implemented steps to restore strategic reserve activity. The Rwandan Ministry of Agriculture's Post-Harvest Task Force has signed into negotiations with private entities to store 7,000 MT of maize and 3,000 MT of beans bought from local farmers. The government plans to create a critical food reserve (based on maize and beans) that could reach 200,000 MT on a permanent basis. North African nations have also engaged in increasing public storage space, including Algeria, Mauritania, and Morocco.

Food stocks were preserved by over 90% of Asian countries (Figure 8.11), and participation of the private sector in stock management expanded over the reference period. Some countries (China, India, Bangladesh, Pakistan, Indonesia, the Philippines, and Vietnam) historically have large reserves of public grain to stabilize domestic prices. Government-owned entities in Indonesia, the Philippines, China, India, and Bangladesh have been controlling the maize and rice markets for decades by creating public reserves (through farmers' procurement or through imports), particularly at times of high prices and releasing stocks into the market to ensure that food prices are affordable to the most vulnerable. In order to sustain buffer stocks in 2008, Sri Lanka restarted its Paddy Marketing Board. Throughout Asia, the role of the private sector throughout asset management has grown. For example, Lao PDR set up a pilot National Rice Reserve as a public-private partnership in 2009, supplying subsidized credit through state-owned banks to millers to maintain a minimum rice stock. In India, the government is introducing the "go-down" (warehouses) storage building system for private entrepreneurs. India's Food Organization offers a 10-year assurance for leasing warehouses built under the program, ensuring a decent return on investment for entrepreneurs. Pakistan has also introduced several public-private pilot collaborations in grain storage ventures, under which the government pays rent to storage owners.

In the Middle East, an increased government intervention and increased investment in sensitive grain holdings was the common trend over the reference period. Many Middle Eastern countries are significantly dependent on food imports and the government's role in food grain purchasing, storage, and distribution has increased over the years. Several countries (such as Oman, Saudi Arabia, and Iraq) are planning to expand their storage capacity (from six months to one year of consumption) (Larson et al., 2012). One exception from the region is Iran, which has privatized most of its wheat business and continued to allow milling firms to purchase most of the country's directly produced over 15 million tons of wheat per year. Only a few countries in LAC preserved public food stocks, while others subsidized private companies or producers for grain storage. State intervention in the food grain sector has been significantly decreased as a result of structural adjustment policies and market deregulation agreements (e.g., North American Free Trade Agreement (NAFTA)), but some countries have adopted initiatives to build or rebuild public grain stocks or encourage private stock operations primarily in response to recent high and unpredictable prices. Venezuela, Nicaragua, Honduras, and Bolivia maintained food stocks as a key element of an interconnected public procurement, storage, and distribution system for food products at subsidized prices. In 2003, Brazil brought back public stocks and reinvigorated CONAB, the national food supply agency, to handle food reserves for both emergency and price stability purposes. CONAB regenerates its inventories through the Food Procurement Program (Programa de Aquisição de Alimentos), which buys food products from smallholder farmers at minimum guaranteed prices. Ecuador In 2007 set up the National Storage Unit, a public agency responsible for overseeing silos for strategic food reserves, looking to buy grain from farmers at guaranteed rates. A few other countries, including the Dominican Republic, Colombia, and Chile, did not have public food stocks, but participated in domestic markets with the goal of incentivizing grain storage by farmers or private firms at the time of harvest when prices are low, and then releasing stocks during the lean season. A collaboration between the Ministry of Agriculture and the public-private company Cotrisa was formed in Chile in 2009 to guarantee that grain storage is subsidized on the support of wheat farmers. The Incentivo al Almacenamiento de Arroz (Incentive for Rice Storage) was also introduced by Colombia throughout the time with the goal of encouraging the storage of rice by private companies or the producers themselves. The Dominican Republic has been running the National Program of Pignoraciones since 2005; supporting rice storage at times of lower producer prices, (the government is setting a price band each year).

8.3.4.3.2 ***Market Institutions***

Many countries with information that is available have taken steps to establish 'modern' market institutions. Warehouse receipt systems (WRSs), commodity exchanges and market information systems (MISs) are among the major areas of growing political interest.

1. **Warehouse Receipt Systems (WRSs):** Although improvement in their use over the reference period has been uneven, overall interest in WRSs has increased. The anticipated advantages include improving farmers' access to credit, building cash, and the forward markets (increasing liquidity and competition), and reducing risks by stabilizing both producers and consumers' prices. WRSs grant ownership privileges to a certain quantity of material of a given value at a specific location to the holder. Because this right can be acquired and sold and used as collateral, WRSs promote credit access, encourages the growth of grades and standards, and plays a critical role in price stability and the creation of future and derivative markets that manage risk. The trust of investors and service providers in these organizations, i.e., in the legal and regulatory system (including licensing) is an important component in order for WRSs to be effective. During the study period, many African countries showed interest in the implementation of WRSs, but lack of trust and enforceable program regulations meant that progress was slow. Domestic exchanges of commodities are often conceived as WRS regulators. For example, under the 2006 WRS Act and the 2007 WRS Regulations, the Uganda Commodity Exchange (UCE), a private registered business, has been appointed by the Uganda government as WRS regulator. By 2012, UCE approved six individual warehouses (primarily for cereals) but the warehouses were reported to operate at an efficiency of less than 20% in the same year due to improper regulatory frameworks and a poor contract enforcement mechanism. In 2007, Zambia developed the Zambian Agricultural Commodity Exchange (ZAMACE) as

a private enterprise body. The function is to provide warehouse managers with certification and inspection. Alone in 2010 (Tembo, 2011), ZAMACE approved eight district warehouses, but an insufficient legislative structure to enforcing contracts, thin markets and financial institutions' refusal to acknowledge receipts for deposited grain as 'commercial paper' (negotiable and transferable instruments) are among the major challenges (Sitko and Jayne, 2011). Tanzania enacted a Warehouse Receipt Legislation and set up a Warehouse Licensing Board, but the project has so far profited greatly only from export crops such as coffee, cotton, and cashew (Onumah, 2010). Kenya and Rwanda's governments are working with the Eastern Africa Grain Council (EAGC) to establish WRSs, but it has proved fruitless to push beyond the Council's pilot activities. South Africa does not have a warehouse act, but the South Africa Future Exchange (SAFEX) provides regulatory oversight of SAFEX supported silo certificates that are most often used by large commercial farmers. To date, the Ghana Grains Council has only accredited five warehouses in Ghana and in 2012 a working group was established to ready the groundwork for a law on warehouse receipts and related regulations (World Bank, 2012d). Many governments in Western Africa use request age or stock credit (Ghana, Burkina Faso, Niger, and Senegal) and third-party probation agreements (Mali) (USAID, 2012a).

In several Asian countries, WRSs has also drawn public awareness, and policymakers have committed to improving the regulatory environment. In Thailand, under the paddy (rice) financing system (first set up until 2008 and brought back at the end of 2011), farmers received loans from the Bank for Agriculture and Agricultural Cooperatives by guaranteeing their rice (deposited in one of the government-run warehouses or with private millers). Nevertheless, due to lack of proper regulatory frameworks, the system resulted in substantial bribery (Jessop et al., 2012). The administration in Cambodia (via Cambodia HARVEST, a project funded by USAID) is working to implement the country's first paddy warehouse receipt program to help rice millers broaden their operations and enable Cambodia to process more rice domestically (USAID, 2012b). In October 2010, India set up the Warehousing Development and Regulatory Authority and in

April 2011 officially introduced the Negotiable WRS (NWRS) (GoI, 2011). The well-structured and effective regulatory agency in Kazakhstan has helped construct confidence in the system (UNCTAD, 2009).

WRSs work in various ways in LAC, but it is difficult for subsistence farmers to access the system. Large grain exporting economies such as Uruguay, Brazil, and Argentina have seen continued investment and public support (e.g., subsidies, and tax incentives) for cooperative-owned warehouses and grain elevators, domestic agribusiness corporations and large international trading houses such as Bunge and Cargill (Ordoñez et al., 2001; Murphy et al., 2012), but subsistence farmers have limited access to such houses. Licensed grain warehouse technicians provide general warehousing services in Brazil, but the reliability of the operation was found to be low as these facilities were quickly developed primarily to manage large public emergency stocks (UNCTAD, 2009). Wealthy banks and the government retain the possession of licensed warehousing companies in Colombia, which helped protect depositors from scam-related losses. In addition, field warehousing (offering warehousing facilities on the property of the client) is the most profitable business in the world (UNCTAD, 2009).

2. **Commodity Exchange Systems (CESs):** As a variable-term response to increased and unpredictable food prices, several countries have placed policy focus on developing and improving agricultural commodity exchanges. Profitable commodity exchange structures, in tandem with WRSs, have the potential to increase the smooth running of agricultural economies by strengthening price creation, facilitating risk management, market accountability, and regional trade, thereby increasing farm production and rural income and improving food security (UNCTAD, 2009). There has been an increasing interest in commodity exchanges in Africa, but there are still a finite number of fully operational exchange markets. Since its inception in May 2007, the Zambia Agricultural Commodity Exchange has experienced multiple changes and has not been operating as an exchange since January 2011 (USAID, 2009). Until now, the position of the Malawi Agricultural Commodities market has been restricted to supplying price information and promoting the

World Food Program (WFP) procurement. The Kenya Commodity Exchange serves only as a price information service. Since 2006, UCE has been reorganized but organizational sustainability has yet to be achieved in the reorganization process (Onumah, 2012). Rather importantly, the Ethiopia Commodity Exchange, formed in 2007 and controlled by the state, has witnessed an enhancement of its export commodity trading operations, in particular, coffee and sesame. Maize, beans, and wheat are also mentioned for trade, but a large amount of these consumer goods cannot be attracted by the market and traded is restricted to spot/ cash exchange (Rashid et al., 2010). Perhaps the most fruitful exchange in Africa is the SAFEX. SAFEX trades futures and options contracts of 200,000 tons of white maize per day on average. The majority of South African sizeable-scale farmers sell their grains through SAFEX, usually through middlemen (Rashid et al., 2010). Excluding SAFEX, exchanges in Africa still need to include the futures market and enough staple trade volumes to provide an appropriate price discovery system.

Regional institutions, as well as several countries in Asia, have been investigating whether the future of rice would help to reduce price volatility. As will be discussed in chapter five below, the Association of Southeast Asian Nations (ASEAN) member states are taking into consideration the effectiveness of creating a market for rice futures in the region. Some member states (e.g., China, India, Pakistan, and Thailand) have one or more commodity exchanges trading in rice and other staple grains but are facing a number of challenges. In 2009, China started transacting futures contracts for rice on the Zhengzhou Commodity Exchange early in order to boost domestic grain pricing and provide more risk control measures for grain traders. Trading volumes, however, have shown substantial fluctuations and prices of the Zhengzhou rice futures contract are not well associated with other Asian rice markets, suggesting considerable baseline risk (McKenzie, 2012). Pakistan Mercantile Exchange Limited started its operations in May 2007 (with rice and wheat traded among commodities), but the amount of trading is limited, and the exchange faces the challenge of involving stakeholders. Thailand's Agricultural Futures Exchange introduced the first white rice futures contract in March 2007, but government market intervention (e.g., warehousing) has overwhelmed private storage and eliminated the private sector's need to use futures markets (McKenzie, 2012). In May 2008, in an effort to contain the price rise in vitally important commodities, the government in India prohibited futures trading in some food commodities but lifted the ban later in 2008. The LAC has motivated market-friendly policies with commodity exchanges (Arias et al., 2011). In the region, at least 10 countries (which include Argentina, Brazil, Chile, Colombia, Costa Rica, El Salvador, Nicaragua, and Venezuela) had at least one exchange of agricultural commodities. Brazil's Bolsa de Mercadorias&Futuros (BM&F) stood out as one of the most notable cases and was listed twelfth worldwide for the number of futures exchanged and/or cleared in 2008 (Arias et al., 2011). In recent decades, BM&F has also implemented several creative frameworks that serve as models to increase small-scale farmers' participation in futures markets (UNCTAD, 2009). Some governments, especially Mexico and Uruguay, do not have an interchange of agricultural commodities, but dependent on neighboring countries (the U.S. for Mexico and Argentina for Uruguay) for price information and hedging.

3. **Market Information Systems (MISs):** As a consequence of the skyrocketing and volatile prices following the food crisis in 2007/08, global, and national interest in market information has increased. Internationally, the Agricultural Market Information System (AMIS) has been championed by the CFS (via its Global Strategic Framework, 2012) and the G20 (Seoul Summit, November 2010) to improve the transparency of the food market and to encourage coordination of policy actions to reduce price volatility. Increased access to better information and communication technologies (ICTs), such as mobile phones and internet-based applications, has made a major contribution to stabilizing staple food prices at national and regional levels. Government-run market information services in Africa have been reproached for their inconsistency and poor robustness, but the policy environments in many countries have empowered the private sector to reap the benefits of the significant increase in inexpensive mobile phone networks and other ICTs to help spread market data in recent years. Many member states in East Africa have a multitude of MISs models: some are financed by

the government, some are private measures, and some are public-private partnerships. In Uganda, Kenya, and Tanzania, both public and private projects have seen the development of mobile technology and other ICTs to help spread market information and provide matching (buyer-to-seller) services. With a mobile penetration rate of 67.2%, Kenya was the leading country in East Africa at the end of 2011. The emerging technology has empowered producers, traders, and other users to access input and output pricing data and to identify and link suppliers, buyers or logistics providers (e.g., storage) and transport companies. Many West African economies have also benefited from the development of market data systems based on ICT, including Burkina Faso, Ghana, Mali, and Nigeria. In North Africa, in 2011, Morocco created a public MIS known as Asaar (prices in Arabic) to provide accurate data on prices of agricultural products using hi-tech tools for data collection and transfer.

Governments in Asian countries developed ICT systems and allowed the private sector and non-governmental organizations (NGOs) to develop various schemes that provide different marketing services. Bangladesh, for example, has ICT-based projects that provide market information and match buyer and seller services via mobile phone, SMS or IVR (interactive voice response). A government scheme in China (established in 2006/07) uses smartphone, SMS, and IVR to provide millions of farmers with data on market prices and technological production. India has one of the largest numbers of ICT-based private and public-owned markets and other information-providing schemes among Asian countries. There are many programs seeking to expand access to agricultural markets through mobile phones, the Internet, telecenters, and IVR. Nearly every country in the LAC has taken measures to improve access to market information for farmers. A number of nations have launched or enlarged a website or mobile market information service, including Bolivia, Chile, Colombia, Costa Rica, Ecuador, Paraguay, and Peru. Bolivia maintains a monitoring system for production and markets, the Sistema de Información a la Producción y los Mercados Nacionales (SISPAM), which tracks the country-wide wholesale and retail prices of agricultural products. Following the world food crisis of 2007/08, SISPAM supported the government to assign price bands, thereby stabilizing domestic food prices such as chicken, potatoes, maize, and soybeans (Bosch et al., 2012). In 2009 and 2008, simultaneously, Ecuador, and Paraguay launched an electronic national information system for key staple prices in major markets (via their Ministries of Food, Livestock, and Fisheries). In 2008, Peru launched a supply and pricing program (Sistema de Abastecimiento y Precios) that provides real-time access to information on volumes, prices, and origins of the country's biggest agricultural and agro-industrial products.

8.4 POLICY COHERENCE, INTEGRATION, AND HARMONIZATION AT NATIONAL AND REGIONAL LEVELS

Consistency in policy is accomplished when policies reinforce each other across a number of domestic policy fields, various agencies, organizations, processes, and actors. It is essential to systematically promote mutually reinforcing actions and strategic planning to achieve more effectively predetermined goals related to food security or agricultural transformation at the national or regional level (OECD, 2012).

8.4.1 National Level Policy Coherence and Integration

The food price crisis of 2007/08 was a critical defining moment for the food and agricultural policy decisions of several countries.

After the recession broke out, many policies that were discarded during the time of market liberalization and trade and structural reforms regained attention. Growing government intervention in food and agricultural production, trade, and consumption. This section focuses on two approaches adopted or revamped by certain countries to:

- Achieve food self-sufficiency; and
- Boost key agricultural commodity exports.

8.4.1.1 Coherence and Development Strategies to Achieve Self-Sufficiency in Nutrition

After 2007/08, the food self-reliance solution (along with food imports to meet national food requirements) has lost its charm and prominence has increased in the food self-sufficiency strategy (Demeke et al., 2009). For a certain part of the world with a massive gap between production and consumption, depending on food imports has become a complex and difficult choice due to the rising price of imported food, declining balance of payments and instability of supply due to export restrictions imposed by major exporters of grain. As a result, many governments have incorporated their production and trade policies in order to become self-sufficient in food. The various measures were designed to ensure high yields for farmers while, in many cases, protecting consumers from high prices. Probably one of the best-known examples in Asia is the Philippines' extensive self-sufficiency plan, namely the food staples self-sufficiency road map (2011–2016). It's directed at:

- Improve grain productivity through improved technology, expansion, and irrigation infrastructure, price support for farmers, enhanced credit guarantee fund and increased insurance cover for crops;
- Boost farm mechanization and post-harvest loss mitigation;
- Strengthening the consumption of rice per capita by increasing table waste and promoting dietary diversification (non-rice production expected to increase by 3.5% annually).

The initiative of the preceding department of agriculture, called FIELDS (2008–2010), used a similar strategy by covering several areas of intervention, including improvement of inputs (organic fertilizers and certified seeds), development of irrigation, formal credit facilities, and technical assistance to farmers. In 2006, China launched a major reform program to reduce agricultural taxes and introduce massive subsidies and other support programs in an effort to maintain a self-sufficiency rate of at least 95% for major grain crops. The sector profits from the policy of the so-called Four Subsidies: Chinese farmers receive subsidies based on their area of production, inputs, and improved seeds used and machinery and equipment used. While being one of Asia's most open economies (the overall tariff regimes have been liberalized in the last decade), China is defending the food grain sector through a tariff quota system. In its approach to agricultural policy, China has thus entered a new age, starting to subsidize rather than tax agriculture. It has also boosted rural infrastructure investment. The new policy of China considers agriculture to be a field that needs help. In order to accomplish food self-sufficiency, Indonesia also championed prices, restricted imports and increased public expenditure on agriculture. Launched in 2008, Morocco's Plan Maroc Vert (PMV) is a good representation of the integrated program of an African country involving a wide range of measures to promote and modernize agriculture. It provided financing and financing facilities, promoted private sector involvement and introduced leveraging alliances (value chain partners) with banks to provide long-term credit and help farmers develop their asset base and manage related risks to growth. In addition, Morocco enacts high tariffs and duties on a wide range of agricultural products. Since 2002, Zambia has supported farmers with aid through the farmer input support program (FISP). This self-targeted program provides a framework for farmers' associations to allocate subsidized inputs to their members. This process has increased the number of beneficiaries reached, the committed budget (from ZMW 193.1 billion in 2007 to ZMW 485 billion in 2011) and the covered plant varieties (soya, cotton, sunflowers, and rice). FISP is complemented by a Food Reserve Agency-managed public procurement program that has run large-scale maize purchasing operations at a guaranteed minimal price. This system of procurement/price support has contributed in recent years to a significant increase in maize production.

In LAC, since 2007, Ecuador's agricultural policy has undergone a profound transition as part of a broader political, sustainable, and agrarian transition that acknowledges agriculture as the core of its rural development, food security, and conservation of the environment. The National Plan for Better Living 2008–2011 and the 2010 Agenda for Productive Transformation (Agenda for Productive Transformation) set two main goals:

- The shift from a main export model economy to a high value-added knowledge economy in harmony with environmental and social protection considerations; and
- A 40% decrease in domestic consumption of soybean, maize, wheat, and barley and the accomplishment of 'food sovereignty.'

To this effect, the government has been implementing concerted policies throughout benefit manufacturers, consumers, and trade. A few of the policy initiatives aimed at food self-sufficiency, particularly importation limitations and price subsidies that impose costs on consumers through drastic rising prices. In order to reverse this detrimental impact, the governments considered commonly offer pro-consumer subsidies and introduce other welfare-state programs to provide the most vulnerable with food security. In Indonesia, the RASKIN program offers rice and other goods to low-income households at a subsidized price. Subsidies are provided in Morocco straight through the value chain to make wheat products affordable, from millers to retail consumers. While a price, setting mechanism on staples is in place in Ecuador and strategic food reserves are retained by a national storage unit that also gets involved for stabilizing prices. Nutrition subsidies in Zambia are often used in conjunction with price control interventions to provide low-income groups with cheap and affordable staple food (e.g., maize meal). Policy on food self-sufficiency involves protectionism policies such as limitations on imports and exports and non-tariff obstacles to isolating domestic food markets from regional and international fluctuating prices. Nevertheless, restricting or prohibiting trade threatens free intra-regional trade agreements and international priorities for food security. Food self-sufficiency legislation is especially at odds with regional-level harmonization policies to accomplish regional food security. For example, some RECs in Africa (e.g., East African Community (EAC), and Common Market for Eastern and Southern Africa, COMESA) showed interest in a maize-free way of achieving regional food security. Nevertheless, the approach only works when tariffs are eliminated and the free trade agenda is followed by harmonized legislation and regulatory frameworks and agreements to eradicate all non-tariff barriers to regional trade (COMESA and EAC, 2003).

Also, the price of a plan for food self-sufficiency can be quite high. Other developing countries face extremely large practical problems in furthering comprehensive and harmonized producer policy support strategies, unlike the examples described here. Such nations also provide agriculture with minimal support without defense from cheap and subsidized imports. Some developing countries often implement conflicting and non-harmonized policies when using numerous measures to keep prices in check for consumers without taking into account the disincentive effect of such policies on producers. For example, many countries in Africa deliver direct and indirect subsidies for grain prices to protect consumers from high prices but have limited and insufficient programs to support prices for producers. The latest OECD research (OECD, 2013) also showed that a random sample of 47 developed and developing countries, producers' support levels tend to be higher in higher-income countries. Even comparatively better-off countries can afford the expense of developing active producers' support programs while offering customers subsidies and other social protection programs.

8.4.1.2 Integrated Policies to Promote Main Commodities Exports

The time after 2007/08 encouraged several countries to go further than national food safety. In order to benefit from high international prices, some food-producing countries have adopted integrated and harmonized policy packages to stimulate the production and export of designated commodities, with comparative advantages for some countries.

The overarching strategy requires a number of specific approaches:

- Offer additional incentives for farmers, particularly through technical and economic assistance, to increase production;
- Establish an encouraging trade atmosphere (post-production infrastructure, storage facilities, highways, etc.) and private investment climate, particularly in R&D and new innovations; and encourage exports by relaxing regulations (quotas and licenses) and requirements (testing and certification, packaging, compliance with international standards, etc.).

Vietnam and, quite recently, Cambodia, among other nations, have adopted a broad export strategy in Asia. Cambodia introduced its Rice Export Policy in 2010, which comprises trade facilitation initiatives by encouraging export procedures along with programs to improve rice production. The latter involves supplying rice farmers with inputs, expanding infrastructure and enhancing land titles to secure land tenure. In Vietnam, a state that in less than two decades switched its designation from a food importer to one of the world's leading exporters (second-largest rice exporter), a recent proclamation by the Prime Minister substituted the ultimate goal of food security with a policy of "implementing international trade responsibilities and ensuring efficient export supplies" (Government of Vietnam, 2010). In LAC, Peru, amongst other nations, has progressively strengthened its policy of export development and trade transparency with an integrated and consistent strategy, already in place since the 1990s. The Ministry of Foreign Trade and Tourism has reasoned with its Plan Estratégico Nacional Exportador 2003–2013 (National Strategic Exporting Plan 2003–2013) for "enthusiastically growing trade on the basis of government and private sector efforts to improve and broaden exports and accomplish competitive integration in international markets." This viewpoint is strongly in line with the perception that significant opportunities (for both national producers and consumers) are created by free trade policy, while being supported by the state's corresponding position in ensuring fair market access for all people. To this effect, the administration has adopted an integrated approach that complements its policy of opening up and promoting trade with steps to help exports, such as credit, logistical support, or development of infrastructure.

In 2007, Uganda introduced the National Export Strategy 2008–2012 (NES) amongst African nations to function as a comprehensive medium-term national plan to revamp the export sector of the country. Tea, fish, coffee, cotton, flowers, and services are the preferential commodities included in the strategy. The NES idiosyncrasies are the high engagement of the private sector in the strategy and the emphasis on the gender aspect in order to create a diverse and competitive export sector with greater female participation. It is anticipated that the government will strengthen Uganda's export ability to compete by developing supply-side capabilities, enhancing the business environment, and decreasing business costs. Key actions recognized to increase the overall atmosphere include delivering appropriate trade support services (market information, trade finance advancement, trade advertisement, and quality management) and strengthening the coherence of export support policies through enhancing institutional capacity and inter-institutional coordination. Moreover, through its National Plan for Export Development and Promotion, Morocco pursues an export strategy. Adopting complementary policy initiatives (trade, development, post-production infrastructure and the general business environment) to encourage agricultural exports seems feasible only for countries with sufficient resources as well as comparative and competitive advantages. Nevertheless, the export development policy is aligned with many RECs' trade and food security policies. Because most nations are food deficits, more open trade policies than food self-sufficiency strategies could be encouraged by appropriate and trustworthy sources of food within REC member countries. National food self-sufficiency is typically contended to be less effective than free regional trade, which tends to increase food availability for deficit regions, stabilizes market prices and provides incentives for regions that produce surpluses.

8.4.1.3 Harmonization of Country-Level Policy Decisions With Regional Economic Communities (RECs)

By promoting trade, Regional Economic Communities (RECs) are set up to promote economic development. Relatively close trade links between REC members encourage countries to resolve barriers created by relatively small domestic market sizes. International trade with food staples improves food security by increasing food accessibility by the free movement of food commodities from a surplus to a deficit area. Within a region, free movement of food can reduce food price volatility by absorbing external or internal price shocks. This section analyzes policy harmonization between national and regional levels in terms of trade-related staple and regional grain stock initiatives policies. The very first sub-section accentuates the evaluation of trade initiatives conducted in Chapter four and evaluates the harmonization and extent of orientation or asymmetry between country-level policy decisions and RECs, explicitly wheat, maize, and rice related export and import measures, while the second examines recent regional stock agreements.

8.4.1.3.1 Harmonization of Trade Policy

1. **Africa:** Pursuing the case of three RECs in Africa, namely SADC, ECOWAS / UEMOA, and EAC, the magnitude to which national trade policies are closely allied with regional trade agreements is investigated.

i. Economic Community of West African States (ECOWAS) and the West African Economic and Monetary Union (WAEMU): The main regional economic organizations in West Africa are the ECOWAS and the Economic and Monetary Union of West Africa (WAEMU, also known as UEMOA). ECOWAS was established in 1975 under the ECOWAS trade liberation scheme (ETLS), started in 1990, to nurture cooperation and interdependence and to promote a free trade area (FTA). UEMOA was founded in 1994 by eight Francophone countries of Western Africa, all of which are also participants of ECOWAS, to support economic integration as a currency union between countries sharing the CFA franc. UEMOA is a federation of customs and currency. ECOWAS and UEMOA have drawn up a joint implementation plan on trade liberalization and convergence of macroeconomic policies. Since 2001, ECOWAS Presidents and prime ministers have been requiring Member States to harmonize their import tariffs with the common external tariff (CET) of the established UEMOA, which was implemented in 1998. Nonetheless, the UEMOA ECOWAS Joint Technical Committee was only established in December 2012 and after a transitional period, (it will officially come into operation in January 2014); ECOWAS countries must follow the external tariff structure of UEMOA and implement other amendments.

- **Policy Alignment and Misalignment:** Several Member States have adopted temporary export restrictions, while generally more harmonized import policies have been registered over the period under consideration. Members of ECOWAS / UEMOA have introduced other export restrictions that clash with their regional agreements. Most of these limitations, however, were short term. In 2007/08, to safeguard food supply to home markets, Togo, Sierra Leone, Senegal, Mali, and Burkina Faso introduced short-term export prohibitions on cereals, including rice and maize. Since 2009, Nigeria has maintained an export restriction on maize. Unofficial export regulations on some staple food crops have been in effect in Burkina Faso and Mali, which are important for the food security of the countries. Such requirements were passed to customs (export bureaucracy) in the form of instructions (Monitoring African Food and Agricultural Policies Project (MAFAP), 2013b). Overall, domestic import policies are aligned with regional obligations, with misalignment documented in just a few cases. After the elimination of import restrictions on staple foods in 2008, Nigeria introduced numerous import tariffs all through the review period. Furthermore, Nigeria increased the efficient duty on imports of wheat grain from 5% to 20% in July 2012 and placed an additional 65% tax on imports of wheat flour, raising the overall duty to 100%. By implementing a broad range of additional taxes and fees on all imports (MAFAP, 2012), Ghana sometimes stopped duty-free imports of goods originating in ECOWAS.

ii. Southern African Development Community (SADC): The SADC was founded in 1992 to promote regional integration and eradicate starvation within the 15 member states, eight of which are among the countries covered by this document. Many treaties (legally enforceable agreements) have been reached between members, including the 1996 Trade Protocol, with a staggered liberalization plan intended to achieve an FTA between members by 2000. The SADC agreement on trade was subsequently revised in 2005, rescheduling the FTA to 2008.

- **Policy Alignment and Misalignment:** Throughout the period 2007–2012, export laws such as temporary export prohibitions were more regularly enforced than import restrictions (e.g., (re) introduction of import tariffs). In so many instances, the export policies of members have been misaligned with SADC FTA. Tanzania, Malawi, Zimbabwe, and Zambia placed partial export bans on basic food items (such as maize and other grains) in 2009/10 and 2011/12. Malawi, Tanzania, and Zambia also used other limits on exports in 2009/10, such as export quotas and licensing systems. On the other end, certain countries' export policies, notably South Africa and Lesotho, were more consistent with SADC FTA. Import policies were misaligned during the comparison period only in some cases. Several delegates strengthened (e.g., Malawi) or re-established tariffs (e.g., Zimbabwe, and Mozambique) that were originally suspended/

reduced. Other participants, such as Tanzania, either reduced (maize) or suspended (wheat) tariffs on imports, in line with SADC FTA.

iii. East African Community (EAC): The EAC is a regional intergovernmental organization founded in 1999 between five countries in Eastern Africa, namely Burundi, Kenya, Rwanda, Tanzania, and Uganda. Ultimately, the EAC aims to improve cooperation and achieve food security between member states; in 2005 and 2010 respectively, a customs union (CU) and a common market were established. Based on a three-band tariff system, the CU applied a common external tariff (CET): 0, 10, and 25%. Nevertheless, EAC's FTA is still not fully in place and is plagued by various cross-country border checks and fees (MAFAP, 2013d).

- **Policy Alignment and Misalignment:** Certain Member States' export restrictions on sensitive products breached EAC treaties, while import tariffs were primarily aligned. Nearly all Member States have introduced export restrictions in the aftermath of the global food crisis of 2007/08. Between 2008 and 2012, Kenya enforced an export ban on maize; likewise, Tanzania implemented protectionist export bans and other restrictions (as shown above, Tanzania is both a member of the SADC and EAC). Uganda, on the other hand, managed to maintain a less restrictive export strategy, i.e., only once issued a temporary export ban on maize, while Rwanda maintained a free export policy.

Import liberalization between member countries has been popular. Wheat tariffs: in 2007 and 2010 respectively, Tanzania, and Rwanda reduced tariffs to zero. Likewise, they were slowly reduced to zero by Uganda (2011) and Kenya (2011). In 2012, the EAC secretariat allowed Kenya to place a 10% import duty on wheat. With relation to tariffs on rice, a lower level of CET has been granted to member countries. Nevertheless, in 2007, Kenya set a preferential rate for Pakistani rice imports and in 2010 aligned, its policy with the negotiated CET. Kenya suspended its CET on maize for maize tariffs, while

Tanzania, Rwanda, and Uganda agreed to conform their policies with the maize policy of the EAC. Broadly speaking, African countries' reaction to the food price crisis of 2007/08 culminated in policy misalignments, especially in relation to export restrictions, which were in some cases proceeded over the period analyzed (especially for SADC and some EAC members). Import restrictions, on the other hand, were less widespread and tariffs were reduced in many cases, indicating a better alignment of national policies with regional commitments. The findings suggest that African countries with food shortages have implemented export restrictions while promoting imports (by removing restrictions); primarily to increase domestic supply and keep prices lower for consumers. While the country's food security problems seem to override regional food security obligations, countries trying to pursue export strategies may be successful in the region (due to limited import restrictions and large deficit levels) (Table 8.14).

Table 8.14. Country Level Trade Policy Alignment vs. REC on Selected Staples (2007–2012)

Region	Selected REC	Covered Members	Agreements	Misalignment
Africa	ECOW-AS/UE-MOA	Liberia, Mali, Burkina Faso, Ghana, Mauritania, Nigeria, Senegal, Sierra Leone, Togo	•Free Trade Area (FTA)* •Customs Union (CU)** in force from January 2014.	Import restrictions: Nigeria, Ghana Export restrictions: Senegal, Sierra Leone, Burkina Faso, Togo, Mali, Nigeria
	SADC	Lesotho, Malawi, Mozambique, Democratic Republic of Congo (DRC), South Africa, Tanzania, Zambia, Zimbabwe	• FTA by 2008 (DRC did not sign it)	Export restrictions: Malawi, Zimbabwe Tanzania, Zambia Import restrictions: Malawi, Zimbabwe, Mozambique
	EAC	Uganda, Kenya, Rwanda, Tanzania,	• CU •Common Market***from 2010	Export restrictions: Kenya, Tanzania, Uganda Import restrictions: Tanzania
Asia	AFTA	Thailand, Vietnam, Indonesia, the Philippines, Cambodia, Lao PDR	• FTA	Export restrictions: Indonesia, Lao PDR, Vietnam, Cambodia Import restrictions: Thailand
	SAFTA	Bangladesh, Bhutan, India, Nepal, Pakistan, Sri Lanka	•FTA by 2016 •Agricultural products are among "sensible" items and a 20% tariff line is applied	Export restrictions: India, Pakistan, Nepal, Bangladesh Import restrictions: none

LAC	MERCO-SUR	Argentina, Brazil, Paraguay (suspended since July 2012), Uruguay	• CU • Possibility of CET temporary exemptions from 2007	Export restrictions: Argentina, Brazil Import restrictions: Argentina, Brazil (nonautomatic licenses and informal barriers)
	CAN	Bolivia, Colombia, Ecuador, Peru	• CU • Andean Price Band System (APBS) for agricultural products	Export restrictions: Ecuador, Bolivia Import restrictions: Colombia
	MCCA	Costa Rica, ElSal-vador, Guatemala, Honduras, Nicaragua	• CU	Export restrictions: Honduras Import restrictions: none
* Free Trade Area (FTA): no import or export restrictions of any kind (tariffs, quotas, bans) among members. ** Customs Union (CU): FTA + common external tariff (CET) in place for non-members. *** Common Market: CU + coordination of various social, fiscal, and monetary policies among members.				

Source: FAO, FAPDA 2013.

2. Asia

i. Association of Southeast Asian Nations (ASEAN) Free Trade Area (FTA): In 1992, the ASEAN Free Trade Area (AFTA) was founded by the ASEAN to facilitate the free movement of goods and services within the bloc. Members are required to qualify an import tariff rate of zero to 5% for commodities originating within ASEAN, called the Common Effective Preferential Tariff (CEPT), without numerical restrictions (non-tariff barriers). AFTA does not qualify a CET and on the basis of its national schedules, each member may impose tariffs on goods from outside the bloc. With ASEAN members, ways to exclude goods from the CEPT are contemplated and include sensitive agricultural products such as rice, among others.

- **Policy Alignment and Misalignment:** In relation to the food crisis of 2007/08, sub-regional trade in certain staple commodities was temporarily impacted at the national level, following the implementation of temporary export restrictions by the region's major rice exporters. There have been some short-term misalignments, particularly in the rice sector, perceived to be the predominant agricultural commodity with high political sensitivity. In 2008, several countries placed provisional export restrictions; Indonesia, Lao PDR, Vietnam, and Cambodia temporarily prohibited exports of rice (the last two countries are major exporters of rice). The limits have been dropped in the years that followed. On the other side, tariff reductions have indicated a degree of policy harmonization between national and REC commitments on most agricultural products. In 2008, Thailand had only one incidence of an import restriction, an import ban on maize.

ii. South Asian Association for Regional Cooperation (SAARC) Free Trade Agreement: The South Asian Free Trade Agreement (SAFTA) was established in Bangladesh, Bhutan, India, Nepal, Pakistan, and Sri Lanka in 2006 as part of the SAARC. The Agreement will begin moving the South Asian region to a FTA with a tariff liberalization program being implemented by 2016. The agreement distinguishes less developed countries (LDCs) from non-LDC member states, providing for unique and differential treatments for the first group, which would include lower tariff reductions and longer implementation periods. Among the most important provisions in the agreement applies to the 'sensitive' industries, including agricultural products, to which a tariff line of 20% is applied without compulsory country list reduction.

- **Policy Alignment and Misalignment:** During the recent increase in food prices, some significant producer countries used extensively export restrictions. India responded to high international food prices in 2007/08 by banning rice, wheat, and maize exports. After a bumper harvest in 2011, sales were only completely resumed. In 2007, Pakistan levied an export tax and eventually a ban on wheat, lifting the ban in 2010 and replacing it with export quotas. Nepal prohibited all food grain exports in 2008, and Bangladesh did the same for rice exports, with the exception of Nepal's wheat ban (lifted in 2010), bans remain in place in both countries today, with only a few export quotas permitted. No member country imposed any import bans, unlike the export bans. The agreement on import tariffs is usually noted, excluding Pakistan, which reintroduced rice import tariffs in 2011. Nonetheless, there is a misalignment about some different agricultural product policies that are included in the sensitive commodity category (negative list). List restriction policies are 'voluntary' (in recent years only India has made significant attempts to reduce the list) and non-tariff barriers (technical, sanitary, and phytosanitary barriers and licensing systems) are still considerable in many SAARC countries.

However, a prevalence of competing bilateral trade agreements in the region has prompted some countries to offer concessions and preferences in the context of those agreements to specific trade partners rather than comply with the provisions required by SAFTA (FAORAP, 2012). Generally speaking, some major producers/exporters in both RECs introduced temporary export restrictions, especially for rice, which is Asia's primary staple. The limitations in AFTA have been shorter than in SAFTA. Also, in SAFTA, formal, and implied limits on imports are relatively broader than in AFTA. However, business opportunities in staple grains are high for exporting countries, as the region has several food-deficit countries as tariff and non-tariff barriers are being reduced or suspended.

3. **Latin America and the Caribbean (LAC)**

i. Southern Common Market: The Southern Common Market (MERCOSUR) is South America's largest trading bloc (aggregate GDP) with two big regional and global food producers. MERCOSUR was formed in 1991 by Brazil, Argentina, Paraguay (banned since July 2012) and Uruguay as an FTA and in 1994 became a CU with a CET. In 2012, Venezuela entered the bloc and Bolivia is on track to join the alliance. MERCOSUR representatives voted in 2007 to permit temporary exceptions for certain sensitive items, including agricultural goods, to the CET.

- **Policy Alignment and Misalignment:** Throughout the research, period, export, and import policies at the country level often contrasted with MERCOSUR's FTA. The main members of the bloc, Argentina, and Brazil, have introduced protectionist measures and restrictions on agricultural products. In 2007/08, Argentina implemented an export ban on wheat and maize, transforming the bans into quotas (opening the grain registry in June 2008 for wheat and in February 2009 for maize, and granting ad-hoc export licenses). In 2008, Brazil implemented a temporary ban on rice exports to protect domestic supplies. Between November 2007 to March 2008, Argentina sharply reduced export taxes on maize and wheat, but gradually reduced them in the following year. It has reported non-automatic licenses and informal import barriers. In 2009, in response to a similar measure implemented by Argentina in 2008, Brazil introduced non-automatic licenses for some fundamental Argentine products, such as wheat flour, wine, oil, processed foods, and other agricultural items. Additionally,

Paraguay, and Uruguay, the bloc's two marginal allies, had an associated trade (export and import) policy of the three staples considered. Overlapping policies also produced complications between partners, prompting diplomatic negotiations to overcome them. Administrations try to resolve their disagreements through national diplomacy and bilateral agreements rather than through MERCOSUR bodies, subverting the supranational capacities of the bloc (Klonsky et al., 2012).

ii. Andean Community (CAN): CAN is a CU that includes Bolivia, Colombia, Ecuador, and Peru from South America and was formed in 1969 with the Cartagena Agreement. The Andean CU has four specific tariff levels: 5, 10, 15, and 20%, depending on the degree of production of the goods, with lower tariffs on raw materials. There are a few exemptions to this CET: a price band system (the Andean Price Band System (APBS)) for agricultural commodities has been adopted since 1994 to protect Andean agricultural products from price fluctuations on the international market and agricultural tariffs are usually higher than non-agricultural products.

- **Policy Alignment and Misalignment:** Block policymakers responded very differently to the crisis of 2007/08, with some countries taking trade restriction measures during and after the crisis. Two countries have adopted export restrictions, especially in the first phase (2007/08). From September 2007 to March 2009, Ecuador temporarily banned exports of rice, while Bolivia banned exports of maize extensively from August 2007 to October 2008, again imposing a temporary ban on maize in 2010. Upon lifting the bans, both countries limited exports of these products by enforcing quotas. Import prohibitions have seldom been registered, while all members have lowered import tariffs. In 2010, only Colombia implemented a temporary ban on imports of grain. All CAN countries have lowered import tariffs, enabling duty-free imports of nearly all of Bolivia's staple food items in 2008, Ecuador's wheat and wheat flour from 2009 to 2011, Colombia's rice in 2007, and Peru's lifting tariffs on staples in 2007 (wheat) and 2011 (maize and rice). CAN members typically followed different policies, with Peru and Colombia attempting to maintain adequate food supply through open trade, while Bolivia and Ecuador replied with increased government involvement and export regulation. After the food shortage of 2007/08, CAN countries also shifted their attention from trade issues to social issues.

iii. Central American Common Market (CACM): The CACM (Mercado ComunCentroamericano (MCCA)) was created in 1960 by Guatemala, Costa Rica, El Honduras, Nicaragua, and Salvador, is now integrated into SICA (Central America Integration System). The MCCA includes an FTA for 96% of the products marketed, and a CET for goods and services.

- **Policy Alignment and Misalignment:** In particular, trade policies are consistent within the bloc, with only one export ban and a few deviations from the CET. The restrictions on exports are limited. The only recorded case was the 2007/08 export ban on maize in Honduras. No member countries enforced import restrictions, whereas all member countries used zero tariffs or temporary lifting of tariffs for some key products during the study period. Maize (2011) and rice (2011); El Salvador lifted tariffs on maize (2010) and on wheat flour (2008 and 2012); Guatemala lifted tariffs on maize (2008, 2009, and 2011), wheat flour (2008, 2009, and 2011) and rice (2008); Costa Rica lifted tariffs on maize (2010 and 2012) and on rice (2011); Honduras on wheat flour (2008 and 2009), and Nicaragua on wheat flour (2008) and white maize (2011). Transaction volumes between Central American countries are high: 49% of agricultural imports in El Salvador and Nicaragua came from members of the MCCA in 2010, 40% for Honduras, 24% for Guatemala and 15% for Costa Rica (FAO, 2011b). Trade barriers and constraints, even after the recession, were limited. Nonetheless, trade policy harmonization shows varying degrees of success between LAC RECs: protectionist export policies and import bans have been adopted by MERCOSUR's major food exporting members and some CAN members, compared to more transparent and aligned trade policies among MCCA countries. Contradictory policies have led to trade issues and undermined MERCOSUR's regional trade, leading to increased state control over CAN trade. By contrast, minimal trade restrictions during the reference period resulted in an expansion of trade between MCCA countries.

8.4.1.3.2 ***Regional Grain Stock Policy Integration***

Political debates have escalated on sustaining strategic reserves at national, regional, and global levels since the exceptional food price surge of 2007/08. A synchronized solution at the supra-national (regional or global) level has drawn new attention amongst the international community, arguing that such interventions can better address emergency situations, particularly in cases of large-scale and catastrophic crises exceeding national borders. Although global stocks are more difficult to control because they adapt to the demands of very different groups of countries, regional food stocks tend to represent a more viable alternative, which have to deal with fewer countries with more similarities, often already connected by a cooperation agreement. Compared to national reserves, establishing regional food stocks has three positive aspects:

1. Large-scale and economies of scale can save costs;
2. Autonomous management could discourage the use of reserves for political gains by governments;
3. Collective bargaining mechanisms can help to prevent trade barriers in major food crises (World Bank, 2012f).

Nevertheless, the development of local stocks has been hampered by a range of policy harmonization and technical issues. One of the key issues to be addressed is:

1. Techniques and guidelines for the storage and release of stocks (necessitating efficient organization, agreement, and cooperation between members on the conditions for determining the volumes to be given by each country; timing and location of storage; and forms of treatment for the release of stocks during crises);
2. Expenditures of establishing and maintaining regional stocks (which are sometimes in addition to existing national reserve costs and involve mobilizing ongoing support from all Member States); and
3. Consequences of stocks for free trade (it is contended that reserves of grain targeted at price stabilization cause inaccuracies of trade in markets and domestic prices). A lack of meaningful and mutual political support in the past has hampered stock-setting at the regional level. Nevertheless, some Asian and African RECs have shown a strong interest in local stocks in recent years. There was no national inventory initiative, on the other hand, in LAC. The key issues currently facing regional inventory agreements in Africa and Asia are listed below.

1. Africa: An illustration of the ECOWAS Federal Policy for Food Stocks

The RAIP 2011–2015 was initiated by ECOWAS members in 2009. As a major aspect of the RAIP, ECOWAS members accepted a Regional Food Inventory Strategy for two main objectives: controlling the demand for important food crops and acting as an emergency reserve and promoting food safety networks in the region. Amid numerous attempts by close ECOWAS associates to set up a regional grain reserve, ECOWAS created a task force to oversee the process and bring the different initiatives together. Creating on actual solutions for a feasibility study on regional food storage potential completed in September 2012 (ECOWAS, 2012), the ECOWAS Task Force formally endorsed the development of the reserve and identified the next steps towards its operationalization by mid-2013. Individual countries decided that ECOWAS, in greater cooperation with UEMOA and CILSS, the Sahel Permanent Inter-State Committee on Drought Control, would lead the implementation of the reserve. The operational management of the reserve would be carried out in close cooperation with RESOGEST (Stocks Offices Management Network) by a specialist ECOWAS organization, the Regional Organization for Agriculture and Food.

The working group agreed to start activities with an initial capacity of 180,000 tons of stocks; one-third of this inventory will be placed in physical reserves, and the remainder in financial reserves. The fund is expected to grow to a total of 410,000 tons of physical and financial assets by its eighth year. The stock release is to be dictated on the basis of the Enhanced Harmonized Framework, the consensus tool for the sub-regional food insecurity analysis (ECOWAS, 2012). Nationally, as previously discussed (chapter four), several West African governments have taken steps to reinforce their national food stocks (following the 2007/08 food crisis) while seeking to build a regional inventory through ECOWAS.

That is not apparent how regional inventory control is synchronized with country inventory and how state dedication to the initiative of the regional stock is maintained as member countries step up their investment to simultaneously create or increase national grain reserves. States with different concentrations of domestic inventories and significant differences in natural disaster susceptibility (e.g., Sahelian countries have drier weather than others) may not show the same level of engagement with regional grain reserves.

2. Asia

i. East Asia Emergency Rice Reserve (EAERR) and Three Emergency Rice Reserve of ASEAN Plus: In East Asia, the tradition of a national emergency reserve for rice has a great history. As recently as 1979, ASEAN governments set up the ASEAN Emergency Rice Reserve (AERR) to create tangible rice reserves, centered on individual countries' charitable donations, which could be used if a member was unable to meet the needs of their citizens through their own production or through foreign rice purchases. The program never became functional, however, and the concept under the ASEAN+3 agreements was revised in 2003. The new EAERR is a pilot project for:

a. Deal with food emergencies;

b. Guaranteeing long-term food security and improving the livelihoods of farmers in ASEAN member countries.

Even though the directorate of the EAERR was set up to function independently and promote rice exchange between countries facing an emergency food requirement and countries keeping reserves, no country has been resorting to the EAERR in the past decade. The ASEAN+3 states agree on an enhanced template, the ASEAN Plus Three Emergency Rice Reserve (APTERR), which entered into force in July 2012, in response to rising and unpredictable prices at the end of 2011. The reserves largely consist of 787,000 tons of rice stocks approved (physically) or allocated by ASEAN+3 countries to meet the region's emergency food needs, plus rice stocks voluntarily contributed to the reserve (unspecified amounts from Japan, China, and Thailand) to be used as a humanitarian response to acute emergencies. During the reference period, all Member States tended to increase their national reserves at the national level to cope with price shocks: this type of policy was generally pursued by the ASEAN+3 countries. It perhaps begins to appear that this developing regional rice reserve initiative's cooperation framework is still too weak to enforce. Indeed, despite countries' relatively improved dedication to make a significant contribution to the reserve, the amount allocated is insufficient to contain a potential domestic crisis in larger countries (such as Indonesia or the Philippines). There are still some serious concerns and shortcomings to be resolved as a result of the two previous local attempts to create a rice emergency reserve:

- **Application Difficulties:** Similar past projects had moderate success due to problems in communication, as well as ambiguous storage systems and cost-sharing between countries.

- **Financial Stability Worries:** The plus three countries are currently the largest donors under the voluntary contribution system.
- **Trade Non-Interference Difficulties:** The program is not structured or encouraged to substitute rice trade between member countries, despite being a trade facilitating mechanism. However, it must comply with WTO treaties banning trade barriers and must only be used in emergencies. In the whole scope, in a region comprising the world's largest rice producers and importers, as well as the largest rice shortfall and exporting countries, recourse to bilateral and regional trade agreements rather than the regional reserve could still be seen as a better solution to food shortages (Trethewie, 2013).

ii. South Asian Food Bank National Cooperation Association: The South Asian Food Bank Association (SFB) was established in April 2007 with two goals:

a. function through normal times, food shortages and emergencies as a regional food security reserve for SAARC members; and
b. Providing regional support for national measures in food security, promoting inter-country partnerships and global integration and resolving regional food shortages through collective action.

The SFB began operating with supplies of 241,580 tons of rice and wheat and subsequently, stocks multiplied to 482,000 tons (each country's commitment doubled accordingly). Countries are obligated to remove the necessary grains during times of food shortage in the event of natural or man-made emergencies. In emergency situations, food grains are released only after discussions have taken place between the Member States concerned on the price of grain (request and release). Discussions are based on existing rules, and the rates provided to members will be at a discount rate relative to the prices of food grain offered to non-members. Closely related to Southeast Asia, in 2007/08, SAARC member countries expanded rapidly their national stockpiles; also, through public-private storage infrastructure schemes, as in India and Sri Lanka. Notwithstanding the alignment of requirements and policies implemented at the country level, the SFB was unable to help any member country tide over any supply shock between 2007 and 2012. As emphasized in the scenario of APTERR, it is challenging to guarantee dedication from very various countries (with different economic status, levels of poverty, production patterns and levels of food deficit) to contribute voluntarily to a regional food reserve. SFB logistics also bear the burden of depositing and delivering food when required: some studies have found that grain storage facilities in South Asian countries are currently insufficient to store the required buffer stock of grains. There is no de-facto food bank without storage facilities in operation, irrespective of any signed policy frameworks. In addition, there are still uncertain procedures for the timely and effective distribution of grain and price negotiations (Robinson, 2011). Finally, developing, and implementing the system seems vulnerable to administrative and political issues: lack of political will to quickly ratify emergency decisions (when the bank must intervene) remains a major constraint (SAARC Summit, 2011).

APPENDICES

Appendix 1: Gender Equality.

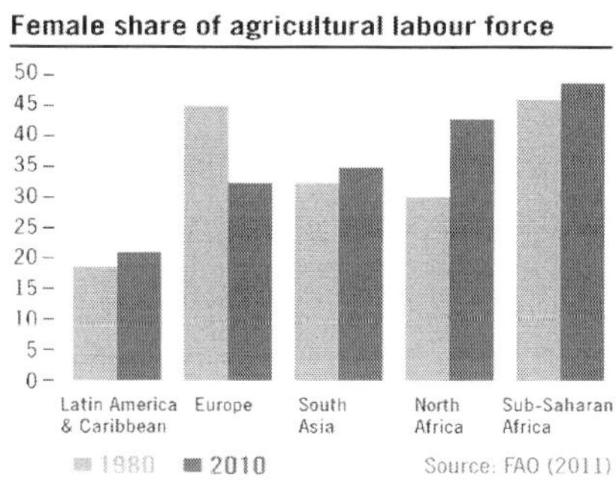

Appendix 2: Elements of Agriculture Policy for Small-Scale Producers in Developing Countries.

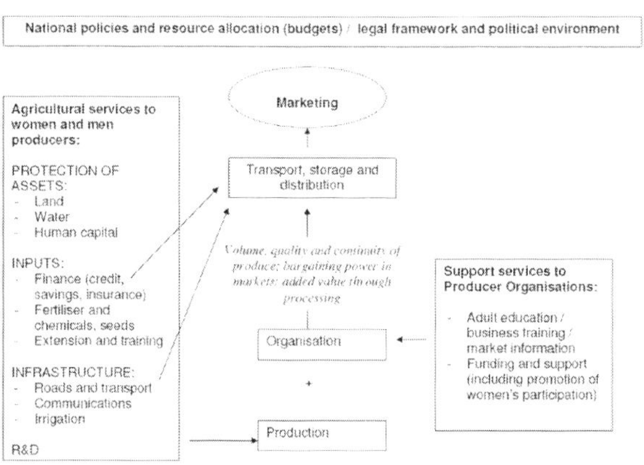

Appendix 3: Realization of gender-equal agriculture and rural community.

Appendix 4: Objectives of common agricultural policy in Europe.

Appendix 5: The impacts of export taxes on agricultural trade.

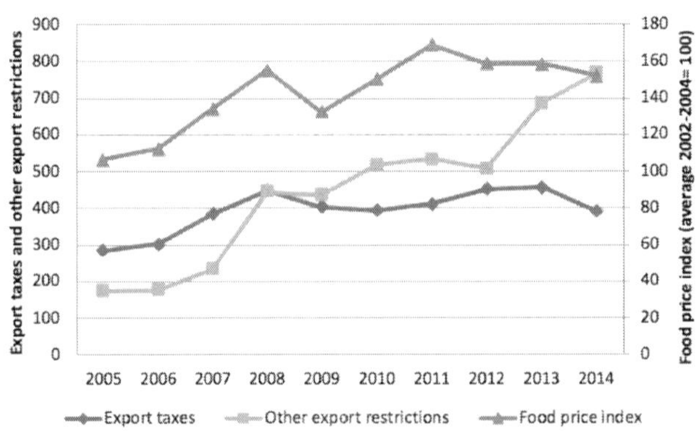

Appendix 6: Trends in Agriculture Sustainability.

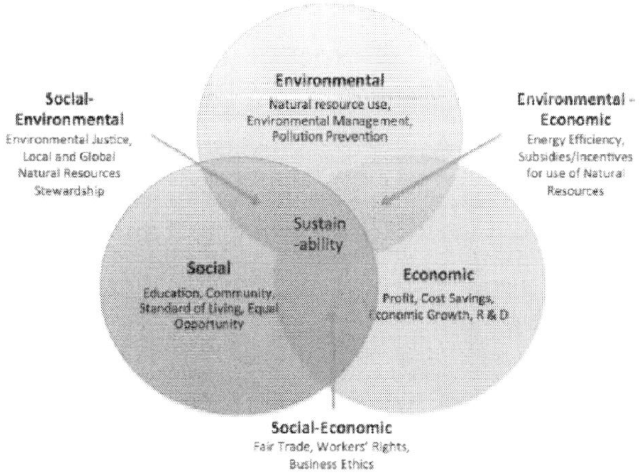

Appendix 7: Harmonization tools of the organic sector.

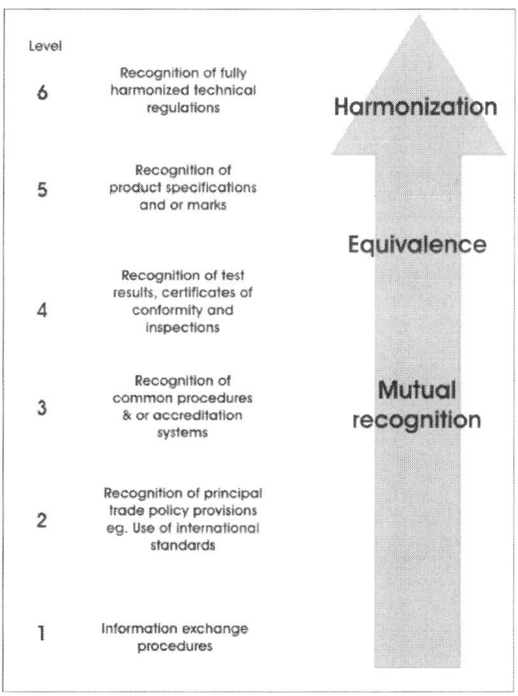

INDEX

A

Additional tax 21
Ad-hoc programs 164
Administration 15
Agribusiness 6
Agricultural Credit Program 167
Agricultural development banks (ADBs) 171
Agricultural environment 3
Agricultural Insurance Act 177
Agricultural land 69
Agricultural loan 168, 169, 170
Agricultural marketing 85
Agricultural mechanization 128
Agricultural output 2
Agricultural policy 84, 87
Agricultural relationships 104
Agricultural supply 71
Agricultural technology 126
Agricultural trade 5, 9
Agricultural value chain 170
Agriculture 2, 3, 5, 9, 11
Agrochemical 140
Alleviate poverty 141
Animal feed 7
Aquaculture 3
Aquatic plants 3
Aquatic species 3
Asymmetric data 52
Atmospheric carbon dioxide 3

B

Behavioral change 85
Biodiversity preservation 3
Biofuels 87
Biopharmaceuticals 87
Bioplastics 87

Budget data 73
Business dynamics 107

C

Cereal production 4
Chemical industry 140
Citizenship 15
Commodity-based basis 67
Commodity market 109
Commodity system 67, 73, 74, 126
Communications 87, 90, 100
Comparative Analysis 18
Comparative productivity 139
Compensating variation 56, 57, 58
Competitive company 60
Competitive performance 50
Comprehensive Africa Agricultural Development Program (CAADP) 183
Computable general equilibrium (CGE) 111
Constant grant function 127
Consumer behavior 46, 53
Consumer behavior theory 46
Consumer prices 89, 96
Consumer surplus 55, 58, 59, 61
Consumption market 66
Conversion curve 62
Cooperative agreements 85
Cost-benefit analysis (CBA) 17
Cost-Effectiveness Analysis (CEA) 17
Cost, insurance, and freight (C.I.F.) 77
Cost-Minimization Analysis (CMA) 17
Cost-Utility Analysis (CUA) 17
Credit guarantee fund trust 169
Credit guarantee schemes (CGSs) 167
Credit market 126
Crop flora 2
Crop production 2, 3
Cross-market effect 109
Crustaceans 3
Cultural diversity 90

D

Decision-making process 66
Defragmentation Program 25
Demand elasticity 55
Demand equilibrium 133, 136
Demand function 53, 54, 55, 61, 105
Democratic Republic of Congo (DRC) 167, 236
Direct collection 73
Direct investment 23
Directly unproductive profit-seeking (DUP) 53
Domestic agricultural 128
Domestic agricultural product 84
Domestic animal 2
Domestic farming laws 84
Domestic food production 86
Domestic market 127, 131
Domestic production 6, 131, 138

E

Economic activity 126
Economic development 107
Economic effect 108
Economic efficiency 49
Economic efficiency theory 49
Economic expert 104, 116
Economic incentive 85, 94
Economic intuition 107
Economic modeling 107

Economic point 69
Economic policy 68
Economic research 66
Economic structure 76
Economic success 106
Economic theory 53, 66
Economic tool 86
economists 49, 50, 55
Elasticity 66, 69, 71, 72
Employment 2, 7
Enterprise 3
Environmental cost 19
Equilibriums 47, 50
Equivalent variation 56, 57, 58
Erosion control 3
European Union 137, 139
Exchange rate 85, 133
Export performance metrics 108
Export subsidies 132
Extreme poverty 106, 107

F

Farm commodity 104, 106
Final market 67
Financial Cooperation 134
Financial development institutions (FDIs) 172
Fiscal policy 85
Fixed assets 71, 72
Food and Agricultural Policy Research Institute (FAPRI) 111
Food and agriculture policy decisions analysis (FAPDA) 162
Food basket 6
Food production , 163, 130, 193
Food quality 20, 32
Food security 163, 176, 182, 218, 223, 227, 229, 230, 231, 232, 234, 235, 236, 244, 245
Food supply 4, 5
Foreign currency 133, 134
Foreign exchange 3, 86
Foreign producer 109
Forest conservation 3
Forest management 87
Forestry 3
Fostering policy 86
Fragmentation 146
Frame Reflection 18

G

Global Bank 6
Global market growth 128
Global policy patterns 163
Global Trade Analysis Project 111
Government intervention 46, 52
Government policy 18
Greenhouse gas emissions 85
Green transition program 165
Gross domestic product (GDP) 3
Guaranteed minimum price (GMP) 174

H

Harm sustainability 22
Health services 90, 98
Household 46
Human beings 2
Human capital 23, 26, 27, 28
Human history 104

I

Income distribution 68
Income generation , 3
Industrial agriculture 2
Industrialization 2
Institutional framework 18, 35
International food trade 5

International human population 2
International market 67, 73
International trade 128
Interpretation 51, 104
Investment 104, 122, 123

J

Jurisdictional territory 14

L

Labor exploitation 141
Labor market 126
Labor production 3
Land productivity 141
Land tenure 126
Large-scale monoculture 2
Legislation 15, 16, 18, 19, 29
Livestock 3
Long-run price trend 127

M

Maize consumption 69
Manufacturing process 66
Marginal cost 60, 61, 62
Marginal price 61
Marginal rate 67
Market-based strategy 86
Market demand 61
Market economy 46, 48
Market equilibrium price 136
Market force 104
Marketing cost 77, 78
Marketing operation 75
Marketing product demand 71
Market intervention 46
Market outcome 66
Market power 50, 109, 122
Market stability 138
Measurement 66
Micro-Agricultural Finance Schemes (MAFISA) 167
Microeconomics 47, 62
Microfinance institutions (MFIs) 168
Microfinance product 168
Minimum support pricing (MSP) 174
Ministry of Finance 85
Modeling development 111
Monetary measure 55, 60, 61
Monopoly position 50
Multi-purpose multi-market 112

N

National agricultural insurance scheme (NAIS) 177
National Cereals and Produce Board (NCPB) 174
National Food Reserve Agency (NFRA) 174
Natural resource 48, 51
New Partnership for African Development (NEPAD) 183
Nutrition 87, 88, 92, 101

O

Open market (OM) 63
Opportunity cost 67, 73, 77
Optimal allocation point 47
Organic farming 19
Organic fruit variety 87
Organization for Economic Co-operation and Development (OECD) 8
Output market 69
Overvaluation 133

P

Pareto criterion 48
Philosophy 14
Physical effect 66
Policy analysis 16, 66
Policy analysis matrix (PAM) 67
Policy-bench marking 18
Policy category 14, 22
Policy decision 69
Policy development 14, 18
Policy framework 86
Policy implication 86
Policy instrument 108, 112
Policymakers 66
Policy-making model 14
Policy monitoring 162
Policy outlines 14
Political colleagues 88
Political interest 19
Politics 14
Population growth 24, 25, 34
Population policy 25
Post-war economy 106
Poverty reduction 87
Price discrimination 113, 114, 115
Price stabilization 173, 174
Producer subsidy equivalent (PSE) 112
Production system 67
Productivity 10
Productivity growth 128, 140
Product surplus 58
Profit distribution 108
Profit-maximizing 60
Program de Desarrollo Territorial Indígena (PDTI) 165
Project management 136
Protectionism 130
Public expenditure 20
Public intervention 52
Public investment 24, 26, 27
Public Investment Policy 86
Public policy 14, 18
Public property 24
Public provision 52
Purchasing power parity (PPP) 133

Q

Quantitative Development Analysis 66
Quantitative testing 107

R

Rapid reductions 104
Rationalizations 105, 135
Realistic analysis 108
Regional agricultural investment plans (RAIPs) 183
Remuneration 137, 146
Resource allocation 67
Resource distribution 14
Resource endowment 76
Resource reimbursement 163
Retail market 70, 75
Risk management 167, 169, 173, 176, 177, 178, 179, 181, 182, 183, 223
Rural community 66
Rural Development 20, 26

S

Sales elasticity 128
Shareholding agreements 145
Shellfish 3
Single market 68
Small and medium-sized enterprises (SMEs) 7
Social outcome 14

Social Policy 15
Social valuation 81
Social welfare 68
Stabilization 26, 30, 135, 137, 138
Stochastic element 111
Subsistence agriculture 2
Supermarkets 85
Supervision 3
Supply and demand 66, 67, 79
Supply control skeptics 106
Supply elasticity 127, 152
Supply management 105, 106, 111
Supply management program 105
Support systems 107
Surplus transformation curves (STCs) 109
Sustainable agriculture 19, 33
Sustainable development 21, 22, 25, 27, 32, 35, 36
Sustainable farming 19, 21, 22, 27, 28, 29, 34

T

Tariff fluctuation 139
Tariffs 131, 132
Taxpayers 108, 109, 110, 116
Total factor productivity (TFP) 10
Transaction fees 89
Transportation 5, 12
Transport policy 85
Treasury management 171

U

Unstable Economy 104
Urbanization 2, 7, 12
Utility function 46, 56

V

Voluntary agreements 86
Voluntary production 111

W

Water quality protection 3
Watershed conservation 3
Weather index insurance (WII) 182
Welfare economics 51
Welfare implication 107, 108, 109
World Bank (WB) 111
World Trade Organization (WTO) 72